THE HOSPITAL
INDUSTRY,
TOURISM AND EUROPE

Perspectives on Policies

Edited by Rhodri Thomas

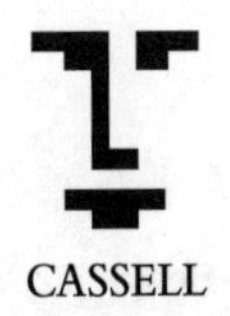

CASSELL

Cassell
Wellington House
125 Strand
London WC2R 0BB

127 West 24th Street
New York
NY 10011

British Library Cataloguing-in-Publication Data

A catalogue record for this book is available from the British Library

ISBN 0-304-33295-X (HB)
0-304-33298-4 (PB)

Typeset by Action Typesetting, Gloucester
Printed and bound in Great Britain by Redwood Books, Trowbridge, Wiltshire

THE HOSPITALITY INDUSTRY, TOURISM AND EUROPE

Perspectives on Policies

CONTENTS

CONTRIBUTORS

Nigel Healey is Jean Monnet Professor of European Economic Studies, Centre for European Economic Studies, University of Leicester.
Howard Hughes is Professor of Tourism, Department of Hotel, Catering and Tourism Management, Manchester Metropolitan University.
David Leslie is Reader in Tourism Studies, Department of Hospitality, Tourism and Leisure Management, Glasgow Caledonian University.
Juliet Lodge is Professor and Director of the Centre for European Studies, University of Leeds.
Rosemary Lucas is Senior Lecturer in Employment Studies, Department of Hotel, Catering and Tourism Management, Manchester Metropolitan University.
Dolf Mogendorff is the former Professor and Head of the Department of Hospitality, Tourism and Leisure Management, Glasgow Caledonian University and is Managing Director, Service Solutions Ltd, Glasgow.
Richard North is a consultant to the food and agricultural industries and a journalist.
David Parsons is Director of Development at the HOST Consultancy and Visiting Professor, Centre for the Study of Small Tourism and Hospitality Firms, School of Tourism and Hospitality Management, Leeds Metropolitan University.
Gordon Robinson is Senior Lecturer and Director of European Business Research, University of Central England Business School.
Heather Smith is Information Officer, North Yorkshire European Community Office, York.
Rhodri Thomas is Principal Lecturer and Co-ordinator of the Centre for the Study of Small Tourism and Hospitality Firms, School of Tourism and Hospitality Management, Leeds Metropolitan University.
Stephen Wanhill is Professor of Tourism, School of Service Industries, Bournemouth University and Head of Tourism Research, Bornholms Forskningscenter, Denmark.
Richard Welford is Professor of Business Economics and Director of the Centre for Corporate Environmental Management, School of Business, University of Huddersfield.

ABBREVIATIONS AND ACRONYMS

ABTA	Association of British Travel Agents
ASC	Assured Safe Catering
BC-Net	Business Co-operation Network
BEUC	Bureau of European Consumer Unions
BHA	British Hospitality Association
BIC	Business Innovation Centre
BRE	Bureau de Rapprochement des Enterprises
BTS	Brevet de Technicien Superieur
CA	Court of Appeal
CEDEFOP	European Centre for the Development of Vocational Training
CET	Common external tariff
COMMET	Community Action Programme for Education and Training in Technology
COPA	Committee of Professional Agricultural Organizations
COREPER	Committee of Permanent Representatives
CP	Co-operation profile
CRP	Common Regional Policy
CRS	Computer reservation systems
CSF	Community Support Framework
DGs	Directorates General
DH	Department of Health
DGXXIII	Directorate General XXIII Enterprise Policy, Distributive Trades, Tourism and Co-operatives
EAGGF	European Agricultural Guidance and Guarantee Fund
EAT	Employment Appeal Tribunal
EC	European Community
ECB	European Central Bank
ECJ	European Court of Justice
ECOFIN	Economics and Finance
ECSC	European Coal and Steel Community
ECU	European currency unit

EDC	European Documentation Centre
EEA	European Economic Area
EEC	European Economic Community
EEIG	European Economic Interest Grouping
EFTA	European Free Trade Association
EIB	European Investment Bank
EIC	European Information Centre
EMI	European Monetary Institute
EMS	European Monetary System
EMU	Economic and monetary union *or* European monetary union
ENVIREG	Regional Action Programme Concerning the Environment
EP	European Parliament
ERDF	European Regional Development Fund
ERM	Exchange Rate Mechanism
ESC	Economic and Social Committee
ESCB	European System of Central Banks
ESF	European Social Fund
ETOA	European Tour Operators Association
ETUC	European Trades Unions Confederation
ETY	European Tourism Year
EU	European Union
EURATOM	European Atomic Energy Community
FIFG	Financial Instrument for Fisheries Guidance
FTA	Free trade area
FTE	Full-time equivalent
GATT	General Agreement on Tariffs and Trade
GDP	Gross domestic product
GNP	Gross national product
HACCP	Hazard Analysis Critical Control Point
HL	House of Lords
HND	Higher National Diploma
HORECA	Hotels, restaurants and cafés
HOTREC	Confederation of National Hotel and Restaurant Associations in the EC
IGC	Intergovernmental Conference
IMPs	Integrated Mediterranean Programmes
INTERREG	Initiative to Promote Co-operation between Border Areas
ITO	Industrial Training Organization
JHA	Justice and home affairs
LACOTS	Local Authorities Coordinating Body on Food and Trading Standards (formerly Local Authority Coordination of Trading Standards)
LEADER	Links between Actions for the Development of the Rural Economy
MEP	Member of the European Parliament
MES	Minimum efficient size
NACE	Nomenclature des Activités de la Communautée Européenne
NTB	Non-tariff barrier
NVQ	National Vocational Qualification
OECD	Organization for Economic Co-operation and Development
OJ	*Official Journal of the European Communities*
OOPEC	Office for Official Publications of the European Community
OP	Operational programme

PR	Proportional representation
QMV	Qualified majority voting
SAD	Single Administration Document
SEA	Single European Act
SEM	Single European market
SMEs	Small and medium-sized enterprises
SPD	Single programming document
TEU	Treaty on European Union
TUPE	Transfer of Undertakings (Protection of Employment) Regulations
TURERA	Trade Union Reform and Employment Rights Act
UNCED	United Nations Conference on the Environment and Development
VET	Vocational education and training
WEU	Western European Union
WTO	World Tourism Organization

PREFACE

The idea for this book came from my involvement with developing European business modules for students on undergraduate and postgraduate courses in hospitality and tourism management. Some very good texts already exist which consider the dynamics of tourism at a European level, while others effectively analyse the sectoral ramifications of internationalization. To date, however, there has been only a partial assessment of the implications of European integration - and the range of policies spawned by that process - for firms in the hospitality industry. This book is intended to overcome that shortfall.

The paucity of publications in this field is perhaps surprising, since it is widely recognized that the European Union is increasingly having an impact on the business environment. Various intitiatives not only prescribe and circumscribe key aspects of business behaviour but also, if the rhetoric is to be believed, create significant opportunities for business development. By bringing together a range of specialists, this volume aims to offer a comprehensive analysis of the current and potential influence of major European Union policies on this sector. More specifically, the book will:

- describe the development, current structure and policy-making process of the European Union, with particular reference to the hospitality industry;
- provide an overview of the industry and analyse its dynamics at a European level;
- describe a series of major policies, examine their rationale and evaluate what they mean for this sector.

By reviewing official sources of information, the final chapter will assist those interested in pursuing their own research or in keeping up to date with developments.

To avoid any ambiguity it is appropriate to explain why 'tourism' appears in the book's title in spite of the overt focus on the hospitality industry. As will become clear from reading the various chapters, it is impossible to explore the impact of European public policy on the hospitality industry without considerable reference to tourism; official initiatives tend not to distinguish between different types of tourism enterprise, and most measures affect tourism businesses and hospitality firms in similar ways. Moreover, the text is clearly relevant to those with an interest in the European tourism industry if for no other reason than that it examines in detail one component of it. This should not be taken to suggest, however, that the considerable parts of the hospitality industry, such as the contract catering sector, which may not be connected with tourism are ignored.

The obvious danger of writing books on European integration is that they may appear to become dated virtually on publication. To overcome this, the contributors examine the general direction of policies and explore the enduring debates rather than merely describing the most recent initiatives. This approach will enable readers to evaluate new proposals for themselves.

Finally, I should like to express my gratitude to the contributors, who have participated enthusiastically and responded to editorial suggestions with good humour and alacrity. Not only has it been a pleasure to work with such a number of distinguished colleagues, but their knowledge and experience have considerably lightened the editorial load. In addition, there are others whose helpful advice and professional support have been much appreciated: Conrad Lashley, Huw Thomas, Vicky Harris and George Holmes. I am also grateful for the guidance offered by Judith Entwisle-Baker, formerly of Cassell, and the secretarial assistance provided by Karen Thackray.

Rhodri Thomas

ONE

The hospitality industry, tourism and European integration: an overview

Rhodri Thomas

INTRODUCTION

The European Union (EU) is the world's largest trading bloc and is becoming increasingly influential in moulding the business environment within its borders. The process of integration has given rise to a series of measures which impact upon the development of the hospitality and tourism industries. Some of these initiatives have been designed with the peculiarities of the sectors concerned in mind, while others have been created to influence businesses more generally.

Many commentators recognize the importance for firms of understanding and monitoring state intervention. For example, Zhao and Merna (1992), in reviewing available empirical studies, generally found a positive relationship between active environmental scanning and enhanced business performance. Moreover, others have drawn particular attention to the importance of assessing the impact of public policies on firms (Go *et al.*, 1992). Lodge's contribution to this volume (Chapter 2) is valuable in this respect. Her chapter not only explains the dynamics of the policy-making process but also draws attention to how organizations wishing to influence the deliberations of policy-makers might do so most effectively.

This chapter provides an overview of the nature and scope of EU policies with particular reference to the hospitality and tourism industries. Following a brief discussion of relevant economic indicators, it offers an outline of the historical development of the EU. The major policy areas as they affect these industries are then reviewed, drawing on the more detailed assessments provided later in this book. It should be recognized, therefore, that what follows is intended to set the scene and to draw attention to linkages between the various areas of activity.

In order to appreciate the context within which much of the policy analysis is set, it is appropriate to provide a brief profile of tourism within the EU. Although it is difficult to be precise, official estimates suggest that tourism represents approximately 5.5 per cent of EU gross national product (GNP), though there are significant variations between member states. Hence, the figure is higher for Greece, Ireland and Portugal and is almost twice the average for Spain and France (Commission, 1994a; 1996a).

Europe is the world's largest tourism market, accounting for some 60 per cent of visitors and 53 per cent of revenue. However, it is losing global market share; a loss of some 10 per cent during the period 1970–92 (Commission, 1994b). Perhaps of greater concern is the fact that various forecasts expect the decline to continue. Thus, it is anticipated that Europeans – who in visiting other countries in the same continent comprise the bulk of international tourists – are becoming increasingly attracted to long-haul destinations and, simultaneously, there is expected to be a reduction in the number of non-European visitors (Jansen-Verbeke and Spec, 1995). In anticipation of what is to follow, the EU is now – rather belatedly – turning its attention to ways of reversing the trends.

Tourism's contribution to employment in Europe is substantial. A recent estimate claims that it is directly responsible for some 9 million jobs, which is about 6 per cent of total employment (Commission, 1996a). Of these, approximately 4 million are in hotels and catering (Commission, 1994a). As is often pointed out, the amount rises significantly when indirect employment generation is considered.

There are trends towards concentration in all sectors associated with these industries. By way of illustration, Long and Richards (1993) point to the growth of travel agency chains and note that the top 10 European tour operators provide 56 per cent of package holiday sales. Statistics for the hospitality industry suggest greater fragmentation. For example, independent hotels comprise 90 per cent of establishments and 80 per cent of rooms within the EU. However, these figures conceal important variations and taken alone may create a false impression of the dynamics which currently obtain in terms of the supply of accommodation. Even taking into account the caution which must be exercised when interpreting official (and for that matter non-official) figures, it is clear that some markets – notably the UK and France – have witnessed increased corporate activity in the 1980s and early 1990s to the extent that chains now control some 20 per cent of room stock in these two countries. Elsewhere, for example Greece, Italy, Denmark and Spain, such structural changes have been far less marked (Litteljohn, 1993; Viceriat, 1993).[1] Both Mogendorff (Chapter 3) and Robinson (Chapter 5) explore these issues in more detail.

HISTORICAL BACKGROUND

A number of theories have been developed which seek to explain European integration. According to the neo-functionalist perspective, for example, the process of integration begins in one non-controversial sector and 'spills over' to other areas, including the political. A central notion is that political elites (including bureaucrats) shift allegiances from the nation state to the new setting. Federalists, by contrast, emphasize the role of governments in the process and highlight, in normative terms, the importance of divisions of authority between levels of government (for a summary of these and other perspectives, see Lodge, 1994, pp. xiii–xxvi). Without wishing to diminish the importance of such debates, the primary aim of this section is to provide a brief account of developments so that readers may appreciate current debates more fully; of course, the likely reasons for events are not ignored.

The idea of a united Europe is not new. However, it is during the post-war period that the institutional foundations which have resulted in the enmeshing of the economic, legal and political systems of member states were laid. As can be seen from Table 1.1,

Table 1.1 Key stages in the development of the EU

Year	*Key developments*
1951	Treaty of Paris is signed, bringing the European Coal and Steel Community (ECSC) into effect from 23 July 1952. Membership comprises Belgium, the Federal Republic of Germany, France, Italy, Luxembourg and the Netherlands.
1957	Treaty of Rome is signed, bringing into effect the European Economic Community (EEC) and the European Atomic Energy Community (EURATOM) from 1 January 1958.
1965	Merger Treaty is signed, with the effect of merging the principal institutions of the three communities from 1967. Henceforth the three communities are known collectively as the European Community (EC).
1973	Denmark, the Irish Republic and the United Kingdom join the EC on 1 January.
1981	Greece joins the EC on 1 January.
1986	Spain and Portugal join the EC on 1 January. The Single European Act (SEA) is signed, coming into effect on 1 July 1987, and introduces the first systematic revisions to the founding treaties.
1992	Treaty on European Union (TEU) is signed (following broad agreement in December 1991 at a meeting in Maastricht in the Netherlands). It entails systematic revisions to, and extension of, the existing treaties. Following ratification, the TEU comes into effect on 1 November 1993. Within the EU, the EC represents one 'pillar' of activities; the others relate to foreign and security policy, and justice and home affairs.
1995	Austria, Sweden and Finland join the EU on 1 January.

Source: Adapted from Bulmer (1994, p. 7).

which provides a summary of the major stages of European integration, the first treaty was signed in 1951 to establish the ECSC. The aim of the ECSC was to create a common market for coal and steel among the six founding members: France, West Germany, Italy, the Netherlands, Belgium and Luxembourg. The impetus for the initiative came from France and Germany. To the former, it offered a means of ensuring peace by integrating key industrial sectors, and to the latter it represented a regaining of control of a vital part of its economy as well as further international rehabilitation.

Although invited to join, the UK declined. Lintner and Mazey (1991), amongst others, suggest three reasons for the refusal. First, Britain's experience during World War II had increased the sense of national pride. Second, the UK's relations with other countries were based on the Churchillian notion of three overlapping circles: the United States, the Commonwealth and Europe. To strengthen one - particularly the last - at the expense of the others was unacceptable. Finally, there was implacable opposition to any supranational initiatives which would weaken the sovereignty of Parliament. At least part of this explanation has a resonance in the 1990s. It is interesting in the light of later developments that Jean Monnet, the architect of the proposed ECSC, in inviting Britain to join in 1950 commented:

> I hope with all my heart that you will join from the start. But if you do not, then we will go ahead without you; and because you are realists you will adjust to the facts when you see that we have succeeded. (quoted in Perry, 1994, p. 3)

Monnet, president of the High Authority of the ECSC (the executive), was instrumental in getting the foreign ministers of the six members to meet at Messina in 1955 to consider further integration. Having agreed a resolution that 'the moment has come to go a step further towards the construction of Europe' (quoted in Nicoll and Salmon, 1990, p. 11), they established an intergovernmental committee chaired by Paul Henri Spaak to examine how the process might be extended. In March 1957 two treaties were signed: one establishing EURATOM, the other the EEC. The former was to encourage and supervise the development of that sector whereas the latter had the more general aims of creating a common market with a common external tariff (CET), the free movement of labour and increased co-ordination of economic and social policies. It should be recognized that, in spite of the apparent economic dimension of these developments, the moves towards integration were then, and have remained, largely political (see, for example, Collins, 1994). In 1965 a further treaty was signed which merged the main institutions of the three Communities, thus creating the Commission and Council of the 'European Communities'.

As with the earlier ECSC, Britain was asked to participate but declined, choosing instead to create in 1960 the European Free Trade Association (EFTA) with Sweden, Norway, Denmark, Austria and Switzerland. Finland, Liechtenstein and Iceland subsequently became members. As its title suggests, this established a free trade area (see Chapter 4) with a much looser intergovernmental forum than the EC and, consequently, posed no threat to national sovereignty.

By 1968, ahead of schedule, the six EC members had successfully removed all tariffs and quotas and had established a CET. Similar progress followed enlargement of the EC in 1973 when the UK, Denmark and Ireland became members, in 1981 with the accession of Greece and in 1986 when Spain and Portugal joined. However, it became increasingly apparent that non-tariff barriers (NTBs) – such as state subsidies, national preferences in public procurement, and differences in direct taxation, technical regulations and standards – prevented the establishment of a true common or single market, as did impediments to the free movement of labour and capital. It is noteworthy that NTBs increased during the 1980s as member states sought to protect domestic industries (for a useful discussion of this point and the scope of NTBs, see Lintner and Mazey, 1991, pp. 42–53). In February 1986, the then 12 member states signed the SEA which took effect from 1 July 1987. Its aim was to establish a genuine single European market (SEM) by the end of 1992, with the free movement of capital, labour, goods and services. In addition, the act formalized other policy aims such as environmental considerations, health and safety at work, research and development, a social dimension and co-operation in economic and monetary policy. The critical institutional development was the increased provision of qualified majority voting (QMV), notably for single market and health and safety measures.[2] This change undoubtedly enabled the process of integration to proceed more rapidly. However, the interpretation of both 'single market' and 'health and safety' has been the source of some controversy, especially in the social policy field (see Chapter 9).

Economic justification for the '1992 programme' came with the publication of an officially sponsored research project into the 'costs of non-Europe', chaired by Paolo Cecchini. Perhaps tellingly, this was initiated *after* the decision was taken in principle to remove NTBs. The findings of the Cecchini Report[3] suggested that the removal of NTBs would in the medium term add 'between four and seven percentage points on the Community's domestic product ... [offer] inflation free growth ... and [generate] very substantial job creation' (Cecchini, 1988, pp. xvii–xix). This view has not gone unchallenged; some argue that the foundations of the analysis are misconceived (for a rigorous and persuasive critique, see Cutler *et al.*, 1989) while others have noted that not all NTBs are covered by the programme (Lintner and Mazey, 1991). Even if Cecchini's analysis is accepted, the benefits will not materialize unless further progress is made towards the integration of markets; a report from the Economic and Social Committee (ESC) recently identified significant obstacles to the free movement of capital, labour, goods and services (Commission, 1995a). Hughes offers an explanation and critical assessment of the theories of economic integration in Chapter 4.

Several important developments occurred from the mid-1980s to the early 1990s, which created an impetus for further integration. First, it became clear that the economic conditions in member states meant that the impact of the SEM would vary significantly.

Second, the unification of Germany in 1990 - which in effect enlarged the EC without a formal accession treaty - heightened the possibility for some of a Europe dominated by that state. Third, there was an increased interest in membership from outside, reinforced by changes in Eastern Europe, which raised questions about the future nature of the EC. It is for these reasons, coupled with a growing interest in economic and monetary union (EMU) and a concern that the social dimension of membership should not be relegated, that further moves towards integration were agreed at the European Council (Heads of State) meeting held at Maastricht in December 1991. The resultant TEU was signed in February 1992 and was finally ratified by November 1993.

Article B of the TEU contains the following five objectives:

- to promote economic and social progress which is balanced and sustainable, in particular through the creation of an area without internal frontiers, through the strengthening of economic and social cohesion and through the establishment of economic and monetary union, ultimately including a single currency;
- to assert its identity on the international scene, in particular through the implementation of a common foreign and security policy including the eventual framing of a common defence policy;
- to strengthen the protection of the rights and interests of the nationals of its Member States through the introduction of a citizenship of the Union;
- to develop close co-operation on justice and home affairs;
- to maintain in full the *acquis communautaire* [acceptance of all previous legislation]. (Council and Commission, 1992, pp. 7–8)

Notwithstanding the five objectives, the TEU is commonly described as being made up of three 'pillars': the EC (as embellished by the TEU itself), common foreign and security policy, and justice and home affairs. In contrast to the EC, the last two are intergovernmental in nature (that is, based on interstate co-operation). The treaty also enshrined the principle of subsidiarity,[4] introduced a co-decision procedure (see Chapter 2), created a Cohesion Fund and set up a Committee of the Regions (see Chapter 7). In addition to the treaty itself, 17 protocols and 33 declarations were agreed and appended to the main text. These include important issues such as the UK's opt-out from social policy provisions. To achieve its objectives the treaty introduced (or developed) more specific policy themes, including tourism. Before discussing these, it is appropriate to comment briefly on the enlargement of the EU subsequent to the Maastricht treaty.

From 1 January 1995, the EU expanded its membership to 15 with the accession of Austria, Sweden and Finland. This had the effect of increasing the population to more than 370 million and its total economic output by some 7 per cent (*Guardian*, 31 December 1994). The assimilation of these countries into the EU posed no significant difficulties because of their relative wealth and advanced social welfare systems. Future enlargement, however, raises critical issues about the nature of further integration and the institutional arrangements of the EU.

The following countries have applied for membership: Turkey, Cyprus, Malta, Switzerland (suspended following rejection in a referendum relating to proposed membership of the European Economic Area (EEA)),[5] Poland and Hungary, with several other European states also keen to join. Turkey's application is problematic for political reasons and on the grounds that it would cause significant economic dislocation, though negotiations have concluded in the creation (subject to ratification) of a customs union (*Guardian*, 8 March 1995). It is expected that, of the remainder, Cyprus and Malta face fewest obstacles to accession (though again there are political questions to be resolved prior to Cyprus's entry).

The EU also has 'Europe Agreements' with several countries, including Poland, Hungary, the Czech and Slovak Republics, Bulgaria and Romania, and is negotiating similar arrangements with other states. These are noteworthy because they represent a pre-accession strategy (implying eventual membership) involving the development of closer economic and political ties (Commission, 1994c). Although the timetable for future enlargement has not been set – it will in part be dependent upon the outcomes of the 1996 Intergovernmental Conference (IGC) – it is clear that gaining full membership will, for some, be a slow process. It is likely, therefore, that this issue will be on the EU's agenda for the foreseeable future.

Enlargement to include Eastern European countries would raise important questions in terms of EU tourism and related policies. Undoubtedly, there is great potential for tourism development but significant investment is required – for example in infrastructure and training – which would probably necessitate resources being diverted from existing programmes. Moreover, the application of the other policy areas discussed below to these countries would be problematic (for a discussion of tourism in Eastern Europe, see Lockwood, 1993; and Hall, 1993).

EU POLICIES AND THE HOSPITALITY AND TOURISM INDUSTRIES

The remaining part of this chapter offers a summary of the implications of European integration for the hospitality and tourism industries by considering the various policies spawned by that process. It draws heavily on the other chapters in the book and readers are, therefore, referred to them for development of the issues.

Perhaps one of the most striking features of any investigation into this area is the relative inactivity of public policy-makers with regard to these major industries. As Robinson (Chapter 5) points out, it took 25 years after the signing of the Treaty of Rome before any serious attempt was made by the Commission to create a degree of coherence in this field. It was not until 1988, for example, that 'Ministers of Tourism' from the member states held their first formal meeting. This is not to suggest that there were no measures of direct relevance – there were in a range of policy areas – but the approach was piecemeal and *ad hoc*. The reasons for the reticence to develop a tourism policy are undoubtedly multifarious, but probably centre on the varying interests of member states (including the perception that individual countries can best deal with the issues pertinent to themselves) and the difficulty of co-ordinating policies for such a fragmented sector.

In 1982 the Commission issued the first comprehensive policy statement on tourism. The 'Initial Guidelines' attempted to draw together the various strands of policy and noted the importance of the sector to the European economy. Although it identified a wide range of policy issues, from freedom of movement of workers and tourists to regional policy, it emphasized three overlapping priority areas: seasonality, alternative forms of tourism (including spatial and temporal considerations) and social tourism.

During the 1980s the European Parliament played a particularly active role in promoting the idea of a tourism policy. This included successfully calling for the designation of 1990 to be European Tourism Year (ETY). Although not a conspicuous success with the wider population, the Commission's assessment of the project was sanguine; amongst other things, it noted its unifying influence on officials and that it had promoted a greater sense of common purpose amongst the agencies involved. The initiative was followed by the 'Community Action Plan to Assist Tourism', which was adopted in large measure by the Council in 1992, and precipitated a three-year plan (1993–6). Robinson (Chapter 5) offers a more detailed description, but by way of illustration, priorities included promoting Europe as a tourist destination, improving the knowledge of the industry, encouraging the staggering of holiday periods, supporting co-operation between regions, strengthening the protection of tourists as consumers, promoting cultural tourism and considering more fully the environmental impact of tourism. Additional considerations, such as the freedom of movement of tourists and workers, are also seen as important.[6] The breadth of these issues, which are dealt with separately below, reinforces earlier observations regarding policy co-ordination. Clearly, regional policy, consumer policy and environmental policy are of direct relevance to the development of tourism but are dealt with by different Directorates General (DGs) which, in turn, have wider concerns than the tourism and hospitality sectors.

Notwithstanding some successes – for example the Package Travel Directive in 1993, environmental measures and the use of regional development funds – Robinson's evaluation of tourism policy is that insufficient attention has been paid to improving the quality of the tourism product and to addressing Europe's declining share of the global market. Failure to deal with such issues does not augur well for the development of the sector into the next century.

The Commission's recent green paper (Commission, 1995c) and its adoption of a multiannual programme (Commission, 1996a) are, arguably, a reflection of growing official recognition of tourism's importance within the EU. The former, produced as part of the preparations for the 1996 intergovernmental conference, provides policy-makers with four options regarding the future role of the EU in this field. The first is to reduce or eliminate European-level involvement. An argument in favour of this option is that the three areas officially considered to be essential to the development of tourism – consumer protection, diversification of the tourism product and transport – would still be dealt with at a European level by various Directorates General (DGs). The second possibility presented is to retain current arrangements whereby EU-level activity is circumscribed by the principle of subsidiarity; generally, EU activity in this context involves encouraging intergovernmental co-operation. The third option is to strengthen EU action within the existing treaties. The appeal of this is that the sectoral effects of a wide range of policies would be more fully considered on a regular basis. The final choice put forward is to strengthen significantly the role of the EU in the development and management of the European tourism industry.

It appears that some leading officials favour increasing the 'competence' of the EU to act in the field of tourism, i.e. option four (HOTREC, 1995). If the final option were adopted, it would have far-reaching consequences for the development of tourism in Europe.[7]

The multiannual programme, which will operate between 1 January 1997 and 31 December 2000, aims to increase the competitiveness of the European tourism industry. Entitled 'Philoxenia' (hospitality), its objectives are to:

- improve knowledge in the field of tourism;
- improve the legislative and financial environments for tourism;
- raise the quality of European tourism (which includes the promotion of sustainable tourism and the removal of obstacles to tourism development);
- increase the number of tourists from third countries.

The programme is the outcome of a review of the Action Plan (Commission, 1996b). At this stage – when many of the details are unclear – it is not possible to offer a sensible judgement about whether the programme is likely to achieve its objectives or not.

The single market and EMU

Even if tourism has been a neglected area, the same observation cannot be made of all other policy fields which have an impact on the industries reviewed here. As has been discussed already, attempts to create a single market in Europe dominated official activity during the mid-1980s and early 1990s. The implications of the programme for the hospitality and tourism industries have, to an extent, been considered by the Commission. It sponsored a research project which culminated in a report entitled *The Impact of Completion of the Internal Market on the Tourism Sector* (Commission, 1993). It is a lengthy, two-volume document which, because much of it is taken up with describing measures in various policy fields, is not as insightful as its bulk would suggest. Displaying significantly more caution than Cecchini (1988), it notes: 'The ultimate impact of the completion of the Single Market on different sectors of the tourism industry is difficult to gauge, and even more difficult to quantify' (Commission, 1993, pp. 9–3).

As Table 1.2 shows, the authors anticipate a range of positive and negative impacts. Although a surprising degree of ambivalence is apparent regarding the effects of many specific policy initiatives, the overall impression is one of optimism. Since, it is argued, the SEM will generate economic growth and the increased prosperity will create greater demand from business and leisure tourists, the negative effects will be mitigated. The corollary of this, of course, is that if the analysis which forecasts growth is flawed (they cite the Cecchini report discussed earlier) then the balance between positive and negative impacts may change. The caveats which they provide – including the probability of unevenly distributed economic gains – are not dealt with. Hughes (Chapter 4) provides a systematic treatment of the debates associated with economic integration. His conclusion is that the effect of the SEM is likely to be positive, but not as great as anticipated by the Commission.

In order to evaluate more thoroughly the implications of European integration it is now necessary to consider separately the policies which have emerged as a result of the process. One major proposal, which many see as the logical extension of the SEM initiative, is for EMU. It has already been noted that the goal of a single currency was one of the five objectives of the TEU. The treaty lays down criteria for the convergence of economies as a prerequisite to participation and sets a target date of 1999 (at the latest) when those eligible will give up their own currency in favour of the 'Euro'. Whether or not this is achieved is ultimately a matter of speculation. For the purposes of this chapter it is more productive to explore the debates relating to the impact of such a move; whether this takes place by the target date, a few years later, has many members or a few is of secondary importance.

Naturally, the Commission anticipates significant benefits to firms from EMU. It frequently notes that a tourist setting out on a round-trip journey to include all member states with 40 Belgian francs at the start would by the end have only some 21 francs left as a consequence of the frequent currency changes, even though nothing had been spent on anything else. The absence of such costs should release resources to be spent on the tourism product (Robinson and Mogendorff, 1993).

Healey (Chapter 6) summarizes the debates surrounding moves towards EMU and

Table 1.2 Official evaluation of single market measures on the hospitality and tourism industries

EC policy proposals / Sector	*Transport*	Removal of physical barriers:	Abolish customs posts	European passport/green disc	Easing of statistical checks	Community visa policy	Motor coaches safety control	Coach cabotage measures	Air transport:	Package 2 measures	Package 3 measures	*Competition*	Control of CRS	State aids	Airport ground handling	*Environment*	Fourth Environmental Action Programme	Fifth Environmental Action Programme (proposed)	Environmental impact assessment	Water, air, noise pollution directives	*Employment*	Freedom of movement for workers	Social security for migrant workers	Standard contracting including:	Maximum working hours	Mimimum working wage	Non-standard conditions re:	Part-time/seasonal occupations	Tourism for all, i.e., horizon and youth programmes	Standardization of professional and vocational qualifications	*Consumer protection*	Package Travel Directive	Overbooking Directive	Fire Safety Directive	Standardized hotel ratings	*Fiscal*	Approximation of VAT	Approximation of excise duty	Abolition of duty free	*Regional development*	Structural funds	IMPs	ENVIREG	INTERREG	LEADER
Transportation services																																													
Car			o	o		o														#																	o				o				
Coach			o	o		o	o	o												#																	#				o				
Rail				o		o																															#				o				
Airline				o		o				o	o			#	o					#													#				#	#	#		o				
Airport			#	#		#									#				#																			#	#		o				
Ferry				o		o																															#	#	#		o				
Tourist operators																																													
Travel agent					o								o	o			o	o		o								o		o		#	#	o	o		#	#	#			o			o
Tour operator					o								o	o			o	o		o								o		o		#	#	o	o		#	#	#			o			o
Accommodation and catering																																													
Hotel (large)													#						#	o		o	o			#		o	#	o							#								o
Hotel (SMEs)					o								o							o		o	o			#		o	#	o				#			#					o	o	o	o
Restaurant (large)																						o	o			#		o	#	o							#								o
Restaurant (SMEs)					o																	o	o			#		o	#	o							#					o	o	o	o

Source: Commission (1993, pp. 7–20).

Key: O – Positive impact # – Negative impact CRS – Computer reservation systems
IMPs – Integrated Mediterranean Programmes ENVIREG – Regional Action Programme Concerning the Environment
INTERREG – Initiative to Promote Co-operation between Border Areas
LEADER – Links between Actions for the Development of the Rural Economy
SMEs – Small and medium-sized enterprises

critically examines their implications from the perspectives of those in the hospitality and tourism sectors. Several potential benefits are acknowledged, including the elimination of risks associated with fluctuating exchange rates and the promotion of international travel. However, he also argues that for those countries which are least integrated into the EU, including the UK and southern member states, there is an increased likelihood of economic instability, which would be detrimental to hospitality firms. His argument is that although the convergence criteria agreed at Maastricht should reduce problems during the transition to EMU, it is still highly probable that the economies of the member states will suffer 'asymmetric shocks' (that is, random changes to aggregate demand or to supply which cause inflation or deflation in *some* member states). The removal of monetary policy from national governments, which EMU implies, means that its use as a 'shock absorber' is removed. As he observes, the countries most likely to be affected are generally those which rely on income from tourism.

In addition, Healey points out that to meet the Maastricht convergence criteria, many countries dependent on tourism would have to increase the revenue raised from taxation and control public expenditure in order to reduce their budget deficits and public debt. It may well be that infrastructure programmes which benefit tourism are curbed and taxation levied on hospitality provision such as eating out. He concludes, therefore, that the potential benefits of EMU may be outweighed by the costs and that a significant number of hospitality firms may be detrimentally affected.

Uneven development and SMEs

In seeking to integrate the economies of member states, the EU has long recognized the need to pay attention to promoting the development of particular regions or, indeed, member states. This concern has resulted in a series of measures, the effectiveness of which is, predictably, the subject of much debate (for contrasting perspectives see, for example, Armstrong, 1994; Cutler *et al.* 1989).

Wanhill (Chapter 7) examines the implications of regional policy from the perspective of tourism and the hospitality industry. In this context, he explains that the policy is used in two ways. First, it provides financial aid to support the development of tourism in specified regions. Thus, the Structural Funds may, for example, be used to promote attractions or enhance tourism infrastructure. By contrast, the second approach is to broaden the economies of those regions which may become too dependent on tourism and suffer as a result of, *inter alia*, seasonality.

Regional policy is implemented via a complex range of programmes. Wanhill clarifies the position by examining in turn each of the major policy initiatives which have sectoral ramifications. This is followed by an explanation of the principles which underlie the allocation of financial aid and a consideration of policy priorities for the period 1994–9. Although a degree of uncertainty remains in some areas, such as the relationship between the public and the private sectors, it is interesting and important to recognize that tourism is likely to attract an increased share of available moneys during the second half of the 1990s. Whether or not these amounts would compensate for any reductions in member states' expenditure precipitated by attempting to achieve EMU's convergence criteria remains to be seen.

A concern that the single market would benefit large firms at the expense of smaller operators has led the Commission and Council to conspicuously support the development of SMEs, through its enterprise policy. Numerous initiatives are included within its remit, but in essence it has three central features. First, there is an attempt to create a favourable business environment. The focus here is on the removal of what are seen to be unnecessary and costly administrative, fiscal and legal burdens (deregulation), which have a disproportionate impact on smaller businesses. The second major plank of policy relates to cross-border co-operation between enterprises, or Europeanization. Finally, there is a commitment to the provision of business information and support (Commission, 1994d). Given the fragmented structure of the industry, it would seem reasonable to suppose that this policy would be particularly relevant to hospitality firms.

Thomas (Chapter 8) reviews the various measures taken, critically examines their rationale, and evaluates their implications for the hospitality industry in the light of available empirical evidence. One of the main arguments is that the case for deregulation is, at best, unproven. Although it is appropriate to consider how state intervention impacts upon businesses, there is little hard evidence to support the notion that current requirements stifle enterprising small firms in this industry. The lack of participation in programmes designed to encourage Europeanization is difficult to interpret. It may signal weaknesses in their promotion but, probably more plausibly, it may be a reflection of the minimal benefits on offer to this sector. The Commission's evaluation of the third element of enterprise policy, the provision of business information and support, is positive. However, it is argued in Chapter 8 that the research which informs this assessment is methodologically flawed, though it is tentatively suggested that some of the services provided are potentially valuable.

Social and environmental concerns

The rhetoric of the Commission has, since the founding treaties, included more broadly based concerns than merely the economic, though over the years this has not been particularly apparent from its actions. More recently, however, policies affecting the regulation, free movement and training of labour, as well as environmental measures, have taken on a new impetus. It is to these that attention is now turned.

Much of the social dimension of EU policy has focused on attempts to regulate the employment process. The rhetoric emphasizes the importance of encouraging 'good' employment practice as an integral part of ensuring economic prosperity. The discourse amongst practitioners has, perhaps not surprisingly, been antipathetic to many of the proposals made by the Commission on the grounds of their cost (see for example BHA, 1995).

Lucas (Chapter 9) explores how existing measures and recent proposals are likely to impact upon hospitality and tourism businesses. She argues that their influence may not be as significant in these sectors as in others which are unionized, because the central actors – employers and workers – will not be familiar with new requirements and may, therefore, miss many of them in practice. Moreover, she draws a distinction between 'direct real' labour costs and 'indirect perceived' ones. The former comprise largely basic pay, national insurance and fringe benefits; it is these, she argues, which are central to employment decisions made by hospitality and tourism businesses. Since much of EU social policy falls into the 'indirect perceived' cost category (for example, the cost of losing cases of discrimination or unfair dismissal), the impact of EU initiatives on these sectors is easily overstated.

Related to the policy developments examined by Lucas are those supply-side initiatives which seek to reduce the social cost of high unemployment by improving vocational education and training (VET). As Parsons (Chapter 10) points out, there is an established record of European support for VET relating to tourism and the hospitality industries, but much of this has been pursued as part of regional or local economic development strategies. This fragmentation of provision makes policy evaluation problematic; a difficulty compounded by official preoccupation with analysing output measures such as completion rates and placement records rather than more sophisticated analyses. As far as EU initiatives are concerned, it is also important to recognize that involvement has been peripheral to national measures and, because of subsidiarity, is likely to remain so.

Parsons reviews hospitality and tourism educational provision in Europe, concentrating on intermediate and advanced level courses. He draws attention to the varying patterns of growth – nationally and sectorally – and highlights comparative strengths and weaknesses. He argues that hospitality and tourism management education in Europe is at a watershed. Although there have been advances, there are also identifiable tensions between providers and some sectors of industry which need to be resolved. The plurality of approaches is not necessarily seen as a weakness. However, he notes that significant benefits would accrue from a wider understanding of national approaches to tourism and hospitality management education.

In addition to the social dimension of EU policy, there has been an increased awareness of the importance of sustainable development. Although environmental considerations were not part of the Treaty of Rome, there has been significant European policy intervention dealing with, *inter alia*, noise, waste, and air and water pollution. As Welford (Chapter 11) explains, the SEA and the Maastricht Treaty strengthened the constitutional basis for initiatives in this field to such an extent that policy makers are now required to consider the environmental impact of all policies.

Tourism is seen as a priority within the fifth environmental action programme, which was introduced in 1992. Welford explores the issues raised by this, noting that the Commission has identified three key areas for action: better management of mass tourism, sustainable tourism development, and modifications of tourist behaviour. Following an outline of EU policy in this field, he discusses the idea of sustainable tourism in more detail. Finally, consideration is given to what firms in the hospitality industry might do in order to improve their environmental performance. Welford argues that this can be achieved by the development of environmental policies, by audits of environmental impacts and through the creation of comprehensive environmental management systems. He concludes by suggesting that firms in the sector are well advised to act in anticipation of future public policy interventions.

Consumer interests

The final two policy areas discussed in the book focus upon EU policies designed to protect consumers of hospitality and tourism services. Leslie (Chapter 12) provides an overview of key consumer policy developments: measures affecting consumer rights, information, safety, the Package Travel Directive and Timeshare Directive as well as other, miscellaneous initiatives. He notes that in some areas, notably the Package Travel Directive, significant progress has been made in protecting consumer interests which should ultimately enhance practice among industry operators. By contrast, action in other spheres, for example standardized information on hotels, has been tentative. This is perhaps surprising at a time when attention is being given to the promotion of a *European* tourism product.

North's contribution (Chapter 13) examines the regulatory framework designed to ensure food safety. Following an outline of the EU's approach – including an explanation of the Hazard Analysis Critical Control Point (HACCP) model, which plays a key role in food safety policy – he offers a systematic critique. Central to his position is the assertion that officials fundamentally misunderstand the HACCP system, confusing hazards with risks. As a consequence, there is a tendency towards excessive control even where risks to food safety are marginal or non-existent. However, North also provides guidelines whereby practitioners, or their advisers, may challenge the interpretation of regulations and, therefore, avoid what are seen as unnecessary burdens.

CONCLUDING COMMENTS

The brief review of developments discussed in this chapter highlights the increasingly pervasive influence of EU policies on the business environment within which hospitality and tourism organizations operate. Although the rhetoric of policy makers points to significant benefits, the actual effects of intervention may fall short of official expectations. For some areas, this implies a need to reconsider how policy instruments might be more effectively deployed to achieve particular aims. In other fields, a more fundamental reassessment may be required of what constitutes desirable goals. Above all, perhaps, the chapter has demonstrated the need for continued analysis and debate of the implications of European integration for the tourism and hospitality sectors.

NOTES

1. The causes of such trends are the subject of some debate, much of which has centred on the efficacy of the structural theory of business demand: cf. Hughes (1993) and Slattery (1994).
2. QMV is a system whereby countries have a differing number of votes depending upon their size. Currently, large countries such as the UK, Germany and France have 10 votes, whereas smaller ones have fewer; for example, Austria and Sweden each has four. A qualified majority is achieved when 62 votes out of 87 are in favour of a proposal.
3. The results of the research are contained in 16 volumes. However, more accessible summaries are Cecchini (1988) and Commission (1988).
4. The TEU inserts a new article (3b) into the EEC treaty which defines subsidiarity as follows:

   > In areas which do not fall within its exclusive competence, the Community shall take action ... only if and in so far as the objectives of the proposed action cannot be sufficiently achieved by the Member States and can therefore, by reason of scale or effects of the proposed action, be better achieved by the Community.
   >
   > (Council and Commission, 1992, pp. 13–14)

   Perhaps not surprisingly, this has been interpreted in a variety of ways (see Collins, 1994, pp. 27–30).
5. The EEA is an agreement between the EU and EFTA with the intention of extend-

ing most of the single market measures to EFTA states (for a discussion see Perry, 1994, pp. 235–41).

6. The so-called 'Schengen countries' – France, Germany, Belgium, the Netherlands, Luxembourg, Italy, Greece, Spain and Portugal – have agreed to the abolition of internal border controls. Austria has submitted an application to participate (March 1995) and Sweden and Finland have not ruled out such a move. The UK, Ireland and Denmark have decided not to join. Although clearly in sympathy with EU objectives, the Schengen Agreements are outside the framework of the EU (see Commission, 1995b).
7. It is interesting that both the Tourism Society and the Confederation of National Hotel and Restaurant Associations in the European Community (HOTREC) have been cautious in their responses to the proposals. The former argues that the real choice facing the EU is between the last two options, preferring the third largely because of the reduced risk of 'restrictive' regulations being imposed on the industry (Robinson, 1995). HOTREC adopts what it considers to be a pragmatic position, choosing to emphasize three preconditions for *any* official action in this field: increased representation from industry during policy deliberations, greater deregulation and, somewhat vaguely, assistance for the tourism industry (HOTREC, 1995).

REFERENCES

Armstrong, H. (1994) 'Community Regional Policy' in Lodge, J. (ed.) *The European Community and the Challenge of the Future*, 2nd edition. London: Pinter, 131–51.

BHA (British Hospitality Association) (1995) 'Europe Presses De-reg Button', *Voice*, **4(2)**, 24–5.

Bulmer, S. (1994) 'History and Institutions of the European Union' in Artis, M.J. and Lee, N. (eds) *The Economics of the European Union: Policy and Analysis*. Oxford: Oxford University Press, 4–31.

Cecchini, P. (1988) *The European Challenge – 1992: The Benefits of a Single Market*. Aldershot: Wildwood House.

Collins, C.D.E. (1994) 'History and Institutions of the EC' in El-Agraa, A.M. (ed.) *The Economics of the European Community*, 4th edition. London: Harvester Wheatsheaf, 21–44.

Commission (Commission of the European Communities) (1988) 'The Economics of 1992', *European Economy*, **35**.

——(1993) *The Impact of Completion of the Internal Market on the Tourism Sector*, DG XXIII. Brussels.

——(1994a) *Report from the Commission to the Council, the European Parliament and the Economic and Social Committee on Community Measures Affecting Tourism*, COM (94) 74 Final.

——(1994b) *Tourism Policy in the EU*, Background Report, ISEC/B24/94.

——(1994c) *The Enlargement of the European Union*, Background Report, ISEC/B19/94.

——(1994d) *Integrated Programme in Favour of SMEs and the Craft Sector*, COM (94) 207 Final.

——(1995a) 'The Working of a Single Market: A Major Challenge', *Frontier Free Europe*. February. Luxembourg: OOPEC.

——(1995b) *The Schengen Agreements*, Background Report, ISEC/B4/95.
——(1995c) *The Role of the Union in the Field of Tourism*, COM (95) 97 Final.
——(1996a) *Proposal for a Council Decision on a First Multiannual Programme to Assist European Tourism 'PHILOXENIA' (1997-2000)*, COM (96) 168 Final.
——(1996b) *Report on the Evaluation of the Action Plan to Assist Tourism*, COM (96) 166 Final.
Council and Commission (Council and Commission of the European Communities) (1992) *Treaty on European Union*. Luxembourg: OOPEC.
Cutler, T., Haslam, C., Williams, J. and Williams, K. (1989) *1992 – The Struggle For Europe*. Oxford: Berg.
Go, F.M., Goulding, P.J. and Litteljohn, D. (1992) 'The International Hospitality Industry and Public Policy' in Teare, R. and Olsen, M. (eds) *International Hospitality Management*. London: Cassell, 36–66.
Hall, D.R. (1993) 'Tourism in Eastern Europe' in Pompl, W. and Lavery, P. (eds) *Tourism in Europe: Structures and Developments*. Wallingford: CAB International, 341–58.
HOTREC (1995) *The HORECA Sector and the European Union*. Brussels: HOTREC.
Hughes, H. (1993) 'The Structural Theory of Business Demand: A Comment', *International Journal of Hospitality Management*, **12(4)**, 309–11.
Jansen-Verbeke, M. and Spee, R. (1995) 'A Regional Analysis of Tourist Flows within Europe', *Tourism Management*, **16(1)**, 73–82.
Lintner, V. and Mazey, S. (1991) *The European Community: Economic and Political Aspects*. London: McGraw-Hill.
Litteljohn, D. (1993) 'Western Europe' in Jones, P. and Pizam, A. (eds) *The International Hospitality Industry*. London: Pitman, 3–24.
Lockwood, A. (1993) 'Eastern Europe and the former Soviet States' in Jones, P. and Pizam, A. (eds) *The International Hospitality Industry*. London: Pitman, 25–37.
Lodge, J. (1994) (ed.) *The European Community and the Challenge of the Future*, 2nd edition. London: Pinter Publishers.
Long, J. and Richards, G. (1993) 'Unification of Europe: Implications for Tourism'. Leisure Studies Winter University. Wageningen: University of Wageningen.
Nicoll, W. and Salmon, T.C. (1990) *Understanding the European Communities*. Hemel Hempstead: Philip Allan.
Perry, K. (1994) *Business and the European Community*. Oxford: Made Simple Books.
Robinson, G. and Mogendorff, D. (1993) 'The European Tourism Industry – Ready for the Single Market?', *International Journal of Hospitality Management*, **12(1)**, 21–31.
Robinson, K. (1995) 'Potential future role of the European Union in the field of tourism', *The Journal of the Tourism Society*, **86**, 12–13.
Slattery, P. (1994) 'The Structural Theory of Business Demand: A Reply to Hughes', *International Journal of Hospitality Management*, **13(2)**, 173–6.
Viceriat, P. (1993) 'Hotel Chains', *European Economy*, **3**, 365–79.
Zhao, J.L. and Merna, M. (1992) 'Impact Analysis and the International Environment' in Teare, R. and Olsen, M. (eds) *International Hospitality Management*. London: Cassell, 3–30.

TWO

The dynamics of decision making in the European Union

Juliet Lodge

INTRODUCTION

This chapter examines how decisions are made in the European Union (EU). It begins by looking at the confusion over the nature of the EU polity, outlines some of the reasons for this, scrutinizes the current set of reasons and shows how decisions are made. It ends with a comment on the problems confronting the EU's decision makers in managing policy and decision making, on the eve of enlargement to include small, Mediterranean, island states and states in Central and Eastern Europe. The dilemmas facing them mean that further institutional and treaty reform is inescapable. Whether this leads the EU to develop itself overtly as a decentralized, heterogeneous and diverse federal system or to abandon its past successes and transform itself into another Council of Europe, unable to legislate on behalf of its people, remains to be seen.

As will become apparent from the discussion of the legislative and policy-making processes below, insider knowledge of what is on the agenda, what official thinking is, who is responsible for what areas of policy formulation and the allocation of funds under specific EU Structural Funds and programmes is vital for tourism organizations seeking to influence outcomes. A premium is placed on good communication between the Commission, the European Parliament (EP) and the various outside bodies interested in EU policy, in shaping and influencing its content, orientation and outcomes. Knowledge of who does what, when, how and why is important. Timing of representations is crucial. Playing a 'European card' rather than a parochial, narrow, national, regional or local one is the precondition of success. Therefore, links across national boundaries with sister groups and interests are critical. Knowing when white and green consultative papers are about to be issued, knowing how to make representations at EU level and through EU umbrella bodies as well as directly through Members of the European Parliament (MEPs) and Commission officials in order to influence the shape that draft policy is taking is important. It is no longer possible to rely solely on national ministers or national MPs. The latter are almost completely ineffective in influencing policy.

BACKGROUND

The system of decision making in the EU is no more impenetrable than that of the member states. Indeed, some would argue that it is a good deal more open. Why then does the tension persist between the myth and the reality of decision making? The notion of a closed and implicitly corrupt Eurocracy contrasts ill with the notion of open, representative and accountable government. The result is confusion. The confusion inheres in trying to square the circle: the EU is not a state, nor is it monolithic. It is not peopled by mandarins perpetrating obscure and arcane practices, nor by politicians comprising a European-level government. The EU is neither a federal state nor a simple and strictly intergovernmental organization. It is a mixture: familiar patterns of government, private and public sector interaction typical of liberal democracies characterize its decision-making practices. While this should provide an anchor and help to begin to make it comprehensible, rhetoric disguises its openness.

The incomplete fit between familiar practices from within a given nation state and the supranational system reveals its complexities, obscures its simplicities and confounds easy comparison with national systems. What characteristics exist that are similar to those with which policy makers in the member states are more or less familiar? First, there is a division of power (albeit an imperfect one) between the executive, legislative and judicial branches of what might loosely be called the EU-level of government. Second, there are horizontal and vertical divisions and lines of communication between policy makers at local, regional, national and supranational levels. Third, there are mechanisms to facilitate interaction and involvement; for example, in the processes of either influencing – via lobbying and bidding for Euro-funds and programmes – or implementing legislative outcomes.

Against this, there can be no doubt that practices confound the extent to which the system is open. Policy makers from within the member states' public and private sectors may be unfamiliar with the routines, standard operating procedures, norms and discipline of diplomatic settings, negotiations, the variety of languages and politico-cultural differences. All may prejudice and cloud understanding of the typical way in which decisions are made.

Moreover, the decision-making system itself, while flexible, has also been subject to some potent changes and reform over the past decade. Numerous legislative procedures exist. Reforms were introduced by the Single European Act (SEA) and then by the Treaty on European Union (TEU). Further reforms are essential at the 1996 Intergovernmental Conference (IGC) if the EU is to be capable of managing its existing agenda and admitting new members.

THE CURRENT SYSTEM

More than eight different legislative procedures exist. They differ vitally in terms of the amount of say in the final outcome the EP, national civil servants and the Council of Ministers have. This chapter will focus on the main legislative procedures. It will not address those procedures in which the Commission has full discretion (mainly over established and agreed technical areas) nor those in which the influence and tendency of national civil servants to claw back authority from the EU level is marked (the so-called comitology arrangements). Nor will it probe the budgetary procedure in which the Council and EP act as the two arms of the EU's budgetary authority. It will focus, therefore, on the consultation, co-operation, co-decision and assent procedures, paying particular attention to the last two, which are likely to become more widespread after the 1996 IGC. What are the rules of the game and who are the main players in the system?

RULES OF THE GAME

The bodies that make policy and legislate on it are the Commission, the Council of Ministers and the EP. The European Court of Justice (ECJ) is the EU's federal court. It interprets the law and adjudicates in cases of disputes and when member states have failed to ensure that legislation is enacted as agreed. Neither the ECJ nor the Court of First Instance will be dealt with here. Nor will the Court of Auditors, which has to scrutinize the EU's finances and requires financial regulatory reporting. But it is essential to remember that European Community (EC) law and EU law take precedence over national law in instances where a conflict between the two may arise. This results not from some draconian power the Court arrogates to itself but from the agreement of the member governments when they decided to create the EC. All member states agree to be bound by the rule of law; all agree to implement legislation passed through the normal legislative procedures; and all agree to implement it even if, during the passage of that legislation, they have either opposed the measure, abstained on the vote or been outvoted in the Council.

The Commission, Council and EP are the legislative actors at the EU level. They are assisted by the Economic and Social Committee (ESC), which has an advisory role, and the Committee of the Regions (established by the TEU), which has a consultative, advisory role but, like the ESC, no power to pass, reject or amend legislation. This is not to say that neither has any influence, merely to underline the fact that formally neither is a legislative organ. The ESC has had some impact on technical proposals but it cannot veto legislation. Nor can the Committee of the Regions. Suggestions that these bodies constitute a third chamber are implausible. Both, instead, have been discussed as candidates for abolition.

Because both are consulted by the Commission, they are the object of some lobbying activity by EU-level umbrella as well as national interest groups, chambers of commerce, local government agencies, professional associations and so on. However, the primary targets of interest group activity remain the Commission (which from its inception encouraged direct links between itself, umbrella Euro-interest groups and union bodies) and the EP, which has come under increasingly intense pressure from lobbyists. Indeed, a list of officially recognized groups was to be set up but it has run into difficulties regarding openness and transparency.

These are the bare bones of the rules of the game. Let us briefly sketch in the composition and roles of the key EU-level institutions.

THE COMMISSION

The Commission is a Eurocracy headed by 17 appointees nominated and appointed by common agreement of the member governments. In practice, big member states have two commissioners apiece and the others one. The EU's further enlargement impels reappraisal of this distribution, and it has been suggested that Commission representation be regionalized so that clusters of small states share a commissioner instead of having one each. Already an implicit hierarchy exists in terms of the portfolios that each commissioner has and the responsibilities under them.

The commissioners are supported by a bureaucracy headed by the secretary general, normally an influential and experienced bureaucrat. The bureaucracy is divided into Directorates General (DGs, each comprising around 250 people) that broadly mirror the administrative responsibilities for given policy areas. These are not entirely self-encapsulated, and sometimes contradictory or not quite compatible initiatives emerge from different DGs on aspects of cognate policy areas. The Commission's size has been much vilified, although it is smaller than many cities' local authorities. The secretariat has over 12,000 officials, translators and interpreters, recruited mainly by competitive examination. National civil servants may also be seconded to these DGs.[1]

The process of selecting the Commission is often protracted and highly political. Commissioners are strictly speaking chosen on the grounds of their general competence and impeccable credentials of independence. But governments deal among themselves over the allocation of the portfolios and the nominees. The aim is usually to strike an ideological balance in the centre ground. The big member states usually appoint commissioners from the governing party or governing coalition members and, where appropriate, the main opposition party. Over the years, more and more senior politicians have been appointed to the Commission.

The selection of the Commission president is especially contentious. The post has usually rotated informally between the big and the small states. The Commission president plays an extremely important role inside the EU and as one of its external representatives. Intense political consultations precede the appointment of the Commission president, whose term of office, nominally two and a half years, usually runs for the full term of the Commission. The renewal of the term of office is plagued with uncertainty, especially when either major initiatives are under way or general elections occur in one of the big member states – and especially in that of which the Commission president may be a national. The Commission president plays a limited role in the distribution of portfolios: the more important ones tend to go to the big member states and/or most experienced and senior members. The EP has a voice in confirming the Commission's appointment (via its vote of investiture on the incoming Commission) and it alone can sack the Commission *en bloc*, by a two-thirds vote of its members – something which has never yet happened. As from 7 January 1995, under the TEU amendments, member governments have also to consult the EP before nominating the Commission president. The president and other commissioners thus nominated are subject to a vote of approval by the EP, after which they are officially appointed by common accord of the member governments.

Powers and responsibilities

The Commission's most vital, political and sensitive task is that of initiating legislation. It also exercises wide-ranging rule-making, supervisory, executive, managerial and bureaucratic functions. Where technical and administrative matters are concerned, it performs the rule-making role associated with national bureaucracies. It has wide executive responsibilities in supervising, monitoring, co-ordinating, ruling on and managing the implementation of EU policies and finances (including structural and non-structural funds, levies, exports refunds, programmes, etc.). Much supervision of EU policy is devolved to local national agencies and the Commission, because of inadequate resources, maintains a watching brief. The efficiency with which it performs such tasks can be seriously impaired by local practices.

The Commission's functions can be broadly grouped under the following headings. It has the following roles:

- to initiate legislation (only exceptionally may other institutions engage in this);
- to administer policy (in some areas, such as agriculture, it has extensive responsibilities, which have been delegated to it by the member governments);
- to act as guardian of the treaty and the *acquis communautaire* (that is, all legislation adopted so far) in ensuring that EU policy forms a consistent whole and that member states fulfil their obligations to implement policy;
- to mediate and conciliate among the member governments, institutions and competing groups in order to promote compromises based, preferably, on the principle of upgrading the common interest rather than on the lowest common denominator;
- to be the watch-dog of the EU in ensuring the proper functioning and development of the common market;
- to represent the EU in third countries and many international organizations;
- to act as the conscience of the EU in proposing legislation derived from the Treaties' goals and/or in view of perceived need.

Appointed *en bloc*, the Commission takes collective responsibility for decisions on a collegiate basis, although individual commissioners assume responsibility for one or more portfolios. The Commission has both political and bureaucratic functions. Politically, the most potent and important power is the right to initiate legislation – a right reserved almost exclusively to the Commission. Once the Commission has tabled a proposal, it is almost inevitable that it will eventually be adopted. This is because the Commission never tables anything lacking broad support and because the Council, in order to reject the draft proposals, has to be unanimous: something that is extremely difficult to achieve. That is why integration is said to be locked in once the Commission has made the initial move.

The Commission exercises its powers in complete independence. It may not seek or follow instructions from individual member governments or other interests (TEU art. 157.2). In theory, commissioners are autonomous and give a solemn undertaking, during a special session of the ECJ, to remain above national politics and the advancement of national interests. In practice, this independence is less than absolute because political realities intrude. While national governments cannot remove commissioners whose policies they dislike, they can refuse to reappoint them.

The Commission is neither a government nor a bureaucracy. It possesses features of both. It has many of the attributes of bureaucracies, and while it is committed to impartiality, it cannot advance integration unless it has political vision and a realistic view of medium-term possibilities. In exercising its functions, it no longer merely executes the Rome Treaty, but interprets the spirit of the Treaties in a bold manner. It is significant that Treaty articles are normally drawn in wide, general terms whose detailed interpretation is left open. The same is true of many Commission programmes and proposals, although these are becoming increasingly detailed. In principle, the parameters for action are set out in the Treaties and then in the work programmes.

Functions

Acting in a bureaucratic capacity, the Commission organizes its work along typical bureaucratic and, hence, hierarchical lines. The hierarchy makes for rigidities, which may result in inadequate co-ordination at horizontal levels – that is, across DGs – and sometimes vertically within them and between the Commission and national administrations. While a commissioner is responsible for a given portfolio, proposals require the endorsement of the whole Commission. The College of Commissioners meets weekly and takes decisions by consensus (by majority vote if necessary).[2]

The Commission president comes into his or her own in respect of sensitive issues that cut across several areas, since he or she is generally responsible, certainly at the political level within the Commission, for promoting consensus and ensuring policy co-ordination. The secretary general has administrative responsibility for co-ordination. In theory, the College is tasked with this too; in practice, issues are thrashed out by the *chefs de cabinet* or by special standing or *ad hoc* co-ordinating committees or task forces.

Proposals are not fashioned out of thin air. They represent the culmination of extensive consultations with leading representatives of Euro-level interest groups, national experts and senior civil servants, and (where appropriate) politicians. (For a discussion of how hospitality organizations might influence the policy-making process, see Thomas, 1996.) The SEA provided for an overhaul of procedures, resulting in a contentious decision on committee procedures colloquially known as 'comitology'. This provides for four main committee procedures under which the Commission is increasingly inhibited by national bureaucracies. These consist of advisory committees; management committees, first set up in 1962 to deal with agriculture, and widely and successfully used; regulatory committees, which extend the management committee procedure to other fields but which also provide for greater appeals to the Council; and a special procedure for commercial policy or actions under safeguard clauses. Comitology at best constitutes an institutional compromise between the need for more effective EU decision making and member governments' desire to maximize national influence at all stages over the Commission's decisions (Docksey and Williams, 1994, p. 121). At worst, it jeopardizes Commission independence and the effectiveness of EU measures, not least because the Council, despite assurances to the contrary, has favoured the resort to the most inhibitory arrangements.

THE COUNCIL OF MINISTERS

Composition

The Council of Ministers comprises ministers (or their substitutes) from the ministries concerned in their own member state with the subject of legislation before them. For example, ministers responsible for tourism industries would be expected to decide on proposals relevant to their sector, agriculture ministers decide on agricultural issues, finance ministers on budgetary matters, and so on. In other words, the Council of Ministers' composition varies according to the subject matter of legislation on the table. Sometimes jumbo Councils are convened (for example, of finance and economics ministers – the so-called ECOFIN Councils) on cognate issues. Increasingly, issues overlap the competence of several ministers, but the Council's work is rarely organized sufficiently effectively to allow all the relevant ministers to be there: all have primary responsibility for domestic politics, which frequently intrude and interfere with timetables and meeting schedules. The result is that legislation becomes protracted or decisions are deferred, pending, for example, the outcome of a national election in which the opposition might be returned victorious, with a different view of a legislative item before the Council. (However, new legislative deadlines do deter the prevarication typical of the 1970s.)

This means that it is important for member governments to organize their own domestic scrutiny of EU draft legislation in such a manner as to ensure that all the relevant domestic ministries have a chance to consult with each other and co-ordinate an appropriate response before the minister, or the minister's deputy, participates in the Council meeting at which the legislative decision is to be taken. It is no good hoping that an item can be postponed or vetoed: the veto is part of political rhetoric. Some decisions have to be taken by unanimous vote – where prescribed by the Treaties – but unanimity may be reached with some members being tactically absent or when the Council president senses that consensus exists. It is only in the very recent past that Council votes have been recorded for perusal. Council sessions by and large remain closed and secret, although a few sessions have been televised as part of the attempt to inject openness into decision making (Lodge, 1994).

The Council presidency

The Council meetings are chaired by a president according to an agreed scheme of rotation. This used to be based on an alphabetically, linguistically correct order, but this changed in the TEU to ensure that member states did not end up dealing with the same legislative cycles when they assumed the presidency – that is, that they were not always in charge of, say, the budgetary phase of the legislative cycle. Now, the guiding principle behind the six-monthly rotation of member states is to ensure that there should not be a period (of, for example, 18 months) in which three new or relatively small member states take on the presidency consecutively. The Council presidency alternates between the big and small states in such a way as to prevent hegemony. It is due to be held from January 1996 as follows:

1996 Italy, then Ireland;
1997 Netherlands, then Luxembourg;
1998 UK, then Austria;
1999 Germany, then Finland;
2000 Portugal, then France;
2001 Sweden, then Belgium;
2002 Spain, then Denmark;
2003 Greece, for the first half (the rest to be decided in the light of further enlargement).

The Council presidency is at the interface of the national and supranational system and has been seen as symptomatic of an embryonic co-operative federal system. The Council presidency has a double role to perform. A key political function involves representing the EU to the outside world (often alongside the Commission president). The critical bureaucratic function that devolves on it rests on its role in policy making, administration, mediation, representation and implementation of decisions taken. The process of reconciling national interests is undertaken both by direct bilateral diplomacy, especially on the eve of important councils and European Councils, and, on a daily basis, by COREPER (see below; Lodge, 1993, pp. 16–17).

When a state holds the Council presidency, it is in a position to display its own country's Euro-credentials. It may also work with the Commission to ensure that issues close to its heart are on the legislative agenda at a given point in the six months in which it holds the post of president. Since the Commission sets the agenda, member governments have to prioritize issues on that agenda by striking a balance between their own priorities and the common good. But this high political role must not be used to the detriment of the daily business of holding and managing the presidency. A Council president, helped by the secretariat, is uniquely placed to fashion consensus and compromise, and to ensure both the smooth running of the legislative procedure and also good co-operation between the Council and the Commission and between the Council and the EP. If the Council presidency's position as impartial referee at Council meetings and its preparatory bodies is hijacked by the preoccupations and priorities of its national government, the member state suffers as well as the EU's legislative process. A heavy price is paid in terms of the loss of credibility as a co-operative player. By contrast, a state that performs the duties of Council president with as much impartiality as possible gains in stature. Given that each presidency is entitled to hold no more than seven informal ministerial meetings designed to permit the pooling of ideas and the freest possible exchange of views, a careful president can use such occasions to promote the EU's agenda while skilfully enhancing the member government's capacity to have a frank input into its overall shape. As a rule the foreign ministers and ministers of agriculture and finance meet once informally during each presidency.

Powers and role

The Council is dependent on the Commission. If the Commission does not submit a proposal for legislation, the Council cannot usually initiate legislation. It can ask the Commission to submit such a proposal, and the institutions may be taken before the ECJ for failure to act where the Treaty prescribes that they must. (This happened to the Council in respect of transport policy some years ago.) Its primary role is to adopt legislation in accordance with the rules of the prescribed legislative procedure (discussed below).

The Council never confronts a draft legislative proposal 'blind'. Before a draft is submitted, the Commission will have consulted widely with national officials, other interests and MEPs about its shape, content and goals. It tries to upgrade the common European interest, which means that states are not usually isolated. But they may be so on some occasions, or they may isolate themselves – as the UK has repeatedly done, without thereby securing gains for itself. Moreover, major initiatives normally require the support of France and Germany to proceed: the Franco-German coalition has been an important source of progress over the years. Indeed, on bolder areas of legislation which have subsequently been incorporated into Treaty amendments (such as justice, home affairs, security and so on), a coalition of the founding member states (France,

Germany, Italy, the Benelux) has resulted in steps being taken by them – with Commission co-operation – before they have been extended to the rest of the EU. The Schengen Agreements are a case in point. The scepticism that deters others from participating early on is often replaced by subsequent recognition of the necessity for further co-operation on new issues by the EU.

The Council has come in for criticism because it acts largely in secret and because it has incompatible roles to play. Comprising national ministers whose first obligation is to present and protect domestic interests, collectively the Council acts as the ultimate branch of the EU's legislature, responsible for adopting proposals that reflect the EU interest rather than that of a particular member state.

Majority voting

Under the European Economic Community (EEC) Treaty, most decisions taken during the first two transitional stages between 1958 and 1965 had to be unanimous. The third stage, in January 1966, foresaw majority voting. At this point, France worried that vital national interests might be sacrificed and provoked a crisis in the EEC, but failed to prevent the principle of majority voting from being applied. The Six did agree to disagree, however: they accepted that where vital national interests were at stake, all efforts should be made to try and achieve consensus. This was embodied in the so-called Luxembourg compromise, which was a statement of principle, not an absolute entitlement to a national veto embodied in a Treaty article – something that many politicians still fail to appreciate. However, during the 1970s, states increasingly procrastinated over proposals, demanding 'consensus', so that the system became paralysed. Only following the reforms introduced through the SEA and the TEU was majority voting, combined with a legislative schedule tied in with deadlines, established. The legislative process was accelerated and rendered more efficient, open and democratic as a result, and majority voting has become the norm in most areas. The Council presidency normally does not even call for a vote to be taken. Instead, it is merely noted that the requisite majority in favour of a Commission proposal (possibly amended as permitted by the legislative procedure) exists.

Following the enlargement of the EU in 1995 to include Austria, Finland and Sweden, the majorities required to pass decisions changed. Now a qualified majority is constituted by 62 votes (from any number of member states) providing that the Council's deliberations are based on a proposal from the Commission. In other cases, those 62 votes must include the votes in favour of a proposal by at least 10 member states. The underlying principle implicit in this rule is that a qualified majority must be one that represents two-thirds of the population of the member states (approximately). This is an important principle to recall because, in the event of further enlargement to the EU, it is conceivable that a majority of member states, all of which would be relatively small, could vote in measures opposed by a minority of states who nevertheless represent the majority of the population of the EU. That is why reforming technical provisions on voting within the Council of Ministers is so contentious and important. It is why the 1996 IGC must examine the issue closely and take steps which will safeguard the position of the big member states.

It may be objected that restoration of the national veto would achieve the same. It would not. It would result in deadlock most of the time and depart from the unique feature of the EU: its capacity, which no other international organization shares in full measure, to pass and implement decisions by consent and directly. There is no question of states being able to opt in or opt out of decisions once passed, because they all have a chance to influence policy and are key players in actually taking the decision on whether draft legislation should be adopted or not.

COREPER

The Council is assisted in its work by the Committee of Permanent Representatives (COREPER). This is divided into COREPER I and COREPER II. The latter comprises national 'ambassadors' to the EU. They work with the Council presidency in planning and managing the Council's work. COREPER I consists of deputy representatives primarily concerned with technical and specialized councils. They prepare decisions for the Council and, under the 'A' points procedure, take decisions which are then endorsed perfunctorily by the Council. Polemical and difficult decisions are always referred to the Council for decision.

COREPER is the gatekeeper between the national and supranational systems: its members represent EU positions to national bureaucracies, and national positions to the EU. It is an extremely important body. The fact that it can take decisions has led to the charge that democracy is being undermined by technocracy.

THE EUROPEAN COUNCIL

The European Council was established in 1974 in order to give heads of government and/or state visibility on the EC's stage at a time when pressure was growing for the appointment, in some member states, of special European ministers, who were viewed suspiciously by some premiers as rivals for public attention. It was formally enshrined in the SEA and the TEU. The TEU confers operational responsibility on the European Council under the common foreign and security policy, or on the Council 'meeting in the composition of the Heads of State or Government' for the establishment and conduct of economic and monetary union (EMU). The European Council has been used in the past as an arbitrator when Council meetings have been deadlocked. It has also been able to give impetus to integration by requesting action, and hence Commission initiatives, in new fields outside the Treaties; but the European Council is essentially an intergovernmental body.

The European Council itself consists of politicians, and its meetings are not attended by either civil servants or national experts. Follow-up work is done and monitored by the foreign ministers (meeting in the Council) and by COREPER members.

THE EUROPEAN PARLIAMENT

Since 1979 the EP has been elected by direct, universal suffrage. Although the original Treaties prescribed direct elections, member governments wrongly equated them with the transition of the EEC to a federal state. After many years of wrangling and a very gradual increase in the EP's powers, elections now take place every five years. The number of dual-mandated MEPs has dropped dramatically, and now serving as an MEP is seen as a legitimate career in itself. The EP's term of office broadly coincides with that of the EU Commission. The seats are allocated on the basis of the population of each of the member states, with the largest being given roughly equal representation. However, Luxembourg's population of 300,000 gets six seats, which means that the 'cost' per seat is in practice uneven, even after the adjustments which led to Germany acquiring 99 seats upon unification compared to France's, the UK's and Italy's 87 seats apiece.

The elections are supposed eventually to be conducted according to a common electoral procedure. All states bar Great Britain use a variant of proportional representation (PR). The British first past the post system severely distorts the overall composition and balance of the EP's party groups.

The organization of the EP's business devolves to the party groups. A specific number of MEPs from a minimum number of states is required for a group to gain official recognition. This is important, as it is designed to inhibit excessive fragmentation along national lines and to encourage European compromises and a European mind-set. Moreover, the party groups have privileges, including speaking time in plenary sessions and positions in the all-important standing committees. So-called 'non-attached' MEPs are in a weak position.

The EP is analogous to continental parliaments in the emphasis that is put on committee work, interparty compromise and upgrading the common interest. It is not a confrontational parliament. Party groups sit in a semicircle along an approximate ideological axis which ranges from Communists on the left to nationalists – and even extreme right-wing politicians – on the right. The centre ground is occupied by the two largest and most powerful groups – the Party of European Socialists and the European People's Party.

The EP's powers have increased over the years. From being a body imbued merely with advisory and supervisory powers – notably *vis-à-vis* the Commission – it has acquired genuine legislative power and authority. This has happened primarily since the 1980s as a result of MEPs' own efforts, guided by Altiero Spinelli, in many respects the architect of the EP's Draft Treaty establishing the EU, which inspired the SEA and the Maastricht Treaty. MEPs have carefully exploited their right to determine their own agenda (something many national parliaments cannot do) and to write their own Rules of Procedure. The latter have been interpreted in such a way as to capitalize on the EP's treaty-given powers and to enhance its capacity to legislate in conjunction with a reasonably sympathetic Commission and often less than helpful Council of Ministers. As a result, the EP now has legislative authority, budgetary powers and authority *vis-à-vis* the Commission, Court of Auditors and Council of Ministers.[3] It has many of the attributes and powers of national parliaments, and even, unlike some national lower houses, the right to reject the budget and to amend it within strict confines. However, it is still not seen as entirely comparable to national parliaments.

National parliaments have been excluded from exercising effective scrutiny over what national ministers do in the Council or over the shape of EU legislation. This occurred because national governments decided to relegate them to the sidelines. For them, European integration was to be an executive process. The advent of Euro-elections has severely compromised this position, and national parliaments are beginning to see that they have an interest in working more closely with the EP in order to assert democratic parliamentary control at national and European level. Unfortunately, this process has been held up in the UK, in particular, by ill-informed prejudice against MEPs and by the House of Commons' legendary rivalry with and hostility towards them. The TEU's introduction of a Committee of the Regions (with consultative status) impelled MPs to reappraise their position, as it became clear that regional representatives, local councillors and city representatives might develop a closer – and potentially more influential – position in relation to the Commission and the Council, through the links they hoped to set up with the EP.

THE LEGISLATIVE PROCEDURES

While the TEU does not meet EP criteria for creating a constitution to supplant the existing treaties, it significantly augmented the potential scope of the EU's popularly elected arm of the legislature. The EP has legislative, budgetary and supervisory powers. It participates in the EU legislative process through four main legislative procedures:

- consultation;
- co-operation;
- assent;
- co-decision.

Until 1980, the EP had only a consultative role in the legislative process, coupled with budgetary powers. The 1980 Isoglucose ruling of the ECJ reinforced its position. It used its Rules of Procedure to acquire an indirect right to initiate legislative proposals (art. 138b) and to participate in shaping the legislative agenda through the Annual Legislative Programme (prepared by the Commission and submitted to the EP) and Joint Declarations (first introduced in 1975 when a conciliation procedure was adopted, primarily for budgetary disagreements). Inter-institutional declarations and agreements have been agreed since then on important issues like budgetary discipline (1988 and 1993) and democracy, transparency and subsidiarity (1993).

Consultative procedure

This provides for a single reading in which the EP has the right to be consulted by the Commission on a draft proposal, but no formal right to reject or amend the proposal. Under this system, it issues an Opinion, which the Commission or Council may more or less safely ignore (and, indeed, in the past they frequently did so).

Co-operation and co-decision procedures

The 1987 SEA introduced the co-operation procedure, which applied to only 10 articles of the EEC treaty but covered extremely important areas, including those central to the realization of the single market programme. This paved the way for an expansion in the co-operation procedure to 15 new fields, following the revisions introduced through the Maastricht Treaty on European Union in 1992. In addition, some of the areas previously subject to the co-operation procedure then became subject to the new co-decision procedure.

The co-decision procedure covers 14 articles, but the TEU provides for the expansion of its field of application on the basis of a proposal from the Commission. This is likely to be addressed by the 1996 IGC. Co-decision provides for a third reading but is otherwise analogous to the co-operation procedure. Special majorities and a conciliation procedure are built in to promote compromise. Among the areas subject to co-decision are: free movement of workers (art. 49), right of establishment (art. 54), mutual recognition of diplomas (art. 57(1)), internal market (art. 100b), education (art. 126(4)), trans-European networks (art. 129d), consumer protection (art. 129a(2)), and environmental programmes (art. 130S(3)).

In essence, the co-operation and co-decision procedures rest on the dual principle that no legislation should be adopted which does not have the approval of the elected representatives of the EU people, and that both the Council and the EP should have a say in the passage of such legislation. Perfect equality between the two bodies of an emergent bicameral legislature has yet to be achieved, but significant advances have been made in a relatively short period of time. The majorities which have to be established in the EP and the Council at various junctures in the first and second readings under the co-operation procedure are designed to ensure that the Council takes notice of MEPs' views. For example, if the EP rejects the Council's common position, the Council has to be unanimous to over-rule the EP's decision, which must happen within a deadline of three months. The overall effect has been to expedite legislation and to engage the Commission, Council and EP in constructive dialogue over legislative details and principles. Between 1987 and April 1993, the Commission accepted 56 per cent of EP amendments at first reading and 47 per cent at second reading; the Council accepted 44 per cent and 25 per cent respectively.

Assent procedure

The assent procedure has also been expanded and used politically. The SEA provided for the EP's assent to the conclusion of association agreements (art. 238) and for the accession of new member states to the EC (art. 237). These have been used politically by MEPs, who have argued against enlargement unless specific institutional changes are introduced to enhance democratic practice, for example.

The TEU extended the assent procedure to all important agreements (that is, those setting up a specific institutional framework, or having important budgetary implications, or requiring the amendment of EC legislation pursuant to the co-decision procedure). The EP has to be consulted on all other agreements (except trade, under art. 113). Nine new articles fall under the assent procedure; these include provisions for a uniform Euro-election procedure (art. 138), the powers of the European Central Bank ((ECB), art. 106(5)), freedom of movement (art. 8a) and the objectives of the Structural Funds (art. 130d). The Council, in effect, cannot adopt a legislative act under the assent procedure unless the EP has approved it.

Further provisions attest to the EP's right to hold other institutions accountable. The following now have to report to or inform the EP: the European Council, the Council, the Council president, the Commission, the Court of Auditors, the ombudsman and the European Monetary Institute (EMI) and the ECB. Additional new rights have codified existing EP practices or given it new powers. They include:

- a right of initiative;
- a formal right of inquiry;

- a formal right to receive petitions;
- a right to appoint/dismiss the ombudsman;
- a right to challenge acts and failures to act by other institutions;
- a right to information before budget discharge;
- rights relating to the appointment of the Commission president and the Commission.

The EP was quick to test out its new investiture powers[4] at the beginning of 1993, when MEPs voted on whether or not to endorse the newly appointed Commission. MEPs condemned the weakness of the Commission's programme,[5] and the Socialists threatened to sack the new Commission. However, in practice, close liaison between the Commission and the EP is the precondition of effective action. The two are mutually dependent: the EP requires the Commission's technical know-how and the Commission needs MEPs to legitimize and lend democratic support to it.

The EP retains its interest in preserving a strong Commission able to act independently of national governments. Any weakening in the Commission's authority (as the SEA and TEU seemed to presage) would undermine further integration. The EP is, therefore, mindful of the need to ensure a balanced distribution of power among the legislative institutions in order to promote legitimacy, reveal the distribution of authority to be just and open, and insert appropriate checks and balances which are not open to arbitrary interpretation and abuse. Subsidiarity does not meet this test.

What MEPs still want - and will press for in the IGC process - is the abolition of the distinction between compulsory and non-compulsory spending. That would increase their legislative influence and power immensely.

THE FUTURE OF THE LEGISLATIVE PROCEDURES

The EP's Institutional Affairs Committee proposed that the legislative procedures be cut to three: the co-operation procedure would be dropped. Co-decision would become the norm. The assent procedure would apply for third-country agreements and enlargement. The consultation procedure (the traditional single reading system which prescribes a right for the EP to be consulted only) would apply to foreign affairs. This represents a minimalist position, since the EU currently uses several different legislative procedures producing over eight different permutations. These contribute to the claim that the system is opaque, undemocratic and whimsical.

The inter-institutional declarations and agreements work on the EP's principle that anything that is not expressly forbidden by the Treaty is allowed. While they may be designed to improve harmonious working and inter-institutional relations, they - and other informal changes - have significant implications over the longer term for constitutional amendments which enhance the EP's authority, its legislative capacity, and its powers of control, scrutiny and supervision. These last are designed to ensure democratic accountability over the EU's executive bodies and *vis-à-vis* the Court of Auditors, the ECJ, the European Council, the EMI, the ECB and the Euro-ombudsman (still to be appointed; see Millar, 1994, p. 35).

Changes in the way in which the EP relates to the Commission, in particular, and the Council of Ministers on operational matters and on a day-to-day basis have helped it significantly to augment its authority, influence and ultimately formal powers. For example, requests for information – questions for oral or written answer, committees of inquiry, petitions – can be and are used politically to enhance openness. In addition, requests to the Commission to explain any refusal to comply with MEPs' opinion or requests that a draft proposal be withdrawn have been used politically to very good effect, in order to expand the scope of the EP's influence and form the basis of treaty revisions. Informal arrangements have become entrenched in treaty modifications.

The kinds of arrangement it now seeks are also likely to inform the institutional changes accepted by member governments at the next and subsequent IGCs. That is why a number of measures sought by the EP – including the introduction of a single legislative procedure – are potentially so important to the evolution and shape of the future EU.

THE ROLE OF INTEREST GROUPS

Clearly, the EU has become increasingly relevant to national private and public sector actors. Out of functional necessity as well as for tactical political reasons, in the past the Commission encouraged direct links between itself and umbrella Euro-level interest groups and trade unions like COPA (for agriculture) and the ETUC (European Trades Unions Confederation). There has recently been an exponential growth in lobbying, which makes for difficulties in communication with the Commission and the other institutions.

More than 500 Euro-associations or Euro-groups exist. Besides these, well over 3,000 interest organizations operate at EU level alongside research and consultancy firms, all of which try to influence policy direction and outcomes. Most national firms employ a variety of lobbying strategies,[6] which enable them to capitalize on national, local and EU-level representation (Bennett, 1991; Burgermeier and Mucchielli, 1991; Danton de Rouffignac, 1990).

Major corporate players enter into direct dialogue with the Commission and can thereby weaken the potency of the relevant sectoral interest group: they tend to have their own individual links with EU officials from the main institutions as well as with MEPs, and ensure that they have a Brussels office to enable them to provide two-way communication in pre-decisional phases of policy formulation within the Commission. Given the Commission's technical information deficit on occasion (a deficit which often exists between agencies and interests; see McLaughlin *et al.*, 1993, p. 201), great care has to be taken to ensure that such links are not used or abused by the corporate and business representatives and lobbyists to transmit skewed information. That could lead to policy being formulated and then heavily criticized by sectoral interest groups, to the detriment of those advocating it both within the Commission and within the corporation or business. Lobbyists work hard to retain their credibility with the Commission and therefore will, when necessary, offer unpalatable advice to their clients on the appropriateness or otherwise of lobbying tactics, timing and content.

Authoritative and representative business groups, however, can expect to have their voice heard by the Commission even though, on occasion, component members of these groups – especially larger players – may try and outflank the official representatives. This was particularly true when American and other multinational corporations entered the Euro-interest representation game, attaching importance to non-collective engagement, rather than collective engagement via the Euro-groups. The latter should not be confused with the European Economic Interest Groupings (EEIGs), whose formation the Commission encouraged. EEIGs combine Euro-businesses (companies, partnerships or sole traders) from at least two member states in order to pool research and development, marketing, or the management of given projects. The EEIG must not be set up to make profits in its own right. It is essentially seen as a facilitative mechanism for capitalizing on expertise across borders.[7]

The logic behind working through EU-level representations is based on the theory that the Commission is entrusted with initiating legislation in the European interest. To discern this interest, it is necessary to have a view of what different national sectors want. Different traditions and competing interests and structures can make it difficult for EU-level groups to reconcile diversity and provide the requisite expertise. Consequently, EU-level representation may be less effective than it appears on the surface, and non-European – and often better-resourced – operators are often equally influential. All, however, are keen to ascertain what the Commission's agenda, priorities and resources for given areas are, and to ensure that these are made as consistent as possible with local interests. To some extent, the Commission and local groups are mutually dependent. But a range of lobbying tactics must be employed and all the key institutions approached in order to affect policy outcomes.

BEYOND MAASTRICHT?

The EP attaches importance to measures to ensure the effective functioning of the TEU commitments in new policy areas, as well as the imperative of addressing unemployment and promoting social integration. Its representatives to the IGC Groupe de Reflexion also have a list of issues that it wishes the IGC to confront, namely to:

- examine the composition of the key institutions (including the question of fewer commissioners, possibly introducing regionally grouped commissioners – one for the Benelux, for example; or creating a hierarchy within the Commission – giving new states junior or shadow status, say; and capping the size of the EP at 700);
- examine working methods (including the questions of the Council presidency and universal majority voting in the Council);
- reform decision making, by adopting co-decision as the norm in place of other legislative procedures;[8]
- restore *unicité*; that is, abolish the current three-pillar structure of the TEU (whereby the common foreign and security policy and justice and home affairs are intergovernmental areas, which precludes effective scrutiny and inputs by the EP, and they elude the surveillance of the ECJ altogether) and bring the Schengen Agreement under the EU's umbrella;
- move towards the establishment of a common defence policy, with the EU taking on the Western European Union's competencies;
- maintain the TEU timetable for a single currency and convergence criteria, increase accountability through the EP, and give a commitment to promoting greater employment;
- end the UK opt-out from the Social Chapter, and support stronger policies to promote social and economic cohesion and equal opportunities;
- give higher priority to environmental, youth, educational, consumer and tourism

policy, and a more closely integrated transport policy;
- re-examine the common fisheries policy (adopted as an amendment);
- make a commitment to public service;
- incorporate a new treaty article in support of the principle of equal treatment and non-discrimination on the grounds of sex, age, religion or disability, and opposing racism and xenophobia, together with a commitment to outlaw capital punishment;
- improve co-operation with national parliaments;
- expand the ECJ's jurisdiction to decisions taken under the pillar structure (should that be retained).

The other institutions have also had an input into the deliberations preparing for the IGC. In response to the invitation of the European Council in Corfu in December 1994, the Commission reported on the operation of the TEU to date. Its report stressed the need for strengthening the EU institutions, with tighter decision making, greater qualified majority voting, streamlining of the TEU's 20 different decision-making procedures, and insistence that in future decision making be subject to the following guiding principles:

- effectiveness (including extension of co-decision);
- democracy (parity between the EP and the Council in legislative matters);
- subsidiarity (avoidance of abusing the principle in order to advance particularistic or national interests);
- openness (specifically transparency and public scrutiny of decision making, notably that of the Council).

Both the Committee of the Regions and the ESC, both of which retain a consultative status in the EU, have sought to improve their position, notably in the legislative process, but without seeking the right to veto or pass legislation (something proposed in the past but rejected as implausible). The ESC wants to gain *de jure* recognition as an EU institution and participate more closely with the Commission in the pre-legislative phase of policy making (for example, in the preparation of Green Papers), and with the Council and EP (notably, sending its *rapporteur* as observer to any Conciliation Committee meetings between the two). It wants its advisory powers concerning EMU to be strengthened, and seeks the right to be informed on justice and home affairs (JHA) and consulted on cultural issues. With an eye on enlargement, it also wants its function in respect of promoting dialogue with economic and social partners under association agreements with third countries to be recognized.

The Committee of the Regions seeks amendment of TEU art. 3(b) (on subsidiarity) to include an explicit reference to the regions and local authorities, and the right to institute proceedings before the ECJ if the principle of subsidiarity is infringed to the disadvantage of the regions. Like the ESC, it wants its status upgraded to that of an official institution, alongside the EP, Commission, Council, ECJ and Court of Auditors. It wants a right of initiative, in co-operation with the Commission, when proposals affecting the powers of local and regional authorities are being drafted. It wants parity with the ESC in respect of its consultative function, and full organizational and budgetary autonomy *vis-à-vis* the ESC.

CONCLUDING COMMENTS

The prospect of further EU enlargement makes institutional reform imperative. The biggest problems to be tackled concern the ways in which policy is made, and the questions of who has access to whom, why and how. What voting rules should obtain? What is the optimum size of the various institutions? What political norms and rules of the game should guide the EU – that is, what is meant by liberal democracy and openness? Should there be an EU bill of rights? Do national governments inhibit openness by restrictive national practices and interpretations of EU commitments, including the notoriously difficult areas related to the vetting of public servants? Resource allocation and redistribution are contentious, and all EU programmes are subject to decision rules and policy-making practices which may seriously weaken the position of the states that pay most into the EU coffers, unless institutional changes and amendments to voting practices are adopted. Whether this impels the construction of a recognizably federal EU remains to be seen. Clearly, many issues cannot be reconciled unless steps are taken which will have the effect of deepening European integration.

NOTES

1. For a detailed study of the Commission see Edwards and Spence (1994).
2. For details see Lodge (1993, pp. 11–12).
3. The European Parliament's budgetary powers were increased by treaty amendment in 1970 and again in 1975. The Maastricht Treaty did not augment them, although MEPs sought change.
4. See arguments presented during the SEA deliberations by the EP Committee on Institutional Affairs (1985).
5. Commission of the European Communities (1993); and the reply on the investiture debate by Commission President Delors.
6. For details see Mazey and Richardson (1993).
7. For further information see Roney (1991).
8. For fuller details see Lodge (1995).

REFERENCES

Bennett, R. (1991) *Selling to Europe*. London: Kogan Page.

Burgermeier, B. and Mucchielli, J.L. (1991) *Multinationals and Europe 1992: Strategies for the Future*. London: Routledge.

Commission of the European Communities (1993) *The Commission's Programme 1993–4*, SEC(93) 58 Final, 26 January.

Danton de Rouffignac, P. (1990) *Presenting Your Case to Europe*. London: Mercury Business Books.

Docksey, C. and Williams, K. (1994) 'The Commission and the Execution of Community Policy' in Edwards, G. and Spence, D. (eds) *The European*

Commission. London: Longman.
Edwards, G. and Spence, D. (eds) (1994) *The European Commission*. London: Longman.
EP Committee on Institutional Affairs (1985) *Working Document on the EP Proposals Submitted to the IGC on the Appointment and Powers of the Commission* (Fanti Report), PE 101.517/1, 28 October.
Lodge, J. (1993) 'EC Policymaking: Institutional Dynamics' in Lodge, J. (ed.) *The European Community and the Challenge of the Future*, 2nd edition. London: Pinter.
——(1994) 'Transparency and Democratic Legitimacy', *Journal of Common Market Studies*, **32**, 343–68.
——(1995) *Institutional Affairs*, Discussion Paper No. 3 by the Jean Monnet Group of Experts in the series 'The European Union and the 1996 IGC: Crisis or Opportunity?'. London: Centre for European Union Studies and the Representation of the European Commission in the UK.
Mazey, S. and Richardson, J. (1993) *Lobbying in the European Community*. Oxford: Oxford University Press.
McLaughlin, A., Jordan, G. and Maloney, W.A. (1993) 'Corporate Lobbying in the EC', *Journal of Common Market Studies*, **31**, 201.
Millar, D. (1994) 'A Weak Ombudsman, a Weaker Parliament', *European Brief*, **2**, 35.
Roney, A. (1991) *The European Community Fact Book*. London: Chamber of Commerce.
Thomas, R. (1996) 'Assessing and Influencing the Policies of the European Union' in Kotas, R., Teare, R., Logie, J., Jayawardena, C. and Bowen, J. (eds) *The International Hospitality Business*. London: Cassell.

THREE

The European hospitality industry

Dolf Mogendorff

INTRODUCTION

This chapter will provide an overview of the current characteristics and trends in the European hospitality industry. While it will mainly be concerned with the hotel sector, it will use the Continental approach in also discussing the restaurant sector. After a section reviewing EU tourism in the context of the hospitality industry, it will profile the hotel sector. It will then go on to look at specific areas of importance to the operation and development of the sector, namely hotel chains, hotel capacity, turnover, occupancy and pricing, and employment characteristics. This will be followed by a briefer section which discusses the restaurant sector in similar format, and the chapter will end with some conclusions on the major trends which will affect the hospitality industry.

The statistics used in this chapter have been gathered from a variety of published sources and often summarized for brevity. Due to the fact that this information has been supplied by various EU member countries, which use different methods of data collection and have varying time lags before publication, the main objective of the analysis is to discern trends, rather than to provide precise comparisons.[1]

TOURISM IN THE EU

Within the broader setting of tourism, Europe has developed rapidly as a major destination for world travel over the last four decades. Akehurst *et al.* (1993), quoting World Tourism Organization (WTO) and Organization for Economic Co-operation and Development (OECD) data, state that, between 1950 and 1991, the annual number of international visitors entering the (then) 12 member states of the European Community (EC) increased by a factor of sixteen, from 17 million to 277 million. These figures include intraregional European tourism (the European tourist holidaying within Europe), attractive because of the relatively short distances between destinations and the very wide variety of landscapes and cultures. According to the WTO (1993a), this accounted for 60.6 per cent of all arrivals in Europe in 1991; indeed, this is a trend that can be seen in almost all the member states in terms of both arrivals and bed-nights, with the exception of Denmark, Germany and the UK. The largest non-European market for visitors to Europe in 1993 was the USA, with 7.6 million visitors; they were also by far the largest spenders, exclusive of airfares, with ECU 12 billion (ETC, 1993).

According to Dawson and Go (1995), and in line with the longer-term trends quoted above, growth in international demand for stays in Europe for the period 1975–84 averaged nearly 6 per cent a year. Since then, however, not only South Asia but also East Asia and the Pacific have overtaken Europe, and estimated growth in international arrivals for 1993–2010 for those two regions is estimated to be 6.1 per cent and 6.8 per cent respectively, while that for Europe is estimated to be a mere 2.7 per cent, the lowest growth rate of any of the world's tourist regions (WTO, 1993b). While such forecast growth rates give some cause for concern, the importance of tourism in the European Union (EU) can be discerned from the fact that, in 1993, eight of the top 20 international destinations were EU member states, and in 1994, Europe held 59.6 per cent of the international share of world tourism (HOTREC, 1995).

Within the EU there are marked differences in international tourist arrivals and growth. France consistently achieved number-one ranking as the world's top international tourist destination, with some 60 million visitors (11.72 per cent) in 1993 – nearly as many visitors as the whole of the East Asia and Pacific area. This represented a growth rate of 6.34 per cent in the period 1985–93. After the USA, Spain and Italy attained third and fourth position with 7.81 per cent and 5.14 per cent of the world market respectively, masking a growth rate of a mere 0.65 per cent for the latter over the period concerned. The UK was placed sixth in both 1985 and 1993, with a share of the world-wide market of some 3.74 per cent in 1993 and a growth rate over the period of 3.61 per cent (WTO, 1995).

In purely European terms, the percentage market share again varies greatly between members. According to WTO figures for international tourist arrivals to Europe in 1992, the EC gained 65.51 per cent of that market. France achieved a 31.06 per cent share of the EC market, followed again by Spain (19.14 per cent) and Italy (14.32 per cent), with the UK taking 9.48 per cent and Luxembourg a mere 0.46 per cent (WTO, 1993a).

Average receipts per tourist arrival grew, in the period 1985–93, from US$288 to US$493 in Europe, a 41.6 per cent increase, second only to East Asia/Pacific with 44.2 per cent. In terms of total receipts (excluding international transport), the USA achieved top position, with a growth rate of 15.56 per cent over that period and a share of world-wide receipts in 1993 of 18.48 per cent. While France, Italy and Spain achieved average annual growth rates of 14.47 per cent, 11.23 per cent and 11.47 per cent respectively, their world market share in 1993 was 7.65 per cent, 6.71 per cent and 6.35 per cent respectively, reflecting perhaps a different client profile and varying relative prices for tourist services in the USA versus European destinations. The UK achieved a 4.4 per cent share of receipts world-wide in 1993, with an average annual growth rate over the period of 8.27 per cent (WTO, 1995).

International tourist receipts in Europe for 1992 (HOTREC, 1995) show that the then EC received a share of 73.87 per cent of the European total, while France received a 20.41 per cent share of the EC market, with Spain (19.59 per cent), Italy (18.40 per cent) and the UK (12.51 per cent) gaining the next three places. When compared with the individual EC market shares of international tourist arrivals in Europe for the same year, as set out above, it can be seen that this confirms the lower average spend for

France, while Spain's share did not differ markedly, and Italy and the UK achieved higher average spends. However, such results need to take into account currency fluctuations, which can make countries more or less expensive as a tourist destination. For example, the large devaluation of sterling in 1992 and its removal from the Exchange Rate Mechanism (ERM) forced many UK citizens to spend their holiday in their home country.

While the above analysis shows the great importance which needs to be attached to international tourism as a source of income for the EU it should be remembered that the great majority of tourism takes place in the form of holidays in the home country. According to Eurostat (1994), more than half the adult population of Europe took a holiday in 1992, of which 60 per cent stayed in their own country.

THE HOTEL SECTOR AS PART OF EUROPEAN TOURISM

The hospitality industry in Europe has grown and developed in parallel with the development of tourism on this continent. Although it is recognized that total demand for hotel accommodation comprises domestic and foreign holiday and business demand, these sources are not differentiated in the following analysis.

Europe led world regions in 1993 with a 43.5 per cent share of world-wide hotel capacity, only the Americas coming close, with 38.2 per cent. However, as with the growth league in international arrivals, its percentage change in terms of number of rooms in the period 1985–93 showed only an 8.8 per cent increase, by far the lowest, with South Asia next at 22.5 per cent and East Asia/Pacific with a massive 79.1 per cent over the same period (WTO, 1995).

In 1993, seven EU countries featured in the top 10 world rankings in terms of international hotel capacity, with Italy, Spain, Germany, France, the UK, Austria and Greece together accounting for 33 per cent of the total, thus, in combination, well exceeding the USA at 25.5 per cent (Federacion Espanola de Hoteles, 1994). Figures on nights spent in hotel accommodation in Europe by international tourists for 1992 make interesting reading, because, in those terms, Spain achieved a 21.09 per cent share of the then EC while the UK came second at 16.82 per cent, Italy came third with 15.97 per cent, and France only achieved fourth place with 15.01 per cent (WTO, 1993a). Thus there appears to be no direct relationship between data on international arrivals (where France achieved first place) and nights spent in hotel accommodation.

What is more, according to the WTO figures, while there was a steady growth in nights spent in Europe during the 1970s and 1980s, local conditions have become much more influential in defining growth. The figures quoted in the HOTREC (1995) report show that, for instance, Greece lost almost 15 per cent of its market in 1991, due to the Gulf War, but bounced back with a 13.6 per cent increase the following year, while Italy had been in constant decline in the period 1989–92. The greatest fluctuations in nights spent have been seen in the performance of Spain in the last few years, where, after a drop of 17.46 per cent between 1989 and 1990, there was an almost matched increase of 14.47 per cent in 1991. This was followed by a small increase of 3.40 per cent in 1992, even though the country was heavily promoted that year because of the Barcelona Olympic Games and the World Exhibition in Seville.

When the hotel industry is viewed as part of the overall structure of the tourist industry, it comprises the largest sector, with 'accommodation' at 32 per cent of total receipts, followed by 'dining' with 25 per cent. Other components consist of shopping (24 per cent), local transport (9 per cent), entertainment (6 per cent) and other activities (4 per cent). In other words, with a combined 57 per cent of total turnover, the hotels, restaurants and cafés (HORECA) sector is by far the largest component of the whole tourism industry.

A PROFILE OF THE HOTEL SECTOR

Throughout the EU the hotel sector comprises establishments which vary from the small bed and breakfast to the large resort or city-centre hotel offering a wide range of services. Viceriat (1993) defines hotels in this context as guest houses, boarding houses, tourist accommodation, and lodgings let by the room with limited hotel services. While the smallest establishments are mostly single-location, family-owned and family-managed, the larger units are often part of an integrated or voluntary chain spanning a number of EU (and other) countries. In full-service, large hotels the range of services can include a wide variety of food and drink venues as well as banqueting, conferencing, shopping, leisure and business facilities. While there has been a decline in small establishments offering accommodation only, this has, to some extent, been overtaken by the development of budget hotels, often operated by chains, where, if food and beverage services are present at all, they are invariably very limited.

Hotel chains

An important aspect of any industry is the extent of its economic concentration; that is, the extent to which its capacity is held by large players. Although, as Viceriat (1993) has pointed out, independent hotels represent almost 80 per cent of capacity in terms of rooms and about 90 per cent of establishments in the EU, there has been an increase in such concentration in recent years, evidencing a maturation of the industry. Such chains can be owner-operated (with subsidiaries) developing growth internally, or franchised or operated under management contract as ways of creating external growth.

Most chains operate varying combinations of these. For example, the French ACCOR group has franchised only about 20 per cent of its total room stock, while the American chain Choice Hotels International's European development strategy is based exclusively on franchising; Hilton International have owned, franchised and management contract properties in their portfolio; while Hyatt Hotels operate their hotel in Birmingham under management contract, but also control the one-third of equity not owned by the City of Birmingham, and Whitbread saw rapid expansion of its portfolio recently through its acquisition of the UK master franchise for Marriott Hotels and Resorts. The importance of such organizations is expressed not just in terms of size but also in the extent to which their strategies affect the shape of the industry, in terms of both systems and products, and the influence they exert on national and EU government policy making.

There are a number of European companies which have expanded rapidly, either organically or through acquisition, and have become major players in both European and world industry terms. Such chains are most highly developed in the UK and France, where they operate approximately 25 per cent and 15 per cent of the market respectively (Viceriat, 1993). For instance, ACCOR of France now operate well over a quarter of a million rooms world-wide and in terms of number of rooms rank first in Europe and fourth in the world (and first in the world in terms of owner-operated hotels). Indeed, the eight top European hotel companies also feature amongst the top 20 hotel organizations world-wide, although in total, European hotel chains control only 25 per cent of international chain capacity. This is because, while North American hotel chains developed to a large extent to fulfil business demand, European hotels developed mainly in response to leisure tourist demand, thus creating a large number of independent (resort) hotels – although currently the ultimate in 'resort' may be Disneyland Paris!

ACCOR is also a prime example of an important, fairly recent, development feature of the industry: multi-tier branding. ACCOR has developed a range of hotel products to satisfy a number of specific markets, from the full-service Sofitel, via three-star Novotel, Mercure and Ibis to the very basic budget hotel Formule 1 brand. Another example of such a trend is Holiday Inns, now owned by British brewing group Bass, with their Holiday Inn, Garden Court and Holiday Inn Express brands. Forte plc (ranked second in Europe) completed a complex rebranding exercise in the early 1990s, and this was followed by the acquisition, in 1995, of Meridien Hotels from Air France, prompting a rebranding of Forte's Grand hotels to the French name before they themselves were taken over by Granada plc in 1996.

The last two companies are examples of the number of large multinational brands which are owned by European companies but own more hotels outside the country where they (or their parent company) are based than in it. Another instance of this structural feature is Hilton International, owned by Ladbroke plc of the UK. They also show examples of the variety of portfolios within which these chains fit – from companies whose sole interest is hotels (another example being Mount Charlotte/Thistle), via those that own or operate hotels as part of a related portfolio with other catering or leisure interests (such as ACCOR), to conglomerates that see a hotel chain merely as one of a number of unrelated investment opportunities (such as Lonrho plc). Some chains, like Holiday Inns and Hilton International, have expanded largely organically, sometimes building new hotels, at other times taking over existing properties. ACCOR has developed its own properties while also acquiring other chains: for instance a large chain of American budget hotels – Motel 6. Apart from developing international brands and multinational companies, some other European organizations have concentrated their development mostly in their country of origin, such as the Dutch chain van der Valk, Club Mediterranée of France, or CenterParcs, again UK-owned but based mostly in the Netherlands. Alternatively, they have taken the strategic decision to remain a purely national brand, such as Stakis plc in the UK.

Budget hotels, serving the short-stay tourist and middle management commercial markets, are continuing to be the fastest-growing sector of the hotel industry in Europe, though still lagging well behind North America. While the original concept very much evolved to be located near motorways, major trunk routes or outlying industrial estates, and certainly developed as low-rise, out-of-town properties in order to control relatively high European land prices and building costs, the latest developments have seen the building of such properties in town centres and at airports, and even as high-rise buildings.

Mixed developments near urban centres have seen composite structures including hotels, offices, entertainment centres and residential housing. Millennium Copthorne Hotels recently opened such a development in Stuttgart, Germany, which includes a 450-room hotel, a restaurant mall, a health spa and a theatre. On the other hand, conversions of existing (but non-hotel) properties have been a recent feature exploited by such companies as Intercontinental (Grand Hotel, Paris), Holiday Inn (Crowne Plaza,

Manchester) and the five-star Swallow Hotel (Birmingham), which was developed from a former office building. Indeed, a number of UK chains now see the value of developing budget hotels in existing or new properties in city centres.

As well as chains of affiliated hotels there are voluntary chains, also known as consortia, which consist of independent hotels (and sometimes small chains) that take common action in terms of purchasing, marketing, recruitment, reservation systems, etc., not least because, in recent years, operating profits in such hotels have been greater than those in their independent counterparts (Commission, 1994). Of the world's top 20, 11 have their head office in EU countries. Utell International is by far the largest, in both European and world terms, with nearly 7,000 hotels in its system, covering nearly 1.5 million rooms. Second in the European league, and third in the world after Best Western, is another UK-based company, Supranational Hotels, with some 600 establishments. This is followed by SRS Hotels Steigenberger of Germany and Logis de France, which, although second in terms of number of hotels, only rank fourth in terms of rooms because they largely concentrate on the smaller unit.

As the HOTREC (1995, p.90) report points out:

> given the traditionally independent nature of the hotel industry in Europe, this type of association allows the hotelier to gain access to a much larger market, thanks to the computerisation of many services, mainly that of central reservation systems ... What has also developed is the creation of 'niche' associations ... This allows the consumer to reserve a room from a distance [in the full knowledge that] it will meet certain expected conditions while it will still preserve a certain individuality and character typical of independent hotels.

However, the recent trend of the number of hotels in Europe decreasing but nights spent increasing may be explained by the increasing rate at which small (family-run) hotels are disappearing. They are finding it ever more difficult to attract venture capital, while capacity is concentrated in chains that make every effort to differentiate their products distinctively, while offering the convenience of standard systems and quality. In future, voluntary chains will expand by finding more partners and by integrating their members' products into European distribution circuits in order to expand their customer base (Viceriat, 1993).

Hotel capacity

In terms of number of establishments, figures for 1993/94 (HOTREC, 1995) show that the UK had the highest number, with 52,200 (including guest houses and bed-and-breakfast establishments), followed by Germany with 38,301, Italy with 34,175, France (19,147) and Austria (18,693), while Spain had a mere 9,734. In terms of number of bedrooms the picture is quite different, showing the UK with a total of 627,214, Germany with 761,384, Italy with 900,753, France with 567,602 and Spain with 533,880 (such figures are not available for Austria). Although more revealing, available sleeper spaces data is too fragmented to be capable of interpretation; however, the above data shows that average unit size varied in inverse proportion to the number of establishments: the UK's average at that time was a mere 12 rooms per establishment, while Germany's was 20, Italy's 26, France's 30 and Spain's 55.

This would appear to provide evidence, for example in the case of Spain, of a relatively young, international, mass tourist industry requiring large, efficient hotels.

Certainly, when these averages are calculated for integrated hotel chains, including franchises, the following picture emerges: the UK 93, Germany 157, Italy 181, France 78 and Spain 166. Thus it can be seen that in Spain, chain-affiliated hotels tend to be large on average, with just over 1,000 establishments being part of such chains in 1993/94 (and similarly Italy, with a mere 147 such hotels); while France, with 2,682 chain hotels, has a much smaller average unit size.

Turnover, occupancy and pricing

The latest available figures (1992/93) (HOTREC, 1995) show that the UK achieved the highest hotel turnover, with a massive ECU 17,576 million and an average turnover per establishment of ECU 499,081, followed by Germany (ECU 15,099 million/ ECU 404,455), France (ECU 9,640 million/ECU 319,655) and Spain (ECU 5,431 million/ECU 558,030). If this is then set against the average number of rooms per hotel in each of those countries, it would appear that average turnover per room was: the UK ECU 41,590, Germany ECU 20,223, France ECU 10,655 and Spain ECU 10,146.

Occupancy rates, on the other hand, show surprisingly similar levels of achievement for some of the main players: while the UK, in 1993, attained an average 53 per cent rate, Germany achieved 61.5 per cent, France 57 per cent and Spain 52.5 per cent that year. Italy, on the other hand, apparently achieved a much lower figure of 38 per cent, while Austria only had a 31 per cent occupancy. While, in the latter case, the low result can at least to some extent be explained by that country's seasonality (and similarly with Italy), this did not seem to affect Spain in the same manner.

One of the reasons why there are differences in occupancy rates is that, in the northern, more prosperous member states of the EU, second holidays and short breaks are now commonplace. This extends tourist seasons and gives hotels an advantage in popularity against other forms of accommodation, although seasonal variations in demand often result in lower prices for 'shoulder' seasons and/or special incentive packages. Such imbalances between supply and demand at different times of year and in different parts of the EU also partially dictate variations in price levels. One of the most useful studies in this area has been the annual Eurocity Survey by consultants Pannell Kerr Forster Associates. Their report, covering trading performance during 1994 of 298 mostly four- and five-star hotels in 26 major cities (PKFA, 1995), found that average room occupancy rose to 67.3 per cent in 1994 for that sample of luxury hotels, an increase of 4.2 per cent compared with 1993.

In terms of price, hoteliers were reported to have found it difficult to raise achieved room rates, which declined 1.5 per cent to £92. While the most expensive hotel rooms were in Paris (which also had the highest yield), followed by London, the latter city had the greatest increase in yield per available room, at 14.3 per cent, followed by Rome at 11.6 per cent, while such revenue for hotels sampled in Berlin rose by a mere 0.2 per cent.

Employment

Throughout the hotel industry, methods that are labour-intensive compared to manufacturing processes have meant that the costs associated with labour are an important part of overall expenditure. The variable demand patterns over time mean that it is difficult to forecast labour requirements, and attempts to overcome such fluctuations have meant the employment of many part-time and female workers, while recruitment and retention continue to be a management concern. Greater mobility and higher expectations within the Single European Market (SEM) might exacerbate such problems when better career opportunities arise in other industries and/or countries.

When labour costs in hotels, expressed as a percentage of turnover, are reviewed for various member states, HOTREC (1995) figures for 1992/93 show that the UK's costs were an average 32 per cent while Germany's (1989) ratio shows it to be 33 per cent, with France at 35 per cent, Italy at 40 per cent and Spain at 38 per cent. Thus, although prices and labour costs in real terms may differ, relative labour costs are seen to be similar, and the greatest direct cost to revenue. In terms of actual numbers, in the period 1993/94 the UK employed 289,200 staff in its hotels, while Germany (in 1987) employed 188,709, France 150,442, Italy 250,000 and Spain 137,277.

Rather than displacing staff, the use of new technology in, for instance, reservation systems and catering technology will require ever-increasing skill levels, while management continue to develop labour-saving and often self-service systems for their customers in order to control labour costs. Thus labour trends will continue to move towards relatively small cores of highly skilled staff supported by more professional management.

THE RESTAURANT SECTOR

This sector, being another constituent part of the hospitality industry, displays characteristics similar to the hotel sector in terms of economic structure, demography, regional variations and, not least, the influence of tourism. The structure of this sector is very diverse and difficult to study, ranging from hotel restaurants to fast-food chains, with *haute cuisine* restaurants, often owner-managed, and roadside cafés also contributing to its size. Industrial and commercial catering in places of work and on various forms of transport have also become an important part of this sector in recent times. Being part of the social fabric of a community, it contributes not only in economic terms but also socially and indeed culturally.

The rapid increase in the number of restaurants in recent years has been engendered by the advent of the two-income family, with more disposable income to be spent on eating out. Competition, created also by the public's demand for new and exotic meal experiences which count as an alternative leisure activity, has forced prices down and made owners and operators much more market-orientated.

Restaurant chains

Restaurant chains originate very much from the USA, from where the concepts of bulk purchasing, systemized production and service, and marketing emanate. This dates largely from the 1950s, with the initial development of fast-food chains such as McDonald's and Burger King, while in Europe the fast-food/popular catering sector historically consisted largely of small, owner-managed operations. It was not until the 1980s that such chains began to achieve serious market penetration in Europe, and expansion now is focused on the EU's southern states. Although limited in menu choice and operating at the popular end of the market, these chains have greatly influenced the shape of the sector, especially with their high-profile marketing and the introduction of franchising on a large scale. This has given rise to a much greater interest in this sector by investors, and it has witnessed large takeovers, mergers and strategic alliances in recent times.

Recent data (Neo-restauration, 1994) shows McDonald's, with some 2,000 restaurants and a massive ECU 4 billion turnover, to be by far the largest player in this field in the EU. Indeed, so successful is this company that it has recently been buying out a number of franchisees, since this provides properties at half the cost of new build. Burger King, as part of Grand Metropolitan of the UK, has expanded rapidly in recent years by first purchasing the counter-service Wimpy chain from United Biscuits (UK) and then expanding aggressively in other European countries. Forte, in order to generate funds for its hotel expansion into Europe, sold off its Gardner Merchant commercial catering division in a management buyout; this was in turn taken over, in 1995, by the French group Sodhexo. Also in that year, Compass (UK) merged with Eurest, the commercial catering interest of ACCOR, to form the largest organization of its kind in the world.

The last company was, until then, also the second-largest EU-based catering organization, with some 600 restaurants. Only Whitbread of the UK was larger in terms of number of establishments, with just over 700, followed by Autogrill SPA of Italy, with some 400 units. As with the hotel sector, there is a preponderance here of UK- and French-owned companies, although German companies (and indeed Swiss) feature strongly. Overall, the vast majority of restaurant and catering chains in Europe are European in origin.

The number of restaurants in Europe (excluding cafés and bars), as notified to HOTREC in 1993/94, show that France, with 103,000 units, achieved top ranking, followed by the UK with 99,900, Italy with 90,590, Germany (1987) with 74,701 and Spain with 53,145.

Turnover

HOTREC (1995) data shows that the UK's restaurants had a combined turnover in 1992/93 of ECU 27,597 billion, followed by France with ECU 16,893 billion, Germany with ECU 16,287 billion and Spain with ECU 11,145 billion, while Italy apparently only achieved a total of ECU 2,022 billion. In terms of average turnover per establishment, these countries are ranked as follows: the UK, Italy, Spain and France (no comparative data being available for Germany). In the EU, the highest average turnover was achieved by Sweden, followed by Austria and Finland.

Employment

In the traditional, owner-managed, small restaurant the trend was that the owner's family was fully employed in the operation. Nowadays, with family size decreasing and other, more lucrative employment opportunities being available which do not have such unsocial hours attached to them, management succession is becoming problematic. In addition, as the HOTREC (1995) report points out, such familial employment distorts relevant statistics; also, labour turnover in restaurants tends to be high, making the collection of accurate data difficult.

Statistics on labour costs as a percentage of turnover appear to vary widely between different member states. While Italy's declared ratio for 1991 was 44 per cent, the UK's for 1993 was 40 per cent, followed by Austria with 38.35 per cent, Sweden with 37 per cent, France with 37 per cent and Germany with a mere 23.9 per cent for 1989 (the Netherlands and Ireland sharing a similarly low figure). In terms of actual employees, the UK declared 295,500 for 1994, with Italy 267,000 (1991), Germany 246,672 (1987), France 242,000 (1993) and Spain 183,621 (1992).

In order to manage the labour force in conditions of fluctuating demand, many operators employ much part-time and female labour, in common with the hotel sector. Such part-time labour often consists of students and immigrants with low specific skill levels. The fast-food chains especially have overcome this skilling issue by, on the one hand, building operations systems which are automated to as high a degree as possible and, on the other hand, developing careful recruitment and retention policies which put a high emphasis on continuous, albeit limited, training.

CONCLUDING COMMENTS

There is no doubt that, in both the hotel and restaurant sectors, concentration of supply into integrated and voluntary chains will continue apace. International and indeed global branding will be a key strategy to gain competitive advantage for organizations, where market share will be of utmost importance.

While the Schengen Agreement will support the free movement of people within the EU (see Chapter 1), transport systems such as the high-speed rail network (TGV), plus an open-skies policy and the Channel Tunnel, will all contribute to an increase in traffic between member states. On the other hand, it is said that, by reducing formalities at internal borders, hotel guest formalities at the point of registration will increase (see Chapters 5 and 12).

In terms of demand, and in common with countries like the USA, the demographic profile of the hospitality customer will change: a generally older population will have more time to spend on leisure and related activities and, possibly, have more disposable income. Southern member states are forecast to develop at a greater pace than their northern counterparts, so catching up with the latter. At the same time, those nation states are forecast to become less important, in favour of a 'Europe of the regions' which accentuates regional characteristics (see Chapter 7). Such a change in perception may also bring with it increased awareness of the environment and more eco-tourism (see Chapter 11).

At the operational level, Crawford-Welch and Tse (1990) forecast that there will be an increase in franchising, and in particular cross-franchising – where a franchisor becomes a franchisee of another concern, or where a number of franchises are held by one franchisee, either within or outside the same organization.

Major changes can be expected in the profile of the industry in Europe over the next decade, not least amongst them the democratization of, opening up of, and opportunities in, the Eastern European countries.

NOTE

1. Particular thanks are due to HOTREC for permission to use data from their recent report (HOTREC, 1995).

REFERENCES

Akehurst, G., Bland, N. and Nevin, M. (1993) 'Tourism Policies in the European Community Member States', *International Journal of Hospitality Management*, **12(1)**, 33–66.

Commission of the European Communities (1994) *Panorama of EU Industry 1994*. Luxembourg: OOPEC.

Crawford-Welch, S. and Tse, E. (1990) 'Mergers, Acquisitions and Alliances in the European Hospitality Industry', *International Journal of Contemporary Hospitality Management*, **2(1)**, 10–16.

Dawson, S. and Go, F.M. (1995) 'Expanding in a Barrier-free Europe', in Go, F.M. and Pine, R. (eds) *Globalisation Strategy in the Hotel Industry*. London: Routledge, 129–67.

ETC (1993) *European Travel Commission Annual Report, 1993*. Paris: ETC.

Eurostat (1994) *EEA Meeting of the Working Group on Tourism Statistics*. Luxembourg: EUROSTAT.

Federacion Espanola de Hoteles (1994) *El Sector Hotelero Espana*. Madrid: FEH.

HOTREC (1995) *The HORECA Sector and the European Union*. Brussels: HOTREC.

Neo-restauration (1994) *CEP Communication No. 280*. Paris: Groupe LSA.

PKFA (1995) *Eurocity Survey 1994*, quoted in *Caterer and Hotelkeeper*, 29 June 1995, and *Financial Times*, 22 June 1995.

Viceriat, P. (1993) 'Hotel Chains', *European Economy*, **3**, 365–79.

WTO (1993a) *Tourisme Internationale en Europe 1970–1992*. Madrid: WTO.

——(1993b) *WTO News*. December.

——(1995) *Tourism in 1994 – Highlights*. Madrid: WTO.

FOUR

Theories of economic integration

Howard Hughes

INTRODUCTION

This chapter is concerned with theories of economic integration as explanations for the development of the European Union (EU). As the pace of integration of economies in Europe increases, it is important to acknowledge the rationale for integration, assess its merits, and recognize and evaluate the consequences for industry. Manufacturing and agricultural industries, in particular, have been long affected by this integration. The service industries to date have been largely unaffected by the EU, but the implications for them are far reaching as the drive towards full integration accelerates. The effects on the hospitality and tourism industries are considered in this chapter after a discussion of the theoretical underpinning of economic integration and of the recent moves towards closer integration within the EU.

There is a presumption in economics, going back to Adam Smith and Ricardo in the late eighteenth and early nineteenth centuries, that universal free trade is more beneficial than a situation where there are barriers to free trade (see the section below on 'Free trade'). Given that the real world is one where there are many such barriers, any move towards the goal of universal free trade may be considered to be beneficial.

There have been many moves towards freeing trade in the world, including those particularly associated with the EU. The movement within post-war Europe has been towards liberalizing trade, but within a select group of countries only. This has usually been regarded as a 'step in the right direction' and an improvement on the previous, more protectionist, situation. The present-day EU originated with moves, just after World War II, to liberalize trade in coal, iron and steel, and it soon became a customs union with a stated intent of progressing to a common market and economic union. The Treaty of Rome 1957 brought into being the European Economic Community (EEC). Although popularly known as the 'Common Market' its form has, for the most part, been that of a customs union (see below). By the end of 1968 the customs union was complete. Determination to accelerate the movement towards the establishment of a common market came with the Single European Act (SEA) 1986. This sought to remove all remaining non-tariff barriers (NTBs) to trade, short of establishing an economic union. The original membership of the EU (West Germany, France, Belgium, the Netherlands, Luxembourg and Italy) has by now expanded to include the UK, Denmark and Ireland (1973), Greece (1981), Spain and Portugal (1986), and Sweden, Finland and Austria (1995).

Largely as a consequence of the establishment of the Common Market, a number of other countries including the UK established a free trade area, the European Free Trade Association (EFTA), in 1960. Several, including the UK, are now members of the EU.

FORMS OF ECONOMIC INTEGRATION

Such limited free trade, or economic integration, may take several forms.

Preferential tariff

A number of countries may show preference to each other by levying lower import duties (tariffs) on goods imported from each other than they do on goods imported from other countries. Thus trade is liberalized, though not necessarily free from tariffs, and is limited in coverage.

Free trade area (FTA)

In this case a number of countries agree to remove tariffs completely on trade between themselves whilst maintaining tariffs on trade with others. Trade is rather more free than is the case under a preferential tariff, but is still limited. Each country is free to fix its own tariff with non-members.

There is a very real practical problem here: the 'problem of origin'. Given that the members are free to maintain their own individual tariffs against non-members, it is unlikely that the tariffs will be at the same level. Countries outside the FTA may find it advantageous, if they wish to sell into a high-tariff market within the FTA, to divert goods initially through a lower-tariff member of the FTA. Those goods can then be traded within the FTA tariff-free. They could reach the consumers of the high-tariff country at a lower cost than if they had been traded directly into that country. This would dilute the intent of the FTA, and the system would need to be 'policed' so that only goods originating from the member countries would be allowed tariff-free access.

Customs union

This is similar to an FTA in that trade is tariff-free between a number of countries and they also maintain tariffs against other countries, but this time at a level which is the same in each country: the common external tariff (CET). This avoids the 'problem of origin'. Each country sacrifices sovereignty by losing freedom to determine its own tariff with non-union countries. Some of the members may, of course, end up with a higher tariff against outside nations than they had previously.

A further issue is that goods imported into the union from outside may be consumed in one union country but may have been imported through another. Even though both countries are within the union, there is an imbalance in as much as the tariff revenues accrue to the importing country but the higher prices are paid by the consuming country. There may be a need, therefore, for a mechanism for reallocating the tariff revenues to the consuming country.

Common market

This goes further than the customs union by freeing trade from NTBs. Additionally, the common market is characterized by the free movement not only of goods but also of the factors of production, such as labour or capital. Barriers to the movement of the factors (or resources) are removed; enterprises can be established in any of the member countries and labour can work in any country.

Economic union

There are several variations on this. The members of a common market may move towards complete economic union and effectively cease to be independent economic units. This would initially involve fixed exchange rates and the co-ordination of fiscal and monetary policies, and ultimately a single currency and common, unified, macro-economic policies – a complete sacrifice of sovereignty in economic matters to supranational union bodies.

FREE TRADE

The view that universal free trade is beneficial is dependent upon a number of assumptions. Many of these may be rather restrictive and unrealistic (see below). There is a presumption in favour of market forces and their operation. Any interference with the forces by protecting trade creates a sub-optimal situation.

The favourable effects of free trade may be represented as in Figure 4.1. Without tariffs the demand curve for a product is *dD*, the supply curve is *S* (perfectly elastic) and equilibrium price is *P*. The supply curve is elastic because each country consumes such a small proportion of the total supply that variations in its demand can be supplied without affecting price. In this situation the consumers' surplus[1] is *dTP*.

The imposition of a tariff, however, raises the supply curve to S_1 and price to P_1. Consumers' surplus is now dRP_1; there has been a loss of consumers' surplus of $P_1\,RTP$. Some of this accrues to government (or to producers as producers' surplus)[2] in the form of tax (tariff) revenue, and may of course be redistributed to the population or the consumer. There is, however, a net loss – a 'deadweight loss' of *RVT*.

If now a country were to join an FTA or a customs union, so that the tariff was reduced, the deadweight loss would be restored. There would be a net gain in consumers' surplus and economic welfare. Price would fall to *OP*, consumption of the product would rise from *Oa* to *Ob* through increased imports, and consumers' surplus would be *dTP* once more (government revenue falls; producers' surplus falls).

This simple analysis illustrates that a move towards free trade is beneficial. However,

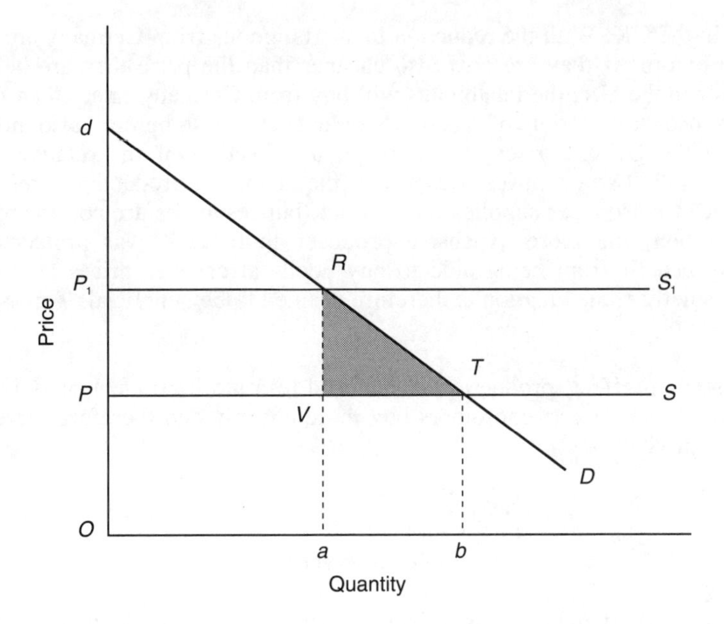

Figure 4.1 Tariffs and trade

a customs union or an FTA is only a second-best situation compared with universal free trade. In addition, the formation of any type of economic integration short of universal free trade may serve to reduce rather than increase economic welfare.

STATIC EFFECTS: TRADE CREATION AND TRADE DIVERSION

It has been suggested (Viner, 1950; Lipsey, 1970) that there may be both trade-creation and trade-diversion effects of economic integration. The net outcome of these two could be less desirable than the previous, less liberal (more protectionist) trade situation. In the process of creating a customs union, the members not only liberalize trade between themselves, they also discriminate against the rest of the world, and this may reduce economic welfare.

The analysis of the trade-creation and trade-diversion effects of a customs union may be considered as the static effects of a union. They are once-and-for-all effects that occur as the union is formed, and are not long-term.

Trade creation

The effect of tariff reduction is to increase the volume of trade between members (see Figure 4.1, where imports rise). Countries are able to specialize and benefits accrue consequently. Production adjusts according to specialization, and costs are reduced by production occurring in the cheapest location.

A hypothetical example may clarify this. Pre-union, consumers in the UK buy goods produced in the UK. With the reduction in tariffs, goods from Germany are cheaper than they were before. If they are now also cheaper than the price they are being produced and sold for in the UK, the inhabitants will buy from Germany rather than from the UK. There has been a creation of trade which did not exist before; also production has dropped in the UK but risen in Germany, a reflection of the relative efficiency of production in the two countries. Resources, the factors of production, are reallocated so that the cheaper producer supplies the product (but resources are not unemployed in the UK); pre-union, the more expensive producer in the UK was protected by tariffs. Consumers benefit from being able to buy goods at cheaper prices than before. *Both* countries benefit; trade creation is therefore deemed to be beneficial. This is the outcome of:

- a production effect: production is switched to a more efficient producer;
- a consumption effect: consumers buy more cheaply and therefore increase demand for the product.

Trade diversion

The effect of a tariff reduction is to increase the volume of trade between the members, but trade may be diverted from the least-cost producer to a higher-cost producer.

Pre-union, it may be that consumers in the UK purchased goods from the USA, as the USA was the most efficient producer and prices reflected this. Following economic integration of the UK and Germany, tariffs between these two will be eliminated and a CET will be imposed on countries such as the USA. The effect could be such that Germany now becomes the producer able to supply the goods at the lowest price, even though it is a higher-cost producer than the USA. Resources are now reallocated in such a way as to reduce economic welfare, since the best (optimal) allocation of resources is no longer achieved. Specialization is not occurring according to comparative advantage.

The prices paid in the UK for the product from Germany could be higher or lower than those paid previously for imports from the USA. If the former, then consumers in the UK could reduce their demand for those products. The effect could be particularly undesirable where the countries now excluded from trade are from the 'third world'. It could be argued, however, that the increased wealth in the customs union would lead to increased demand for production from the rest of the world. Whereas the consumption effect would be similar to that under trade creation – that is, lower prices in the UK and therefore increase in consumption – the production effects are the reverse. (The magnitude of the consumption effects might be such as to outweigh the production effects.)

NET EFFECTS

An evaluation of any form of economic integration depends, therefore, on the net outcome of the trade-creation and trade-diversion effects. Ostensibly the net outcome will be beneficial if the trade creation effects exceed the latter effect (see Swann, 1992a; Nevin, 1990; Lintner and Mazey, 1991).

There is more likely to be a beneficial outcome if economies, pre-union, produce similar products but with dissimilar efficiencies. Following union, there can be a rationalization of production towards the more efficient producers, and similarly if they are at comparable stages of economic development. The opportunities for a beneficial outcome are also likely to be greater the greater the differences are in costs of production.

Also, the higher the initial pre-union tariffs are, the greater the gains are likely to be. Producers can produce inefficiently and charge high prices when protected by high tariffs. The union will expose these producers to competition from low-cost union producers, and prices could fall considerably.

Given the discussion of trade diversion, it would seem that a low CET against the rest of the world would be more beneficial than a high one. A high CET is likely to lead to trade diversion. Similarly, the more comprehensive the union, in terms of world trade and production covered, the more beneficial it is likely to be; trade creation is likely to outweigh trade diversion. Trade diversion is likely to be less, the more likely the lowest cost producers are to be in the union.

It is clear too that even where overall a union is beneficial, some individual members of the union may benefit more than others, and some may actually be worse off than previously, perhaps due to unemployment in the process of adjustment. The implicit assumption is that the gains outweigh the losses and the gainers compensate the losers. The reality may be quite different.

LIMITATIONS OF ANALYSIS

The above static analysis is itself subject to particular reservations (see Lintner and Mazey, 1991; Nevin, 1990). The discussion assumes that transport costs are zero or negligible; transport costs will affect prices and therefore decisions of producers and consumers, and even though Germany may be the least-cost producer, post-union, it may still be possible to import and sell goods from the USA at a lower price than Germany's. The cost of transport from the USA might be low enough to outweigh the effect of a high tariff barrier.

Also, the analysis is conducted on the assumption that markets, both domestic and international, are perfectly competitive, with all of the assumptions this entails, including perfectly elastic supply curves. Factors of production (resources) are assumed to be fully mobile and substitutable within countries (but not between them), and the process of adjustment is assumed to be instantaneous and costless. Firms and industries in countries adjust their production without problem to the new circumstances post-union, increasing or decreasing output appropriately. If resources are not mobile then the full static benefits cannot be achieved.

There is also an assumption that the basis of trade is comparative advantage (and differing factor endowments), though more recent developments in trade theory offer explanations using more complex factors. The benefits associated with trade creation are based on the assumption that specialization occurs according to comparative advantage; the reality might be quite different when influences such as product differentiation, economies of scale, transport costs and factor mobility are taken into account.

The analysis is partial equilibrium analysis (Nevin, 1990), with the effects examined in one market and generalized to the whole economy. For this to hold, each market needs to be small. The analysis is also conducted in terms of economic efficiency and economic welfare. The costs of adjustment, in particular, are ignored, as are influences on growth and the distribution of income.

None the less, despite the possible negative effects and the shortcomings in the analysis, it is clear that a move towards limited free trade may be sought by many countries, perhaps for political reasons. In addition, countries may settle for a situation which is second-best to universal free trade, if only because it is recognized that the latter situation is unlikely. Universal free trade is clearly impractical, not only because of the ideological differences between countries but also because of the adjustments that would be necessary domestically, especially in terms of the disappearance of some firms and industries previously protected by tariffs.

DYNAMIC EFFECTS

Notwithstanding the supposed static effects of trade creation and diversion, it is also claimed that there are other effects which are of a dynamic nature. This implies that they are not of a once-and-for-all nature but are longer-term, less obvious and less direct. They are the effects that persist through time and are difficult to measure. They may well be of much greater importance than the static ones, and may be such as to more than compensate for any negative static effects. These dynamic effects may take several forms.

Increased competition

As a consequence of the reduction in tariff protection, domestic firms are faced with competition from foreign producers. Static, partial equilibrium analysis suggests that the least efficient firms will disappear and specialization by country will result. In practice, firms may react to increased competition by seeking to reduce any inefficiency, lowering costs and prices as a consequence. Firms that were previously in a protected and strong position (perhaps monopolistic) will now operate in a more competitive market and are not likely to be passive.

The very threat of increased competition may be such as to encourage businesses to reduce *X*-inefficiency and over-staffing, etc. Increased efficiency may also be achieved by introducing new investment.

There may be a psychological effect in that actual entry into a customs union alters business people's attitudes and perceptions of the market environment. The effect may be to make them more aware of the nature and extent of competition, less complacent, more competitive and more aware of threats and opportunities.

Economies of scale

It may be that the national markets that existed pre-union were not large enough for domestic firms to exploit economies of scale fully. Post-union, a larger market is now available. Those firms that are able to serve that larger market and survive may be able to operate at a scale where the minimum costs of production are achievable. Production is no longer split between several countries in less than optimal plants, but is now concentrated in one country, with the opportunity to produce in larger, better plants.

It is possible, however, given particular tariff situations, that output becomes concentrated in the least efficient producing country, especially as prices could, pre-union and immediately after union, be lower in the least efficient country. Consumers would buy from the least efficient country, forestalling any opportunity for industry in the more efficient country to achieve economies of scale (and therefore the lowest prices).

Terms of trade

Terms of trade are the price obtained for exports relative to those paid for imports. It is beneficial if prices of exports rise relative to those of imports, since it implies that a given volume of imports can be bought with fewer export sales; this is an improvement in the terms of trade.

Membership of a customs union will result in lower import prices for some members. Paradoxically, a tariff may have had the effect of keeping import prices down through restricting demand; the greater volume of demand for imports post-union may force prices up.

The members of a customs union, when acting together, may be able to achieve favourable terms of trade against the rest of the world. The combined trade and economic power of the union may be enormous, and weaker individual (especially many 'third world') countries may be disadvantaged.

Investment

Investment may be stimulated by economic integration. The rise in output itself may give rise to such an increase, and this new investment will usually embody the latest technology and raise productivity. The influence of increased investment on the level of aggregate demand will be to increase the rate of economic growth of the economy.

It is evident, then, that trade creation is not a necessary condition for an increase in economic welfare for members of a customs union. Even if the volume of trade falls, economic welfare may be increased through the dynamic effects identified above. Similarly, gains through trade creation could be outweighed by adverse dynamic effects. Losers and gainers within the union will need to negotiate (directly or through agencies such as governments) about compensation for any losses incurred.

EMPIRICAL STUDIES

The foregoing discussion has been theoretical in the sense that it has not been based on evidence of what actually happens. There have been, however, a number of studies that have attempted to measure the effects. These empirical studies have usually concentrated on the static effects and net trade creation, though increased trade flow is not, in itself, a measure of increased economic welfare. Also, isolating static from dynamic effects is difficult.

It is not particularly easy to assess the volume and value of net trade creation. Most studies have been *ex-post* rather than *ex-ante*. The former involves comparing the actual pattern of trade after union with what it would have been without the union. A major difficulty is causation, as there will have been many simultaneous influences on trade patterns.

Attributing any changes solely to the union may be difficult. Additionally, the approach requires an assumption about what the situation would have been without the union.

Studies of the EU vary enormously in conclusions and methods of calculation. (For details, see Nevin, 1990; McDonald and Dearden, 1992; Vickerman, 1992; Swann, 1992a.) All suggest that trade creation, which is especially evident in manufacturing, has outweighed trade diversion, which is especially evident in agriculture, but that the benefits are relatively small – equivalent to about 2 per cent of EU gross domestic product (GDP) (Swann, 1992a). In terms of economic welfare, this is less than 1 per cent of EU GDP.

Ex-ante studies predict, pre-event, the likely outcome of union or of changes in the union (see Cecchini, 1988, discussed below). These are crucially dependent on estimates of elasticity of demand and supply.

There have been relatively few studies of dynamic effects largely because of the complex factors at work.

SINGLE EUROPEAN MARKET

It has been observed earlier that the EU had existed as a customs union for many years (since 1968) and movement towards a common market was slow. The EU agreed in 1986, by the SEA, to accelerate this process and establish a single European market (SEM) by the end of 1992.

Having made the decision to move more swiftly to accomplish the common market, a major study was initiated by the EU to examine the consequences. (Perhaps it would have been more logical to have undertaken the study first.) This study (Cecchini, 1988) estimated that the costs of not achieving the common market (the costs of 'non-Europe') were equivalent to about 5 per cent of the EU's GDP. Cecchini identified a number of barriers to trade which remained, and which needed to be removed if the full potential of the common market were to be realized.

Although most tariffs and quotas had already been eliminated, some remained, but the most significant were NTBs. These may be classified in a number of ways.

Cost-increasing barriers

Customs formalities, such as VAT assessments and verification of technical regulation requirements, delayed the movement of goods and added to costs. The documents required for this were numerous, and varied according to the country concerned. The transportation of goods across several frontiers could require many sets of documents. In 1988, the requirement for numerous documents was replaced by the introduction of the Single Administration Document (SAD). This replaced about 70 separate forms and was itself abolished in January 1993.

To meet the different technical requirements in the different countries (see below), producers of goods would need to modify their products, often quite significantly. This is costly and also restricts the ability to achieve long production runs and economies of scale.

Some members of the EU had already progressed to a border-free relationship since 1990 – the Schengen Group of France, Germany, Belgium, the Netherlands, Luxembourg and Italy.

Market-entry restrictions

There were a number of barriers which made it difficult or impossible for firms to enter certain markets. Member countries frequently had their own technical regulations and standards for products. These may have been legal requirements, to protect health and safety, or minimum standards set by national testing organizations. The nature of these regulations and standards was sometimes such that products which could legally be sold in one country could not be in another. The effect was to protect domestic firms from competition from foreign firms, with possible resultant *X*-inefficiency and monopoly profits.

Products such as televisions, washing machines and cars may have had to be modified several times in order to meet the requirements of the individual states. Costs were therefore increased and firms were unable to operate with a Europe-wide range and achieve economies of scale. However, earlier attempts to ensure common standards for all products had been abandoned in favour of 'mutual recognition'. The *Cassis de Dijon* ruling (1979) by the European Court of Justice (ECJ) had already established that goods legally manufactured and sold in one member country could only be precluded in others to protect consumer interests such as safety or environmental concerns. It was this principle that was to be confirmed by the SEM. In the case of food, the EU has moved to a situation where it seeks only guarantees that the food is fit to eat and is adequately labelled to inform consumer choice.

A further restriction has been member governments showing preference or restricting opportunities to domestic firms in placing contracts (discriminatory public procurement), especially in telecommunications, power generation, railways and defence.

Entry into many services was also difficult; a variety of rules and regulations covered legal, banking, insurance and other financial services, and also transport. In particular, many countries limited the ability of non-nationals to establish themselves in services.

Restrictions on capital movements had similar limiting effects. National systems of accounting, corporate law and taxation differed and had comparable consequences.

Member states imposed different requirements for transport hauliers and vehicles; they set different quotas on the number of journeys that could be made by foreign hauliers. These quotas were abandoned in 1993, allowing hauliers to operate freely throughout the EU. All modes of transport were to be deregulated.

The mobility of labour is much less than that of capital. There are obvious difficulties, such as language and culture, and mobility is further restricted by limited recognition of qualifications and differing tax and social security systems. The intent of the SEM has been to establish the 'equivalence' of qualifications, so that each state recognizes the diplomas, degrees and other qualifications awarded by other members, and thus recognizes the entitlement to practise a vocation or profession in any of the member states (see Chapter 10).

Market-distorting activities

The effect of taxation and subsidies is to distort prices from those which would be determined by market forces. Thus products, whether goods or services, would be sold at prices that were not reflective of their true costs of production, and competition would not be on an 'equal' basis.

Some subsidies are subtle, such as regional aid. The most evident tax problem is VAT. This is common to all EU countries, but is levied at different rates in the individual countries, and its coverage is not common throughout the EU. It distorts prices and has required, in the past, costly and complex checks at frontiers. Full harmonization throughout the EU would remove this obstacle. There are, however, no plans for this. It is accepted (Lintner and Mazey, 1991) that some variation in VAT is consistent with a customs union; experience in the USA suggests a 5–6 per cent variation. The EU sought therefore to achieve two bands of VAT: 14–20 per cent, and a lower rate of 4–9 per cent on food, books, children's clothes, etc.

Excise duties also vary between member states. Some uniformity has been aimed for, but it has proved very difficult to achieve. Associated with this has been an intent to abolish 'duty-free' sales. In a single market, there should be no opportunity for such sales, as all are 'internal'. These plans have been abandoned for the time being.

Governments have continued to give aid to non-member countries on condition that a proportion of it is spent in the donor country. They have, too, negotiated individual agreements with countries regarding trade; the Multi-Fibre Agreement, limiting textile imports, is conducted separately by each member.

EFFECTS OF THE SINGLE EUROPEAN MARKET

Cecchini estimated that there would be a number of gains from achieving the SEM. These may be classified in a number of ways but, in total, they were estimated to be between 5.8 per cent and 6.4 per cent of EU GDP at 1988 prices (see Table 4.1).

Table 4.1 Summary of effects of the SEM

Micro:	*% of EU GDP*
Direct	
Removal of barriers affecting trade	0.2–0.3
Removal of barriers affecting production	2.0–2.4
Indirect	
Exploiting economies of scale	2.1
Intensified competition	1.6
Total	4.3–6.4
	(Mid-point: 5.3)
Macro (on the assumption of neutral fiscal policies):	
GDP	4.5%
Consumer prices	-6.1%
Employment	+1.8m
Budget balance change*	2.2%
External balance*	1.0%

* % points of GDP
Source: Cecchini (1988).

The 'barrier' (static welfare) effects of removing border controls and delays and of eliminating technical standards and public procurement obstacles would be once-and-for-all and achievable in the short term. The elimination of the barriers to trade (frontier controls) would have a relatively minor impact of between 0.2 per cent and 0.3 per cent of GDP. A gain of between 2.0 per cent and 2.4 per cent would result from the easing of barriers to production (technical and regulatory, etc.).

Other (quasi-dynamic, market integration) effects would take longer to work through, involving the restructuring of production, the resultant economies of scale and the impact of increased competitive pressure. These longer-term benefits were believed to be equivalent to 2.1 per cent and 1.6 per cent of GDP respectively.

Essentially the SEM would give a boost to the supply side of the economy, resulting in lower costs and prices and, consequently, a rise in demand. Economies of scale and increased competition would reduce *X*-inefficiency and would stimulate research and development and innovation to reduce production costs further and improve non-price characteristics.

These supply-side effects would have macro-economic effects in the form of reduced inflation, improved trade balances and reduced government budget deficits (see Table 4.1). Governments would thus have the opportunity to boost aggregate demand in their economies to reach higher levels of non-inflationary growth. The benefits at this level were estimated to be very significant effects of the SEM. A number of scenarios were considered which were dependent upon the reaction of governments to the possibility of reflation. In the long term there would be an increase of 4.5 per cent of GDP and an extra 1.8 million jobs. If, however, governments recognized the full potential for faster growth, the gains could be 7 per cent of GDP and an extra 5 million jobs.

RESERVATIONS

Despite what has been claimed for the SEM, a number of obstacles to completion remain, and there are shortcomings in the Cecchini analysis.

The Cecchini estimates do not take into account the costs incurred in the process of achieving the SEM (El-Agraa, 1994). The distribution of gains and costs between member states and between individuals or groups is not addressed either; estimates were for the EU as a whole.

It may also be that the Cecchini estimates are over-generous (Swann, 1992b). They are considerably higher than those of any previous studies, though they do include some quasi-dynamic effects. These, of course, are the most difficult to quantify and are dependent upon many factors.

The 'barrier' effects may be based on rather unrealistic assumptions, including that efficiency gains are passed on to the consumer and displaced resources are swiftly re-employed elsewhere (Baimbridge and Burkitt, 1991), and that restructuring the economy will occur without long-term unemployment. The mobility of labour is, though, likely to be restricted by cultural, language and social security differences. The 'barrier' effect benefits are small, and it has been suggested that far greater benefits could be obtained through reform of the EU's Common Agricultural Policy (Baimbridge and Burkitt, 1991).

The achievement of the economies of scale (minimum efficient size (MES)) in the SEM assumes that the European market is relatively homogeneous and that a standardized product can be sold throughout Europe. For many products, markets will remain small, and national cultural differences will restrict the ability to achieve MES. The implication is that many European firms are 'too small', but there is no strong evidence for this (McDonald and Dearden, 1992). There is a view (Vickerman, 1992) that the NTBs have actually been low (see Cecchini, 1988) and firms have sought economies of scale across borders already. Whatever such economies are possible have been achieved; firms that are able to operate on a European scale are probably already doing so. In addition, the actual cost savings in achieving MES may be over-represented (McDonald and Dearden, 1992). Any move towards realizing economies of scale through larger plant and firm size may well lead to reduced competition and increased *X*-inefficiency – the negation of the positive effects envisaged within the SEM.

Some observers consider, however, that the Cecchini estimates are pessimistic. Baldwin (1989) (see Vickerman, 1992; El-Agraa, 1994) estimated that gains could be up to twice or even five times those identified in Cecchini. The basis for this was the view that the impact is a permanent enhancement of long-term growth derived from an on-going increase in savings and investment. Smith and Venables (1988) (quoted in Hitiris, 1994) suggested that the welfare benefits of modifying oligopolistic practices brought about by increased competition could significantly exceed the Cecchini estimates.

There are political problems associated with the fact that not all members of the EU are equally enthusiastic about the developments. As a consequence, there are delays in implementation and a reluctance to comply with all of the requirements of the SEA. Some member states have succeeded in obtaining adjustment periods beyond 1992. The SEM may well increase conflict between states (McDonald and Dearden, 1992), since all will not see it as in their best interests to comply and the market will need to be 'policed'. The Cecchini gains depend on all states adhering to the rules of the game. All member states would have to resist the temptation to introduce measures to alleviate the hardship associated with structural changes. Firms would have to compete and not merge or collude their way out of trouble.

A common market is a step towards an economic union. It is possible that the full benefits of a common market cannot be achieved if member states continue to adopt their own independent macro-economic policies. There are moves, of course, towards economic union, but this is proving difficult to achieve. By operating independently member states can continue, in effect, to create barriers to trade. Nation states will go on implementing their own tax and legal systems, so that a single 'business environment' will not be achieved.

The macro-effects are dependent upon the prior achievement of the micro-benefits (which are not certain anyway). The macro-effects also depend on the EU countries taking co-ordinated action to reflate their economies. It is doubtful whether the political will exists to do this, and without mechanisms of co-ordination (involving sacrifice of national sovereignty) it is unlikely to occur.

From the wider perspective, the completion of the SEM may harm the growth of free trade in the world as a whole (McDonald and Dearden, 1992). Its effect could be considerable trade diversion. Its competitive pressures may lead some of the weaker EU states to seek increased protection from nations outside the EU. There is too a lack of common policy for external trade (Dudley with Martens, 1993), so that individual nations continue with bilateral agreements. It is possible, however, that the stimulus that the SEM gives to economic activity in the EU could induce more imports from the rest of the world.

The 'barrier' effects are small and the 'market integration' effects may be over-estimated and/or over-optimistic. The main effect may be psychological, in turning the attention of firms towards the European market.

EFFECTS ON TOURISM AND THE HOSPITALITY INDUSTRY

Some concern has been expressed about the effects of the SEM on tourism and the hospitality industry. VAT has been a particular anxiety, with the industry wishing to ensure lower rates on hospitality and tourism and to avoid the imposition of VAT on air fares and inclusive tours (Gauldie, 1988). There has been unease too about the impact on airline and airport revenues of the abolition of 'duty-frees'. Tour operators and travel agents have had some reservations about legislation affecting responsibility for proper performance of the contract with the client.

There has been a consensus, however, that the net impact on tourism and the hospitality industry would be beneficial. In particular, a more prosperous population would travel more and there would be more business travel. Yet even before 1992, barriers to movement were few and routes had been opened up to larger numbers of airlines. It was therefore unlikely that the effects would be dramatic; developments would rather be steady and long-term. (For discussions of possible impact see Gauldie, 1988; Castan *et al.*, 1990; HOTREC, 1989.)

The most significant effects were believed to arise from transport deregulation. This should increase competition and reduce costs. It was unlikely that deregulation of international passenger air transport would in itself guarantee substantial gains, since there are already airline agreements and mergers, and these need to be controlled. Non-price competitive strategies (including computer reservation systems (CRS)) would need to be examined and if necessary regulated. There was also a need for appropriate and corresponding air-traffic control, and airport development and capacity policies.

There has been resistance to deregulation. Governments have often had a vested interest in state-owned airlines, and since governments in both countries relating to a flight need to agree, the process can be slow. The main problems relate to '5th freedom rights' (passengers carried from one state to another by the airline of a third state) and cabotage (carriage of passengers within one country by the airline of another) (Vickerman, 1992).

The USA and Canadian experiences of deregulation do not inspire optimism. Airlines have withdrawn from the least profitable routes and developed networks from hubs. This makes for more roundabout journeys for passengers. The effect of increased competition has been a restructuring of the industry, with fewer carriers and the possibility of less competition in future.

With respect to road transport, it was envisaged that there would be more flexibility, especially in allowing foreign coaches to bring passengers into and through the UK and to pick up UK passengers (Van Kraay, 1993).

CONCLUDING COMMENTS

There is a strong body of thought that free trade is 'a good thing', and moves towards it, even on a limited scale, have been common throughout the world (and not only in Europe). The economic benefits of free trade are, however, based on a set of restrictive assumptions associated with perfect competition and comparative advantage. By removing the barriers to trade, countries are able to specialize according to comparative advantage, with the consequent benefits of reduced costs and increased consumption.

The economic benefits, in reality, may be matters of some dispute. This is especially true in the case of geographically limited free trade blocs of countries, such as customs unions or common markets. In these circumstances it is possible, even on the basis of the conventional restrictive assumptions, for the net effect to be less beneficial than the situation pre-union, because of trade diversion. Trade may be diverted from least-cost to higher-cost producers. In addition there are many dynamic forces whose impacts, by their very nature, are less measurable and less certain. The outcome of economic integration is dependent on a complex interaction of static and dynamic effects, each of which is difficult to demonstrate in practice. It is arguable too whether the total impact of economic integration can be assessed, given the many variables that influence economies' progress. The process of isolating the influence of economic integration on economic development and economic welfare is subject to significant conceptual difficulties.

Despite the problems associated with confirming, in practice, the advantages of free trade, there has been considerable development of limited FTAs, customs unions and common markets, in addition to moves towards universal free trade, such as through the General Agreement on Tariffs and Trade (GATT). Some of the developments may owe more to political vision, ideology and alliance than to rational and justifiable economic grounds.

The move within the EU towards the SEM reflects the faith in free trade. The SEM programme is seen as a necessary acceleration of the process of moving from customs union to common market, with the ultimate objective of economic union. The achievement of the full benefits of free trade can occur only if the remaining obstacles to free trade are removed. These obstacles were mostly NTBs, which are more difficult to identify and, in practice, to remove. None the less, the move towards freer trade is inexorable and, by exposing economies to more international competitive forces, it is believed that opportunities for adding to economic welfare will be increased.

NOTES

1. Consumers' surplus (*dTP*) is the excess of total utility (satisfaction) derived by consumers from buying a product (*dTbO*) over the total market value paid (*PTbO*).
2. Producers' surplus (P_1RVP) is the excess of receipts (P_1RaO) over costs (*PVaO*).

REFERENCES

Baimbridge, M. and Burkitt, B. (1991) 'The Cecchini Report and the Impact of 1992', *European Research*, **2(5)**, 16–19.

Castan, A., Varmo, A. and Gabard, L. (1990) *1993 and Beyond: The Impact of EC Legislation on the Hotel, Catering, and Tourism Industries*. Cergy-Pontoise Cedex: Institute de Management Hotelier International, Cornell-Essec.

Cecchini, P. (1988) *The European Challenge – 1992: The Benefits of a Single Market*. Aldershot: Wildwood House.

Dudley, J., with Martens, H. (1993) *1993 and Beyond: New Strategies for the Enlarged Single Market*. London: Kogan Page.

El-Agraa, A. (1994) *The Economics of the European Community*, 4th edition. Hemel Hempstead: Harvester Wheatsheaf.

Gauldie, R. (1988) '1992 and the European Travel Industry', *Travel and Tourism Analyst*, **3**, 66–78.

Hitiris, T. (1994) *European Community Economics*, 3rd edition. Hemel Hempstead: Harvester Wheatsheaf.
HOTREC (1989) *White Paper. The 1992 Challenge for the Hotel, Restaurant and Café Industry*. Paris: Confederation of National Hotel and Restaurant Associations in the European Community.
Lintner, V. and Mazey, S. (1991) *The European Community: Economic and Political Aspects*. London: McGraw-Hill.
Lipsey, R. (1970) *The Theory of Customs Unions: General Equilibrium Analysis*. London: Weidenfeld and Nicholson.
McDonald, F. and Dearden, S. (1992) (eds) *European Economic Integration*. London: Longman.
Nevin, E. (1990) *The Economics of Europe*. London: Macmillan.
Swann, D. (1992a) *The Economics of the Common Market*, 7th edition. London: Penguin.
——(1992b) (ed.) *The Single European Market and Beyond*. London: Routledge.
Van Kraay, F. (1993) *Tourism and the Hotel and Catering Industries in the EC*. London: Athlone Press.
Vickerman, R. (1992) *The Single European Market*. Hemel Hempstead: Harvester Wheatsheaf.
Viner, J. (1950) *The Customs Union Issue*. New York: Carnegie Endowment for International Peace.

FIVE

Tourism policy

Gordon Robinson

INTRODUCTION

Tourism as a policy priority seems to have crept up on the decision makers of the European Union (EU). Historically, a matter left to the member states, tourism has largely been by-passed by the EU's treaties and excluded from the competence of its institutions. Despite tourism's economic and social importance, it has only been in the last 10 years or so that any effort has been made to formulate and execute policy at the EU level. Indeed, any formal mention of tourism as one of the EU's fundamental objectives had to wait until 1992, with the passage of the Treaty on European Union (TEU). Even here, however, the reference was very weak, and any stronger commitment will have to await the outcome of the Intergovernmental Conference (IGC) in 1996, when the achievements of tourism policy so far will be reviewed and decisions made about its future possible development.

This chapter traces the development of tourism policy from the early 1980s, when the first coherent attempts were made to define its objectives. It examines the reasons for the massive growth in the industry and evaluates the economic impact it has had on the member states. It looks at the major challenges which are presented to policy makers, particularly the one posed by the stark geographic and seasonal demand for the product usually characterized as 'mass tourism'. It concludes with an evaluation of the achievements and failures of policy, and argues that in the context of the global challenge to Europe's competitive position the EU should not surrender its present status as the world's premier tourist market, now under very serious threat from the United States and Asia-Pacific.

TOURISM AND EUROPEAN UNION

In terms of the wealth which it generates, tourism in the EU is as important as transport and energy and much more important than agriculture, yet it has never been given a very high priority. Where development has taken place, it has been slow, episodic and fragmentary. Despite the fact that countries like Italy and France, founder members of the European Community (EC), have always done well from tourism, 25 years went by after the signing of the Treaty of Rome before any attempt was made to define policy in this field.

Tourism has been very much the poor relation of other concerns such as fiscal policy, transport, regional policy, and freedom of movement, all of which have had a considerable impact on it. It has suffered from a lack of attention and focus, and as a result policy development has tended to take place in related areas such as consumer affairs or the environment. Thus, for a long time, tourism has been partly substituted by other policy concerns and even to some extent colonized by them. This has meant that tourism policy has tended to develop almost in disguise or by proxy.

Giving the sector greater prominence has been impeded by a lack of consensus among the member states, some of which have benefited much more from tourism than others, while all of them have been reluctant to let the EU develop an integrating role by adding tourism to its sphere of competence.

The character of the industry itself has not helped. It is a complex network of businesses engaged in the provision of accommodation, restauration, travel facilities and services and entertainment (Commission, 1994c). It involves a myriad of activities including those of nation states, airlines, travel companies, hotel chains, and the food, drinks and financial services industries. It is made up of more than one million microenterprises which on average employ nine or fewer workers, a large part of whom are seasonal or part-time. Needless to say, this has created an environment uncongenial to the development, implementation or enforcement of policy.

It is now well over a decade since the first attempt was made to define a tourism policy, yet it is still not being taken seriously, and this despite the sector's manifest social, economic and cultural importance. Predicted to grow at 4 per cent a year between now and the year 2000 (*Financial Times*, 1 March 1995), tourism is now the world's biggest industry and will form the largest sector of economic activity in the EU by the year 2000. The EU's Economic and Social Committee (ESC) has recently argued that:

> it would be difficult to identify any other human activity which has, in such a short space of time, developed in such a marked manner and had such far-reaching effects.
> (ESC, 1992, p. 43)

The figures speak for themselves. In 1990 the world travel and tourism industry had a gross output of US$2450 billion, which included US$1.2 billion of purchases of goods and services from other industries. According to Wharton Econometric Forecasting Associates, world travel and tourism grew at an annual rate of 8.7 per cent in 1990 and was expected to generate more than US$3,000 billion in 1992 (*Financial Times*, 21 September 1991). The very fact that the 1994 Berlin travel and trade fair had 167 international exhibitors is an indication of how global the industry has become.

In 1990 travel and tourism accounted for more than one-third of all international trade in services and close to 5 per cent of trade in goods and services in the Organization for Economic Co-operation and Development (OECD) (OECD, 1992), while 5 per cent of all EU foreign trade was accounted for by tourism in the same year (Commission, 1991).

The sheer growth in the industry is evident from the fact that in the period 1960–90, the number of visits by foreign tourists to the EC grew six-fold, from 69 million to 429 million, while the income that it generated increased 37-fold (ESC, 1992).

EUROPE'S PLACE IN WORLD TOURISM

Even though Europe's share is falling, it still holds the largest slice of the world tourist market and has five out of the top seven most popular destinations in the world. The attraction of Europe, with its natural and cultural richness and diversity, has been well summed up as follows: in no other part of the world is it possible to find 'within such a short radius so many different cultures, so much history and such a melting pot of nations' (HOTREC, 1990).

At the time of writing, Europe is the destination for 64 per cent of all tourists, including intra-European travellers, and it collects 55 per cent of world-wide tourist income. This compares with the 1970 figure of 71 per cent and 63 per cent respectively. This decline has occurred despite the rise in the number of tourists visiting the EU, which has doubled over the last 10 years. The relative fall in global share has been going on since 1985, and EU observers fear that it could turn into an actual deficit in the near future (ESC, 1992).

The reasons for this are not hard to find. The revolution in transport, the development of tourism in other parts of the world and the growth in real disposable incomes are all drawing European travellers to more distant destinations. In 1993, for example, about a third of a million Germans visited Thailand, and they were second only to the Japanese in the amount that they spent (*Bangkok Post*, 1994). The EU concedes that one of the main reasons for this loss of market share is the progressive drop in the price–quality ratio of its tourism product, and the fact that 'certain aspects of the tourism products on offer, in comparison with other destinations, no longer match the preferences and new concerns of consumers, be they from the [EU] or elsewhere' (ESC, 1992, p. 45).

THE ROLE OF TOURISM IN THE EU'S ECONOMY

The rising importance of tourism is mirrored in the economic structures of the EU's member states. Tourism is now a key part of the EU's economy. It absorbs 7.5 per cent of all capital expenditure and 12 per cent of consumer spending (EP, 1993). In 1988 its share of gross national product (GNP) ranged from 9.4 per cent in the case of Spain to 9.0 per cent in France and 7.3 per cent in Greece. At the other end of the scale, it represented only 1.3 per cent of the GNP of the Netherlands, and 3 per cent of Belgian GNP (Eurostat, 1989).

The role of tourism in the national economy is well illustrated by the case of Britain. Even though its share in GNP (between 4 per cent and 5 per cent) is fractionally below the EU average of 5.5 per cent, its importance to the economy should not be underestimated. Britain is fifth in the league of world overseas tourism earners. In 1990, according to the Department of Employment, it attracted a record 18 million overseas visitors. Tourism of all kinds contributed some £25 billion to the economy, provided some 1.5 million jobs and was creating employment at double the rate of other sectors (Baty and Templeton, 1991).

According to the British Tourist Authority's figures, tourism was the fourth most important export earner, ahead of traditional industries such as iron and steel, textiles and even petroleum products (British Tourist Authority, 1991). In Scotland, it is the single most important sector, generating £1.6 billion-worth of business in 1991 and employing 150,000 people. In the same year, Welsh tourism netted slightly less, at a record £1.5 billion (Department of Employment, n.d.), while the West Midlands alone saw a turnover of £1 billion, which put tourism on a par with the motor vehicle industry.

In 1994 the World Travel and Tourism Council calculated that tourism would represent 12.3 per cent of UK gross domestic product (GDP) and was in fact generating a trade surplus rather than the deficit of £3.5 billion argued by the government's figures (*Financial Times*, 24 September 1994). While in Britain as a whole the tourism and leisure industries employ 10 per cent of the workforce, in some parts of the country dependence on the industry is considerably greater. In Cornwall, for instance, one in five of all workers are employed in the industry, while on the Isle of Wight it is one in every two (*Financial Times*, 10 November 1991).

Within the EU, tourism represents something like 8 per cent of all private consumption, and when the multiplier effect is taken into account this rises to 10 per cent (Commission, 1987). The total number of workers supported by tourism is not easy to calculate since different data-gathering methods are used and much of the work is seasonal and marginal. However, there is broad agreement on a figure of between 7 and 8 million, of which about half work in the hotel and catering trade (EP, 1993) and 20–30 per cent are part-time. Other calculations suggest that if all tourist activity were to cease, between 10 per cent and 12 per cent of the EU's workforce would lose their jobs (Commission, 1991; HOTREC, 1990). Of the 1.2 million firms in the sector, 95 per cent employ nine workers or fewer, representing some 60 per cent of the total workforce (EP, 1993). Because of its very evident North–South flow, tourism has a major redistributive effect on wealth within the EU, which is particularly beneficial to the poorer Mediterranean countries. Germany, the UK and the Netherlands are the big purchasers of EU tourism services, with Germany alone spending about a third of the EU total in 1993. This expenditure has been encouraged by the long-term rise in the DM, particularly against many of the Southern currencies, which has led to a fall in the relative price of their tourism product. The average Germany family sets aside some DM 200 per month for holidays, and a recent poll discovered that in areas where families would find it hardest to reduce expenditure, holidays came second only to such basics as food, housing and clothing (*Financial Times*, 21 November 1994). The main beneficiaries of this and other internationally generated revenue in 1991 were, in rank order, France, Italy, Spain and the UK (EP, 1993), and Spain alone accounted for 43 per cent of all UK holiday sales in 1994 (*Financial Times*, 18 November 1994).

The importance of tourism to the national economies is further underlined by the share which it has in the export of goods and services. In the case of Spain, which in 1992 was the third most popular tourist destination in the world, tourism receipts comprised 22.7 per cent of all export earnings in 1989, while the figure for Greece was 16.3 per cent (Eurostat, 1989). In Ireland, where the trade has benefited from its environmentally friendly image, tourism receipts made up half of the balance of payments surplus in 1990 (*Financial Times*, 1 November 1991). In Portugal in 1993 it accounted for 25 per cent of all export earnings and covered 50 per cent of the visible trade deficit (*Financial Times*, 14 March 1994).

EUROPEAN UNION TOURISM DEMAND

Within the EU the habits of mass, popular tourism have become well entrenched. Encouraged by rising disposable incomes, fewer hours at work, earlier retirement, and a revolution in both land and air transport which has made it easier to carry more people further, faster and more cheaply than ever before, tourism has become a well-established part of people's habits and needs. Even though 40 per cent of the EU population still does not travel away for its holidays, for those who can it has come to form an important extension of their social rights and expectations.

The scale of the phenomenon can be gauged from the fact that in 1990, 180 million EU citizens took a holiday away from their usual residence, to which must be added journeys for professional and educational reasons (EP, 1990). This movement is narrowly concentrated in terms of both destination and season; two-thirds go away in July and August and more than half to the seaside (Commission, 1987). In Holland, for example, nearly one-third of the entire population leaves the country in high summer, while in Britain it has been calculated that 10 million people will either leave or arrive on peak holiday weekends (Butt Philip, 1989). In Portugal half of all tourism income is earned in the period from July to September (*Financial Times*, 14 March 1994).

This seasonal concentration has created a major problem. Dubbed 'mass tourism', this is the blight of unregulated and often unplanned growth of tourism facilities, pressure on the infrastructure, congestion, pollution, double-booking, overcharging, and social, cultural and, above all, environmental degradation. It is a negative and ugly phenomenon, which is largely responsible for the decline in the price–quality ratio of the EU's tourism product. As a consequence, it has become enemy number one of most tourism planners at the EU level.

So far the Mediterranean has been its principal victim. Because of its geographical characteristics, the waters of the Mediterranean are only completely renewed every 80 years. It is a major seaway and is heavily used by shipping, which, in any one year, will discharge some 330,000 tonnes of oil. In addition, ships continue to wash out their tanks and dump rubbish overboard. The Hellenic Marine Environment Protection Association has calculated that it takes over 400 years for a plastic bottle to dissolve in sea water, while even a bus ticket will last four weeks before disintegrating completely (*Financial Times*, 20 November 1991). Yet it is on this region than an ever-growing number of visitors converge.

According to the ESC, the Mediterranean receives more than 100 million tourists annually, a figure which some estimate will double by the end of the decade. Unless urgent steps are taken, the consequences could be disastrous. In 1990 the European Parliament (EP) drew attention to the effect which unsustainable demand was having on the area's 'fragile ecological equilibrium ... seriously endangered by saturation and devastation' (EP, 1990).

Unfortunately, the Mediterranean is not an isolated case. Concern has also been expressed about the Baltic, which shares many of the Mediterranean's geophysical characteristics, and there is a growing worry about the Alps. Not only are they suffering the effects of acid rain caused by the increasing volume of trans-Alpine traffic, but they are also having to contend with recreational pressure of Mediterranean proportions. Every year they are visited by over 110 million people (*Financial Times*, 4 March 1995), while in the winter about 50 million tourists make use of more than 120,000 km of ski-slopes. The result is deforestation, increased risk of avalanche, floods and the destruction of the flora. Presently, about one-fifth of the Alpine forest is suffering from pollution or mismanagement. It is little wonder that calls are being made for 'serious measures ... to halt the alarming destruction of woodland and the mountain agriculture of the "natural alpine area" whose ecological balance is being seriously endangered' (EP, 1990). In response, the EU in 1991 established an Alpine Convention, whose aim was to safeguard and protect the region.

Tourism's Midas touch is also being felt in other parts of the EU. As an English Tourism Board (1991) study wryly pointed out with regard to the quality of the tourism experience, 'few of the ten million annual visitors to the Notre Dame in Paris can feel any sense of quiet contemplation', a sensation which must be equally rare for the fewer than 400 inhabitants of the Devon town of Clovelly, annually overwhelmed by some 400,000 visitors.

THE DEVELOPMENT OF EUROPEAN UNION TOURISM POLICY

Prelude to the *Initial Guidelines on Tourism* (1982)

The first attempt at a comprehensive statement of tourism policy, made in 1982, was preceded by a plethora of 'proxy' measures. In 1968 came the first detailed provisions concerning workers in hotels, cafés and restaurants (Council, 1968). In 1975, the European Regional Development Fund (ERDF) was set up, and even though it did not concern itself directly with tourism it did nevertheless create a policy framework and resources which could be used to promote it. At the end of 1975, a directive concerning the quality of bathing water was issued (Council, 1975). The following year also saw a law on the discharge of dangerous substances into the aquatic environment (Council, 1976), and in the wake of the *Amoco Cadiz* disaster off the coast of Brittany in 1978, the Community initiated an action programme on the control and reduction of pollution caused by hydrocarbons released into the sea (June 1978). At about the same time the Community augmented its commitment to the Bonn Agreement for cooperation in dealing with pollution of the north sea by oil (1969), with support for the Barcelona Convention of 1976 for the protection of the Mediterranean against pollution, and the Athens Protocol for the defence of the Mediterranean against land-based pollution (May 1980).

The European Summit of May 1977 saw a significant strengthening of policy on the environment, while in 1979 the Council passed a measure on the conservation of wild birds (Council, 1979). In total, between 1973 and 1984, the Council of Ministers issued 63 legal instruments concerning water and air pollution, waste, noise, chemical products and the protection of nature.

Pressure from public opinion, particularly on the question of the environment, and from the EP on the issue of the protection of Europe's cultural heritage, combined with a growing realization of the scale of tourism's importance, encouraged the Commission to pull all of these threads together in its *Initial Guidelines on a Community Policy on Tourism* of 1982 (Commission, 1982).

The *Initial Guidelines on a Community Policy on Tourism*

This document represented the first comprehensive attempt to take stock of tourism's importance and to situate it in the context of other related fields of policy. It identified the key issues and highlighted the major problems of policy development and implementation. Despite its shortcomings, which the EP and the ESC were not slow to point out, it acted as a marker for debate and action in years to come.

The key policy issues which it identified were as follows:

- The freedom of movement of tourists and the protection of their interests. Particular attention was paid to the inhibiting role of customs and police checks, the social security provision for tourists, and their protection in terms of both their physical safety (hazards in places where they stay) and their interests as consumers (rights regarding travel agents, etc.).
- The working conditions of those in the industry. Here the *Guidelines* referred to the rights of establishment and freedom to provide services, vocational training of people in the industry, and the mutual recognition of their professional qualifications.
- The impact on tourism policy of transport and regional policy and the importance of environmental and cultural protection.

In terms of the further development of policy, the Commission argued that while there was no disputing the fact that the main responsibility remained with the member states, there was nevertheless a need for a number of common rules and a better co-ordination of policy. This co-ordination would in its turn, be more effective if the Council of Ministers were more proactive, as many of the Commission's previous proposals had been left unresolved for a considerable time. Political reality, however, dictated that the central authorities of the EC should not go too far in seeking to co-ordinate national policies, 'because each of these reflects the very different situations of the Member States. Nor should [they] try to solve problems that could be better dealt with at the national or even regional level' (Commission, 1982, p. 6).

The *Guidelines* identified three key priorities for action. The first was the tackling of tourism's acute seasonality, which was leading not only to the blight of mass tourism in the summer but also to the under-use of resources at other times of the year. The 'habit of regarding one or two months of the year as the holiday season', it argued, would 'have to be overcome and this means that the public must be offered new "products" and the poorer sections of society encouraged to take advantage of off-season prices' (Commission, 1982, p. 7). The staggering of industrial and school holidays was seen as a major priority.

Seasonality could also be mitigated by the development of alternative forms of tourism. The intention was not only to lure people away from the beaches in the peak periods but also to encourage new forms of leisure, such as out-of-season cultural tourism and rural tourism.

The *Guidelines'* final priority was that of 'social tourism'. The growth of tourism in recent years, the Commission argued, should not hide the fact that large sections of society were still not benefiting from it. Special attention should be paid to 'young workers and pensioners, who would, if encouraged, take holidays during the low season. They are prime targets for the staggering of the tourist season, which will enable better use to be made of investments in tourism' (Commission, 1982, p. 7).

FROM THE *INITIAL GUIDELINES* TO EUROPEAN TOURISM YEAR 1990

This period marks a significant transition in the development of tourism policy, which was largely brought about by the unintended enhancement it was given by the implementation of the Single Market Programme from 1986 onwards. This not only aroused a recognition of tourism's economic importance but also alerted the EC to the role it could play in the development of a more politically and culturally unified community. It was recognized that increased freedom of movement and greater acquaintance of EC citizens with each other's culture could act as a catalyst for the revolution in attitudes on which the project of the single market critically depended for its success. There was, in addition, a growing awareness of the contribution which tourism was making to the Community's role in the world economy, and particularly the part which it could play in arresting the decline in its competitiveness, which was becoming a matter of increasing concern.

The fleshing out of policy now began to gather pace. A particularly important part was played by the EP, which constantly urged the Council of Ministers to act with greater speed and determination. In 1983, it adopted a resolution based on the Viehoff Report, which called not only for greater priority to be given to tourism but also for greater protection of tourists in terms of the safety and hygiene standards of their accommodation. It also suggested further action to harmonize the qualifications of the workers in the industry, and made proposals for harmonized classification of hotels (EP, 1984).

This last proposal was picked up by the Council in 1986, when it recommended the standardization of information symbols in hotels and called for a Community-wide grading system (Council, 1986a). In the same year it established a consultation and co-operation procedure in the field of tourism (Council, 1986b), and adopted a resolution which asked the member states to encourage a better spread of holidays and the creation of alternative destinations for tourists.

More importantly, it set up the Advisory Committee on Tourism. The role of the Committee, which was to report annually to the Commission, was to facilitate consultation and exchanges of opinion between states and, where appropriate, to encourage co-operation, particularly on the question of the provision of services for tourists. Important though all these measures were, they failed to satisfy the EP. The McMillan Scott Report a year later argued that the measures adopted by the Council still fell 'far short of what is desired and needed' (EP, 1987).

Progress was, however, being made. In a very significant development, all of the national ministers responsible for tourism held their first formal meeting in December 1988. They adopted an action programme which highlighted the integrative role which tourism could play in the formation of a large area without frontiers, and in the creation of a true 'people's Europe'. Even more significant was the call made by the EP, with the support of the Commission, to have 1990 designated as European Tourism Year (ETY), a request which was later endorsed by the Council (Council, 1989).

European Tourism Year 1990

The chief objectives of ETY were to facilitate intra-Community tourism, promote tourism from abroad, improve the working conditions of those in the industry, encourage a better seasonal and geographic distribution, and improve awareness of the sector.

The Commission agreed to allocate resources to projects which promoted a better quality of tourism, while financial support was also committed to publicity campaigns about low-season travel and cultural, social and rural tourism. As part of ETY, the Commission undertook to co-ordinate and encourage funding from other programmes, such as the Integrated Mediterranean Programmes (IMPs) and the Regional Development Fund, and also to support assistance from the European Investment Bank (EIB), whose role was particularly important for the development of large-scale tourist complexes and the financing of structural improvements. Finally, ETY was envisaged as a springboard for future developments and as an opportunity to consolidate and develop, in a long-term strategic framework, various activities in the field of tourism.

Despite the fact that ETY made very little discernible public impact, the Commission saw it as a success. It maintained ETY had brought together disparate elements of the Brussels bureaucracy which were more used to competing than co-operating with one another. Departments responsible for information, the environment, and social and regional policy had all come together to plan and execute specific ETY objectives. At the same time, links between national and local administrators, trade associations and representatives of the industry had been improved, as was the connection between all of them and the Commission (Commission, 1991).

A second argument for its success, the Commission believed, was that ETY had highlighted the need for a broader European policy dimension. Particularly successful in this regard had been the new insights gained into rural and environmental or 'ecological' tourism. Significant progress had also been made in the field of cultural tourism, and projects attracting financial support from the Commission included those which had designed and promoted European cultural itineraries. These, particularly, had fostered greater co-operation and exchange of experience and information between the different regions of Europe.

Thirdly, the Commission argued that ETY had stimulated a transnational and collaborative approach to the industry's development. It had demonstrated that co-operation of this kind exerted a multiplier effect, particularly in as yet undeveloped areas (for example, urban tourism) or where the need for the transfer of know-how and experience was considerable, as in the case of co-operation with Central and Eastern Europe.

Finally, ETY had been a success because it enabled operators, promoters, customers and governments to gain a greater awareness of the importance of tourism as an asset for the Community. By raising the profile of tourism and by giving the industry a common focus, while trying to create, even if only fleetingly and imperfectly, a greater sense of common interest, ETY had responded to one of the industry's greatest problems: its heterogeneity, disparity and lack of common purpose.

Although the EP and the ESC did not wholly share the Commission's enthusiasm for its handiwork, they did nevertheless feel that ETY had been sufficiently productive to encourage it to develop a more considered, comprehensive and better organized policy. In response to suggestions along these lines made by the tourism ministers at their meetings in Milan in 1990 and Nordwijk in 1991, the Commission set its hand to this task. The result was the 1991 *Action Plan*.

THE *ACTION PLAN* AND THE CHALLENGES TO EUROPEAN TOURISM IN THE 1990S

Described by the Commission as the most significant measure launched at the Community level on tourism (Commission, 1994a), the *Community Action Plan to Assist*

Tourism (Commission, 1991) is a long, densely argued and wide-ranging response to the challenges to EC tourism as it entered the 1990s. Even though the scope of the proposals was limited by the Council, it is much more thorough and wide-ranging than the *Initial Guidelines*. It reflects not only the great changes which had occurred in tourism in the intervening decade but also the progress which had been made in the development of policy. Its aim was to:

> cover all aspects of tourism and ... to achieve an all-round improvement in the quality and competitiveness of tourism facilities and services [and] facilitate awareness of the demand for tourism and support efforts to satisfy [it]. (p. 15)

It pulled together major strands of policy, only three of which will be dealt with here: the need to tackle the continuing problem of mass tourism; the requirement to co-ordinate policy in a complex and growing industry; and the necessity of promoting Europe as a tourist destination.

The Commission recognized that the tourism product had to be revitalized if Europe was to hold its own in world markets ever more characterized by sophisticated and demanding clienteles. The dash to the seaside in midsummer, no less a problem now than it had been a decade before, had to be dealt with more decisively by the offer of new destinations and experiences. Of these, rural and cultural tourism had the most to offer.

The Commission had already begun to develop a strategy for rural tourism the year previously (Commission, 1990) and the *Action Plan* built on this. It argued that rural tourism was a 'natural alternative to mass tourism [with a] great potential authenticity, local culture, architectural heritage, and personal contacts between local people and tourists' (p. 23). It proposed to improve rural tourism by generating more information about it at both the European and local levels, and also by helping the sector's operators. These proposals were additional to those of 1990, when it had called for more training and an increase in and better orchestration of investment in this sector.

As has already been seen, cultural tourism had acquitted itself well in ETY. It had become a growing sector of activity, pulling in an increasing volume of tourists from both within and outside the Community. It was an area where tourist businesses benefited from:

> customers attracted by services external to the industry itself. Largely because of the diversity of customers, the development of different forms of cultural tourism also contributed to the staggering of tourist visits, to a better balance in intra-Community tourist flows and to the promotion of new tourist destinations.
>
> (Commission, 1991, p. 24)

In order to promote cultural tourism, the Commission proposed further encouragement to research and the exchange of information, a European prize for the best cultural tourism product, and a number of schemes, some already begun during ETY, for improving access to, and the quality of, museums.

Cultural tourism, as well as other emergent sectors such as urban, social and environmental tourism, had, however, to be placed in a coherently organized context. The necessary precondition was a deepening of the knowledge of the industry, or what the Commission termed gaining an 'accurate as possible picture of the present situation and the development problems faced in all areas of the ... industry' (p. 16). This had already begun the previous year, when the Council had adopted a two-year programme for developing tourism statistics (Council, 1990), and the *Action Plan* suggested that this should be taken onwards, with detailed studies on questions such as the forward analysis of various forms of tourism and the ways of promoting them. To make this effective, the member states were asked to collaborate closely, while the outcome of the work was to be published and disseminated as widely as possible in order to create a documentary base on tourism's essential features.

Perhaps more importantly, the Commission suggested strengthening policy co-ordination between the different sectors of the industry. This was vital, given the rapidly changing business and social environment in which it found itself. The Commission advised that the policies of the member states should be better co-ordinated through the Advisory Committee on Tourism, which should meet more frequently and regularly. Lastly, in order to improve the strategic effectiveness of policy, it suggested that a tourism impact assessment should be made, so that the consequences of all Community policies on the industry could be analysed during the various stages of their development.

The Commission finally turned its attention to possible remedies for the Community's loss of market share. It suggested a number of measures, the first of which was the strengthening of the competitive position of EC firms in third markets. This could be done not only by operators combining their efforts but also by securing reciprocal agreements with those countries which had done well out of the growth of European tourism. These should be encouraged to offer similarly advantageous conditions to EU firms. It argued that the emphasis of promotion ought to be changed and greater advantage be taken of US and Pacific markets. It also felt that the opportunities offered by the creation of the single market and the opening up of Eastern Europe should be given greater recognition.

The *Action Plan* was then sent to the other institutions of the Community for their comments. While pleased with the initiative, they were generally less impressed with many of its proposals. It was accused of vagueness, lack of clear priorities, failure to assess previous measures before proposing new ones, and, according to the ESC, even pusillanimity in its suggestions for global marketing (ESC, 1992; EP, 1992). Having done the round of the institutions, it was then sent to the Council of Ministers, where its main proposals were accepted in July 1992 (Council, 1992).

The Council adopted 11 key points, of which the top six for action were:

- improving knowledge of the industry and ensuring greater consistency of Community measures;
- staggering of holidays;
- transnational measures to support co-operation between border regions;
- the protection of tourists' consumer rights;
- cultural tourism;
- tourism's environmental impact.

It instituted a three-year plan to begin in 1993 with what the EP called a minuscule budget of ECU 18 million (EP, 1993). It also stipulated that the Commission should make an annual evaluation of the *Plan* and provide a final report on it no later than June 1996. If the Council was happy with the progress which had been made, it would agree to its further extension.

TOURISM POLICY TOWARDS THE YEAR 2000: CHALLENGE AND RESPONSE

With the approach of the new millennium, tourism policy makers face two clear, interrelated challenges. The first is the growth, evolution and differentiation of demand within Europe itself, while the second is the emergence of new international destinations.

Short of an economic downturn of the kind not seen since the 1930s, there seems little reason to doubt that tourism will continue to grow in importance. Indeed, a recent report predicts an increase in real disposable income of the average European of 20–25 per cent in the next few years alone (Commission, 1993a). The World Tourism Organization (WTO) predicts an annual growth rate of world tourism of just below 4 per cent for the rest of this decade, and in Europe the number of international arrivals is expected to grow by some 60 million during the same period.

This is not just a quantitative challenge to Europe's already overstretched tourism capacity; it is a major qualitative one as well. Whole new sectors of demand are developing, one of which is the 'senior travel market'. Created by the trend towards ever earlier retirement, the 55-year-old-plus tourist now takes 20 per cent of all trips in Europe, and this is expected to grow rapidly in the years to come. The plain fact is that the tourist of the future is likely to be very different from the one of the past. The average European holiday maker, it has been argued, will have very little in common with his or her counterpart of 20 or even 10 years ago (Commission, 1993a).

Future demand is likely to be for products which are more activity- and health-oriented, reflecting the lifestyle changes presently going on in Europe and the developed world. This poses a particular threat to some of Europe's mature, if not yet senescent, products. As awareness grows of the dangers of over-exposure to the sun, and as holiday makers vote with their wallets against resorts which seem to be unperturbed by overcrowding and rowdyism, a number of Mediterranean 'sun, sea and sand' resorts are likely to be at risk. Destinations developed to cater almost exclusively for this kind of customer seem particularly threatened. As the Commission itself has pointed out, there is an analogy with the difficulties that affected Northern European resorts when there was a shift to the Mediterranean. In this case, however, it might be much harder to avoid the consequences, since dependence on tourism is far higher.

International competition and the trend towards long haul, which is being facilitated by the revolution in air transport, are the other major challenges to the industry. New long-haul business is widening the horizons of European travellers and taking important business away. All things being equal, this ought to be compensated by growing purchasing power in the new source markets of Japan and Asia-Pacific, already targeted by the Commission in the *Action Plan*. That this has not happened, however, is largely due to the ability of the US, the world's most popular tourist destination, to cream it off instead.

Through the appeal of its mega-attractions, its ability to present itself to European travellers as a medium- rather than a long-haul destination, and through the sheer volume of its capacity (13 of the world's 20 largest hotel chains are based in the US), the United States presents a formidable challenge. This is happening at the same time as Asia-Pacific's role is growing. The fact that this part of the world has increased its share of global tourist receipts from 2.9 per cent in 1960 to 15.5 per cent in 1992 (Commission, 1994c) has been ominously compared with the entry of Japanese electronics firms into Europe in the early 1960s (Commission, 1993a). Both of these developments could not be more serious for the European tourist industry.

CONCLUDING COMMENTS

How adequately, then, have the EU's policy makers responded to the multiple challenges which the sector faces? On balance the answer must be that progress has been very inadequate. Indeed, in some respects the problems of the sector are developing more rapidly than are the solutions, particularly in the areas of product quality and global share. The EP, which has been the most exasperated and consistent critic of the slowness of progress, has even accused the Commission of having a tourism policy in words only (EP, 1993). On key questions such as the staggering of holidays, already identified as a major problem in the *Initial Guidelines*, virtually nothing has been done.

Rather than bringing all the elements of a tourism policy together under one roof, the Commission has allowed more powerful directorates general to formulate tourism-related policies instead. Experience has shown that to be effective Directorate General XXIII Enterprise Policy, Distributive Trades, Tourism and Co-operatives (DGXXIII), in which tourism presently finds itself, needs to be organizationally and politically strengthened and given an increase in its resources. Tourism policy clearly needs to have greater priority and be more comprehensive, better co-ordinated and more wholeheartedly supported both financially and politically than it has hitherto.

All of this should not, however, obscure the progress which has been made. There has been a growing awareness of the industry's importance at all levels and a steady accretion of policy. The Package Travel Directive of 1993, even though it was developed in the related area of consumer affairs, is a good example of this (see Chapter 12). ETY and the 1991 *Action Plan* have created parameters within which other developments have taken place, while issues placed on the agenda by the Commission, such as tourism's negative effect on the environment, have won a response from some quarters of the industry.

There are now very modest budgetary measures in place which in turn are being augmented by help from the Regional Development Fund, the Cohesion Fund (of importance to Spain, Portugal, Greece and Ireland), and the European Social Fund (see Chapter 7). In addition, support is given through programmes such as the Regional Action Programme Concerning the Environment (ENVIREG) and money from the EIB. This, for example, funds infrastructural developments in transport, telecommunications and environmental protection, as well as part-financing projects such as conference and exhibition centres, all of which have an impact on the tourist industry.

It should also be noted that after a very long battle tourism has been included as one of the EU's spheres of activity, under art. 3t of the TEU. The Commission has attempted to further concentrate minds with the publication of its 1995 *Green Paper on Tourism* (Commission, 1995). Indeed, in April 1996 it proposed the First Multiannual Programme to assist European Tourism (1997–2000). Named Philoxenia (hospitality) it aims to 'stimulate the quality and competitiveness of European tourism taking into account the balanced and sustainable development of the sector, the satisfaction of the tourists' needs and the rational use of the natural, cultural and infrastructural resources' (Commission, 1996). Whether or not the Council takes its cue from this and incorporates tourism as one of the EU's competences (at present tourism is dealt with under the catch-all art. 235 of the EEC Treaty), will have to wait until the outcome of the IGC in 1997.

What then of the future? In a context where tourists are becoming more mobile and sophisticated, the main challenge to the EU is to develop a more differentiated and environmentally sensitive product, which will capitalize on Europe's cultural and natural uniqueness and at the same time even out the ebb and flow of demand, which is having such damaging consequences. Given the projections of tourism's future growth, made in the context of the secular and global revolution in the relationship between work and leisure, there is little doubt that it is one of the major economic and business challenges which the EU faces. Given its worrying decline in other key areas of competitiveness, it is one which it can ill afford not to recognize or meet.

REFERENCES

Bangkok Post (1994) 'Mid-Year Review', 30 June.
Baty, B. and Templeton, R. (1991) 'Tourism and the Tourist Industry in 1990', *Employment Gazette*, September.
British Tourist Authority (1991) *Digest of Tourist Statistics*. London: BTA.
Butt Philip, A. (1989) *European Border Controls: Who Needs Them?* London: Royal Institute for International Affairs.
Commission (Commission of the European Communities) (1982) *Initial Guidelines on a Community Policy on Tourism*, COM(82) 235 Final.
—(1987) 'The European Community and Tourism'. *European File*. Luxembourg: OOPEC.
—(1990) *Community Action Plan to Promote Rural Tourism*, COM(90) 438 Final.
—(1991) *Community Action Plan to Assist Tourism*, COM(91) 97 Final.
—(1993) *The Evolution in Holiday Travel Facilities and in the Flow of Tourism Inside and Outside the European Community. Part 1. Main Findings*. Directorate General XXIII, Tourism Unit.
—(1994a) *Report from the Commission to the Council, the European Parliament and the Economic and Social Committee on Community Measures Affecting Tourism*, COM(94) 74 Final.
—(1994b) *Tourism Policy in the EU,* Background Report, ISEC/B24/94.
—(1994c) *Panorama of EU Industry*. Luxembourg: OOPEC.
—(1995) *The Role of the Union in the Field of Tourism.* Commission Green Paper, COM(95) 97 Final.
—(1996) *'Philoxenia' - The First Multiannual Programme for European Tourism*, (IP/96/366) Press Release, London.
Council (Council of the European Communities) (1968) Directive 68/367/EEC of 15 October 1968 Laying Down Detailed Provision Concerning Transitional Measures in Respect of the Activities of Self-employed Persons in the Personal Services Sector.
—(1975) Directive 75/160/EEC of 8 December 1975 Concerning the Quality of Bathing Water.
—(1976) Directive 76/464/EEC of 4 May 1976 on Pollution Caused by Certain Dangerous Substances Discharged into the Aquatic Environment of the Community.
—(1979) Directive 79/409/EEC on the Conservation of Wild Birds.
—(1986a) Recommendation of 22 December 1986 on Standardised Information in Existing Hotels (86/665/EEC).
—(1986b) Decision of 22 December 1986 Establishing a Consultation and Cooperation Procedure in the Field of Tourism (86/664/EEC).
—(1989) Decision on an Action Programme for European Tourism Year (89/46/EEC).
—(1990) Decision of 17 December 1990 on the Implementation of a Two Year

Programme (1991–1992) for Developing Community Tourism Statistics (90/665/EEC).
——(1992) Decision of 13 July 1992 on a Community Action Plan to Assist Tourism (92/421/EEC).
Council and Commission (Council and Commission of the European Communities) (1992) *Treaty on European Union*. Luxembourg: OOPEC.
Department of Employment (n.d.) *Tourism into the '90's. A Summary of Key Facts*. London: HMSO.
Department of Employment/English Tourist Board (1991) *Tourism and the Environment: Maintaining the Balance*. London: HMSO.
EP (European Parliament) (1984) Resolution on Community Policy on Tourism. 16 January.
——(1987) *Report Drawn up on Behalf of the Committee on Youth, Culture, Education, Information and Sport* (McMillan Scott Report). PE/115.349, 1987.
——(1990) Resolution on the Measures Needed to Protect the Environment from the Potential Damage Caused by Mass Tourism, as Part of the European Year of Tourism. 17 September.
——(1992) *Proposals for a Council Decision on a Community Action Plan to Assist Tourism*. OJC 67, 16.3.92, pp. 235–47.
——(1993) *Tourism on the Road towards 2000. Rapporteur* P. Cornelissen. PE 206.166/Fin.
ESC (Economic and Social Committee) (1992) Opinion on the Community Action Plan to Assist Tourism. 24 February.
Eurostat (1989) *Tourism in Europe: Trends*. Luxembourg: OOPEC.
HOTREC (1990) *The 1992 Challenges for the Hotel, Restaurant and Café Industry*. Paris: HOTREC.
OECD (1992) *Report on Tourism Policy and International Tourism*. Paris: OECD.

SIX

Monetary union

Nigel Healey

INTRODUCTION

In December 1991, the member states of the European Union (EU) took the historic step of pledging themselves to the creation of a monetary union before the end of the century. The Maastricht Treaty envisages the creation of a European Central Bank (ECB), issuing a single currency and making monetary policy for all 15 member states. Few issues in the EU's history have excited such controversy. Political reaction has been especially marked in Britain, where the prospect of giving up the pound in favour of a single EU currency has split the Conservative government and polarized popular opinion between so-called 'Euro-enthusiasts' and 'Euro-sceptics'.

Yet, taken at face value, the objective of a single currency appears to offer unambiguous benefits to European producers and consumers. Monetary union would eliminate exchange rate risk on intra-EU imports and exports, promoting cross-border trade and investment. These potential benefits would apply, *a fortiori*, to the hospitality industry, where a high proportion of total value-added is internationally traded. Over 20 million foreign tourists visit Britain each year, for example; a similar number go abroad for business or leisure. Exchange rate volatility currently distorts relative prices, adversely affecting the competitiveness of the tourist industry in states with appreciating currencies and eroding the purchasing power of potential business travellers and holiday makers in states with depreciating currencies.

This chapter examines the implications of European monetary union (EMU) for the hospitality industry. It begins by defining monetary union and reviews the economic costs and benefits of adopting a common currency. It then considers the precise nature of the monetary union envisaged in the Maastricht Treaty, going on to discuss the likely ramifications for the hotel and catering sectors.

WHAT IS MONETARY UNION?

In technical terms, a 'monetary union' consists of an arrangement between participating countries in which:

- bilateral exchange rates (that is, the exchange rates between one member state and another) are permanently fixed, with no margins for permissible fluctuations;
- there are no institutional barriers (such as legal controls) to the free movement of capital across national frontiers.

For a genuine monetary union, both of these conditions must be simultaneously fulfilled. For example, prior to German reunification in 1990, the East German currency (the Ostmark) had been fixed at a 1:1 exchange rate against the West German Deutschmark since 1949, but this arrangement did *not* constitute a monetary union. The exchange rate was entirely artificial and applied only to official transactions within East Germany; state regulations outlawed unofficial currency trading and prohibited the import or export of Ostmarks. In West Germany, where illegally smuggled Ostmarks could be freely traded, the market exchange rate averaged approximately OM5:DM1 in the year before reunification.

In addition to irrevocably fixed exchange rates and the abolition of all capital controls (which have already been removed under the EU's '1992' programme – see Cecchini, 1988; Healey, 1992a), the form of monetary union agreed in Maastricht involves replacing national currencies with a common currency. Although monetary union technically requires no more than permanently fixed, bilateral exchange rates, moving to a common currency has the advantage of eliminating the transactions costs of switching between national currencies (Zis, 1995). The adoption of a single currency also helps to make the monetary union more permanent, by increasing the costs to participating states of withdrawing from the arrangement (Delors, 1989).

THE BENEFITS AND COSTS OF MONETARY UNION

Economics textbooks typically characterize exchange rate systems as 'fixed' or 'floating' and, on this basis, monetary union can be seen as the 'hardest' form of fixed exchange rate regime – that is, an arrangement in which the value of national currencies can neither fluctuate within bands nor be periodically realigned. To a large extent, therefore, the economic arguments for and against EMU are an extension of the long-running 'fixed versus floating rates' debate (for example, Artus and Young, 1979; de Grauwe, 1988; Krugman, 1989), which turns on whether the economic benefits of stabilizing the exchange rate (reduced exchange rate uncertainty) outweigh the costs of giving up exchange rate flexibility (sacrificing 'monetary sovereignty'). The additional dimension of EMU is the transition to a single currency, which provides the extra benefit of eliminating transactions costs over and above reduced exchange rate uncertainty. The following sections examine the main benefits and costs of EMU in turn (see also Barrell, 1992; Begg, 1991; Eichengreen, 1990; Emerson, 1992; Healey and Levine, 1992a; Goodhart, 1991).

Reduced exchange rate uncertainty

EMU would clearly end the uncertainty that exchange rate fluctuations presently bring to intra-EU trade and investment. While it is true that increasingly sophisticated financial institutions provide a form of insurance against exchange rate uncertainty, these 'hedging' facilities are not costless, and their cost reflects the potential savings to the EU of adopting a single currency. Moreover, for long time horizons, so-called 'forward' facilities are not universally available (Levine, 1990).

Such considerations have a special importance for members of the EU, the *raison d'être* of which is to facilitate cross-border movements of goods, services, labour and capital. Advocates of EMU argue that the potential gains from membership of the EU cannot be realized in the long term unless countries are able to exploit fully their own, unique comparative advantages (Jenkins, 1978; Brittan, 1991). To achieve this, economic resources – land, labour, capital and enterprise – must be transferred from less efficient to more efficient sectors, and the commercial decisions which make such reallocations possible depend critically upon expectations of the future. Since uncertainty about the future course of intra-EU exchange rates may inhibit the restructuring of production by which the potential gains from greater trade are translated into reality, EMU should therefore accelerate economic integration within the EU (Artis, 1989; European Commission, 1990).

Transactions costs

Business and leisure travellers are all too familiar with the transaction costs involved in changing currencies. These charges are made by banks to reflect their deployment of resources (such as personnel and equipment), as well as the opportunity costs of holding stocks of foreign exchange (that is, the interest forgone). For tourists dealing in small retail amounts, these charges can easily amount to 10 per cent of the value of the currency changed. One independent estimate suggests that, for the EU as a whole, eliminating transactions costs by the adoption of a single currency would yield savings of 2–3 per cent of total EU gross domestic product (GDP) (Artis, 1989).

The costs of sacrificing monetary sovereignty

For member states, EMU would entail the complete sacrifice of 'monetary sovereignty' – that is, the ability to make independent monetary policy at a national level. Of course, for those member states presently within the European Monetary System (EMS), the capacity to make monetary policy with a view to influencing domestic economic conditions is already limited. The need to maintain their exchange rates within the present ±15 per cent target bands against other EMS currencies means that there is reduced scope to use interest rates for domestic policy purposes (see van der Ploeg, 1989). Nevertheless, as events in 1992–3 graphically illustrated, under the EMS arrangements member states can, if the constraints on domestic policy making become intolerable, realign their target rates or even leave the EMS. Moreover, given the width of the margins for permissible fluctuations, provided exchange rates are suitably positioned in their bands, quite large domestically inspired changes in interest rates can be made without driving exchange rates out of their trading bands.

Under EMU, all such discretion would be eliminated. The power to make monetary policy would be transferred to a new ECB, which would set a common EU interest rate and issue a single EU currency. National central banks would simply become the regional agencies of the ECB, with no independent power to alter local monetary conditions. The primary cost of EMU therefore centres on the cost of surrendering monetary sovereignty and accepting a common monetary stance, set by a central policy-making body. The obvious danger is that the monetary stance – and the implied common inflation rate – chosen by the ECB might be inappropriate for certain member states. But for these costs to be significant, it is necessary that:

- accepting the common monetary stance results in a sub-optimal unemployment–inflation mix that persists in the long run (that is, there is significant price and wage inflexibility in the economy); and
- there are recurrent divergences in economic conditions in different member states, so that a common monetary stance necessarily becomes inappropriate at one time or another for the needs of one or more member states.

Consider each condition in turn. Traditional economic theory suggests that there is a trade-off between (lower) unemployment and (higher) inflation. Under such circumstances, there is no reason to believe that each country in the EU would have the same relative preferences between these two policy objectives. Southern states, for example, have tended to give greater weight to minimizing unemployment, while Northern states, notably Germany, have made price stability their main priority. If each country were forced to accept a common inflation rate under EMU, there is a danger that individual governments might be unable to achieve their desired objectives for unemployment. For example, the monetary stance adopted by the ECB might be regarded as inappropriately restrictive by a Southern state, resulting in higher unemployment (lower inflation) than the country's government would otherwise choose.

For the costs of monetary union to persist over time, however, there must exist a stable, *long-run* trade-off between inflation and unemployment, so that tighter monetary policy translates into permanently (rather than transitorily) higher unemployment. Although the EU economies are clearly plagued – to a greater or lesser extent – by price and wage inflexibility, which prevents unemployment from putting downward pressure on wages and so restoring equilibrium, the consensus view amongst economists is that such inflexibility is an essentially short-run phenomenon; that is, eventually prices and wages adjust and, in the long run, unemployment tends to a 'natural rate', which is independent of the rate of inflation (see Friedman, 1968). If this is true, it follows that sacrificing monetary sovereignty might mean nothing worse than accepting, in the long run, the rate of inflation implied by the monetary stance of the EU as a whole – with no lasting implications for the rate of unemployment. Provided that all members of the EU agree to make zero inflation the central objective of monetary policy, EMU should accordingly be compatible with both 'full' employment (that is, unemployment at the natural rate) and price stability in the long run.

A shared commitment to zero inflation in the long run does not, however, mean that the costs of sacrificing monetary sovereignty are self-evidently trivial. The 1980–1 and 1990–2 recessions in Britain graphically illustrated that the short-run costs of reducing inflation in terms of higher unemployment can be significant. Thus, if member states were to create EMU at a time when one or more had an entrenched inflation rate well above zero, then the attempt to impose a common, non-inflationary monetary policy could lead to serious unemployment in the higher-inflation states (CEPR, 1991). While such unemployment would be essentially transitional, the social and economic costs of 'settling into' EMU might be so high as to force such high-inflation countries to withdraw. For this reason, economists have generally argued that member states should achieve a high degree of inflation 'convergence' prior to joining EMU, thereby minimizing the unemployment costs of membership, rather than entering with differential rates and relying on the disciplining effects of EMU (via higher unemployment) to force inflation convergence *ex-post*.

The problem of asymmetric 'shocks'

The analysis above suggests that, in the long run, sacrificing monetary sovereignty is costless, since monetary policy has no lasting effect on unemployment. Moreover, if member states can bring their inflation rates into line with each other (preferably at zero inflation) prior to the creation of EMU, then the transitional, short-run costs of moving to a common, non-inflationary monetary policy can be minimized.

However, even if all member states were to join EMU with zero inflation, thereafter being subject to a common, non-inflationary monetary stance, their inflation performances might not *continue* to be completely identical over time. Random supply-side 'shocks', as well as unexpected changes in aggregate demand (such as a sudden fall in national savings ratios), might cause sudden bouts of inflation or deflation within individual member states. If these shocks were 'asymmetric', in the sense that they affected some member states more than others, then because EMU obliges each member of the EU to adhere to the same monetary policy, countries hit by such shocks would be unable to use monetary policy to stabilize their economies. The result of EMU might thus be *increased* instability in the real economies of certain states (Bayoumi and Eichengreen, 1992; Minford and Rastogi, 1990; Minford, 1995).

In the face of recurrent asymmetric shocks, therefore, the prior convergence of inflation performance is not a sufficient condition for minimizing the costs of EMU membership. Years after joining, certain member states might continue to be plagued by periodic bouts of inflation and unemployment, as localized supply-side or demand-side shocks temporarily drove their inflation performance away from that of the rest of the EU. Under such circumstances, EMU might thus impose significant economic costs on member states. Economic theory suggests that, in the absence of a monetary policy 'stabilizer', these costs might be alleviated in one of two other ways: either by the asymmetric shock being quickly and smoothly transmitted to the rest of the EU, or via fiscal transfers between the unaffected and affected member states. Let us consider each possibility in turn.

Optimum currency areas

If member economies were perfectly integrated, so that to all intents and purposes they could be treated as a single market, the problem of asymmetric shocks would be greatly eased (Mundell, 1961). Under such circumstances, the free movement of goods, services, labour and capital would quickly spread the effects of a localized deflationary or inflationary shock from the country initially affected to the rest of the EU, so that no individual country would be disproportionately affected. There would accordingly be no incentive for countries (initially) unaffected by, say, an inflationary oil price rise to force their more vulnerable partners to maintain a restrictive common monetary policy (de Grauwe, 1994).

At present, however, the EU remains a collection of segmented national economies (de Grauwe and Vanhaverbeke, 1991). If the EU were perfectly integrated (and its markets competitive), then the prices of products in different member states, measured in any given currency, would be the same – a principle known as 'the law of one price'. Table 6.1, which shows the prices in different EU countries of various products, confirms that this condition is not yet satisfied. Although the EU's '1992' programme is intended to create a genuine common market in goods, services, labour and capital, it is clear that the capacity of asymmetric shocks to destabilize a future EMU could be a significant problem well into the next century (Feldstein, 1992).

Table 6.1 Prices in the EU (common currency, Belgian price = 100)

Country	*German cars*	*Pharmaceuticals*	*Life insurance*	*Domestic appliances*
Belgium	100	100	100	100
France	115	78	75	130
Germany	127	174	59	117
Italy	129	80	102	110
Netherlands	n/a	164	51	105
Britain	142	114	39	93

Source: European Economy.

Fiscal transfers

Within nation states, the problem of localized shocks is also moderated by the centralization of the fiscal system. Residents and businesses pay taxes to a central government and receive, in return, state expenditures on social security, health, education, etc. As a consequence, an asymmetric shock which strikes a particular region of the country alters the pattern of inter-regional fiscal transfers in a way which helps to stabilize demand and employment in the affected area (MacDougall, 1977). For example, suppose there were a collapse in oil prices. This development would have an especially marked impact on Scotland, which is heavily dependent on the oil industry in the North Sea for income and employment. The ensuing localized recession would lead to lower taxes being paid by Scottish workers and businesses (especially in the oil and oil-related industries) to central government in London, and would increase the total demands of Scottish citizens on public spending programmes, as claims for unemployment-related benefits increased. The original fall in Scottish income would thus be partially compensated by a change in the balance of fiscal transfers, with payments to central government falling and receipts from central government increasing. In this way, an integrated, centralized fiscal system helps to stabilize income and employment in regions affected by specific economic shocks.

In the EU at present, however, the stabilizing function of the central budget is extremely limited. Despite recent increases in the size of the budget, total EU expenditure amounts to no more than 1.27 per cent of the EU's GDP, in contrast to public spending within member states, which accounts for approximately 50 per cent of GDP on the average. Moreover, although the EU has fiscal instruments like the European Social Fund (ESF) and the European Regional Development Fund (ERDF) (see Chapter 7), these account for less than 25 per cent of total spending, which is dominated by the Common Agricultural Policy. They are, in any case, directed towards equalizing structural differences in living standards rather than correcting short-term fluctuations in income and employment. In other words, as presently constructed, the EU's central budget is too small and too inappropriately designed to provide any stabilizing influence for member states suffering from asymmetric shocks.

THE POLITICAL DIMENSIONS OF EMU

It is now well known that the effectiveness of monetary policy depends critically upon the political and institutional context within which policy decisions are formulated and executed. No discussion of the benefits and costs of EMU is complete without considering the constitutional framework within which future EU monetary policy is to be made. Modern economic theory suggests that if the ultimate power over monetary policy is vested with democratic governments (or a central EU body representing their interests, like the Council of Ministers), the outcome is likely to be higher inflation than if it is delegated to an independent central bank (for example, Kydland and Prescott, 1977; Barro and Gordon, 1983; Alesina, 1989; Alesina and Grilli, 1991).

In contrast to the political pressures which bear upon elected governments, a constitutionally independent central bank has no incentive to depart from the socially optimal objective of price stability. Delegating control of monetary policy to an independent central bank might therefore insulate the policy-making process from electoral considerations. International evidence confirms that there is a strong relationship between the degree of central bank independence and inflation. A related benefit of an independent central bank is that it may serve to make monetary policy announcements more 'credible', reducing the unemployment costs of fighting inflation. As the term suggests, 'credibility' refers to the extent to which people believe the pronouncements of a policy-making body. Inflationary expectations will only adjust favourably to the official announcement of a tightening of monetary policy if wage bargainers believe the policy changes will be carried through. Given the political incentives for an elected government to renege on promises of price stability as election time looms, the private sector is unlikely to pay much heed to the declared intentions of politicians. A central bank which is constitutionally independent of the government and bound by a statutory obligation to fight inflation, on the other hand, is liable to command much greater credibility, giving it the ability to achieve stable prices at a lower cost in terms of unemployment than a government taking exactly the same policy stance.

The dimensions of central bank independence

There are two dimensions of central bank independence. First, the central bank must be politically independent, in the sense that its decisions should not be subject to the approval or direction of the government. Ideally, the government of the day should not be able to 'rig' the bank's policy-making executive by appointing either the governor or its senior staff. To the extent that the government has the power to make such appointments, the interests of political independence would best be served by having lengthy, secure terms of tenure for key executives, spread out so that only a small proportion fell due for renewal within the lifetime of any one government. Mandatory government representatives on the bank's executive also militate against political independence. Table 6.2 sets out the main dimensions of political independence, ranking EU central banks on this basis.

Table 6.2 Measures of political independence

Central bank	*1*	*2*	*3*	*4*	*5*	*6*	*7*	*8*	*9*
Germany		*		*	*	*	*	*	6
Netherlands		*		*	*	*	*	*	6
Italy	*	*	*		*				4
Denmark		*					*	*	3
Ireland		*				*		*	3
France		*		*					2
Greece			*					*	2
Spain				*	*				2
Belgium				*					1
Portugal					*				1
Britain					*				1

Key:
1 Governor not appointed by government
2 Governor appointed for 5+ years
3 Executive not appointed by government
4 Executive appointed for 5+ years
5 No mandatory government representative on executive
6 No government approval of policy decision required
7 Statutory requirement for central bank to pursue price stability
8 Explicit conflicts between central bank and government possible
9 Index of political independence (sum of asterisks in each row)

Source: Alesina and Grilli (1991).

Second, the central bank should be economically independent, in the sense that it is able to execute monetary policy without being blown off-course by government actions. For example, in many countries, the government has an account with its national central bank, which it can effectively overdraw at will – thereby increasing the money supply. Central banks may also be obliged to buy any issue of government bonds that is not taken up by the general public, with the same effect on the money supply. Under such circumstances, a tight monetary policy could be undermined by an increase in the budget deficit. Some instruments of monetary policy may also be under the control of the government. For example, historically British governments have imposed both qualitative and quantitative controls on commercial bank lending. Table 6.3 shows how 11 of the national central banks of the EU member states presently rank on the main dimensions of economic independence.

THE MAASTRICHT TREATY

Reflecting concern over the constitutional status of the new ECB, the Maastricht Treaty (Council of Ministers, 1992) requires the proposed European central banking system to be constitutionally independent of elected governments and legally bound to maintain price stability within the EU. Although collectively termed the ECB, the system will comprise:

- the ECB, which will have a president and an executive of six members appointed by the European Council for eight-year terms, and a governing council (the executive plus governors of the national central banks from participating member states);

Table 6.3 Measures of economic independence

Central bank	*1*	*2*	*3*	*4*	*5*	*6*	*7*	*8*	*9*
Germany	*	*	*	*	*	*	*	*	8
Belgium		*	*	*	*	*		*	6
Britain	*	*	*	*		*	*		6
Denmark		*			*	*	*		4
France				*	*	*	*		4
Ireland		*	*	*		*			4
Netherlands				*	*	*	*		4
Spain				*	*			*	3
Greece				*		*			2
Portugal				*		*			2
Italy				*					1

Key
1 Government credit from central bank not automatic
2 Government credit from central bank at market interest rate
3 Government credit from central bank for temporary period only
4 Government credit from central bank limited in amount
5 Central bank does not take up unsold government bond issues
6 Discount rate set by central bank
7 No government qualitative controls on commercial bank lending since 1980
8 No government quantitative controls on bank lending since 1980
9 Index of economic independence (sum of asterisks in each row)

Source: Alesina and Grilli (1991).

- the European System of Central Banks (ESCB), consisting of participating national central banks, which will act as regional agents in carrying out the policy instructions of the ECB.

To the extent that all the significant decision-making power will reside at the centre with the ECB, the use of the term 'ECB' to describe the system as a whole is retained in what follows. Tables 6.4 and 6.5 show that on all indices of political and economic independence the proposed ECB will be identical to the German Bundesbank, which is presently the most independent of all EU central banks (see Tables 6.2 and 6.3 above).

Table 6.4 Measures of political independence

Central bank	*1*	*2*	*3*	*4*	*5*	*6*	*7*	*8*	*9*
ECB		*		*	*	*	*	*	6
Germany		*		*	*	*	*	*	6

Note: Key as Table 6.2 above.
Source: Alesina and Grilli (1991).

Table 6.5 Measures of economic independence

Central bank	*1*	*2*	*3*	*4*	*5*	*6*	*7*	*8*	*9*
ECB	*	*	*	*	*	*	*	*	8
Germany	*	*	*	*	*	*	*	*	8

Note: Key as Table 6.3 above.
Source: Alesina and Grilli (1991).

Since the ECB will embrace, and operate through, national central banks, the Maastricht Treaty requires that the latter end their present links with their national governments, becoming fully politically and economically independent before they may be admitted to the ESCB (Harden, 1990; Lomax, 1991; Healey, 1992b). Article 7 of the

Treaty, for example, specifically forbids any national central bank in the ESCB seeking or taking instructions from any other EU institution, including its national government.

To minimize the transitional unemployment costs of EMU to the historically high-inflation countries of the EU (such as Britain, Italy, Spain, Portugal and Greece), the Treaty envisages that the move to a single currency will depend on the fulfilment of certain 'convergence criteria' (see Bank of England, 1992). The logic of these conditions is that, if satisfied, the short-run costs of giving up monetary sovereignty will be modest and, by implication, outweighed by the likely benefits. The three indicators of inflation convergence are as follows:

- Successful candidates must have inflation rates no more than 1.5 per cent above the average of the three EU countries with the lowest inflation rates.
- Long-term interest rates should be no more than 2 per cent above the average of the three countries with the lowest rates.
- A national currency must not have been devalued and must have remained within the 'normal' (±15 per cent) bands of the EMS for the previous two years.

With the exception of the second point, these three criteria are self-explanatory. The significance of the second lies in the fact that long-term interest rates provide a guide to the financial markets' expectations of inflation in the longer term. Put simply, today's long-term interest rate is a weighted average of expected future short-term interest rates. If investors expect inflation to be high in the future, they will expect short-term interest rates to be correspondingly high in the future as well. The long-term interest rate will accordingly be higher than in a country where inflation is expected to remain low in the future.

THE IMPLICATIONS OF EMU FOR PUBLIC FINANCES

The Maastricht Treaty contains two further convergence criteria which impose limits on public finances, namely that:

- national budget deficits must be less than 3 per cent of GDP;
- the national debt must be less than 60 per cent of GDP (or at least satisfactorily falling towards this level).

The rationale of these fiscal criteria stems from the implications of creating an independent ECB with a statutory responsibility for maintaining price stability for national governments. Not only would an independent ECB end the ability of member governments to manipulate the business cycle for electoral purposes, but it would also constrain national public finances in two ways (see Healey and Levine, 1992b). First, the right to issue 'fiat' money (that is, notes and coin) is to be transferred from national governments to the ECB, so that 'seigniorage' profits would be lost to member governments (Grilli, 1989; Drazen, 1989). Such seigniorage profits stem from the fact that governments presently 'sell' newly created currency to their national banking systems for its full face value, while the actual production costs of printing notes and minting coins are much lower.

Table 6.6 shows that the Southern Mediterranean countries of Greece, Portugal and Spain would be particularly adversely affected by the loss of seigniorage profits. At

Table 6.6 Seigniorage revenue as a percentage of GDP

Country	Seigniorage revenue, 1994
Belgium	0.60
Britain	0.30
Denmark	0.32
France	0.40
Germany	0.57
Greece	1.37
Italy	0.74
Ireland	0.47
Luxembourg	0.16
Netherlands	0.60
Portugal	1.63
Spain	1.07

Source: Bank for International Settlements.

present, these countries have relatively undeveloped financial systems, which means that their currency ratios (that is, currency as a proportion of the money stock) are higher than in Northern states. This region also suffers relatively high inflation rates, which continuously erode the real value of currency in circulation, obliging the private sector to hold ever larger cash balances for transaction purposes. Against the backdrop of inflation, the seigniorage profits from currency issue afford a significant source of revenue for national governments; the higher the currency ratio and the higher the rate of inflation, the greater the importance of the seigniorage revenue as a means of financing government expenditure.

The second implication of EMU for national public finances is that the requirement of economic independence for the ECB will deny governments the right of automatic, unlimited access to central bank credit (Demopoulos *et al.*, 1987). In contrast to the present arrangements within many member states, national governments will no longer be able to finance budget deficits – or refinance maturing government debt – by selling bonds to their central banks and increasing the money supply. To the extent that both the loss of seigniorage revenues and the ending of automatic credit facilities will make it more difficult for national governments to finance large budget deficits and refinance large national debts (that is, as fixed-term bonds mature), the Maastricht Treaty requires that member states should control their budget deficits, limiting them to not more than 3 per cent of GDP, and stabilize their public debt:GDP ratios (at or below 60 per cent) prior to joining EMU.

THE ROLE OF THE CONVERGENCE CRITERIA

If at least seven member states meet all five prerequisites by the end of 1996, this group may set a date for a more limited EMU that – initially at least – will exclude the other EU countries. The remaining states may then join as and when their circumstances allow. Should the 1996 conference fail to set a date for EMU, it will be reconvened in 1998. At this time, if at least two member states meet the prerequisites agreed at Maastricht, those that qualify will automatically adopt a common currency in 1999, leaving the others to apply for membership in due course.

Table 6.7 shows the situation at the end of 1994, together with the convergence criteria which would have applied had the decision on creating EMU been taken at that time. It shows that of the then twelve member states, only Luxembourg met all five conditions. A combination of recession and turmoil in the foreign exchange markets between 1991 and 1994 has undoubtedly set back the cause of monetary unification (Temperton, 1993). Economic recovery in Europe should, however, improve the state of national public finances in the medium term, while exchange rate stability is likely to return as the dislocation caused by German reunification (which drove up German interest rates and triggered the tensions within the EMS) is unwound. Nevertheless, Table 6.7 highlights the huge efforts that the Southern states, in particular, would need to make in order to participate in a future EMU.

THE IMPLICATIONS OF EMU FOR THE HOSPITALITY INDUSTRY

The economies of the EU are characterized by significant price and wage inflexibility. They remain nationally segmented and are only weakly linked via the EU's central budget. It is against this backdrop that the likely implications of EMU for the hospitality industry must be considered. While the introduction of a single currency would greatly benefit the industry by eliminating exchange rate risk and promoting international travel between member states, there is a significant threat of greater, rather than reduced, volatility in national economies, which may adversely affect the industry.

The key problem is that, while the Maastricht convergence criteria will reduce the transitional costs of 'settling into' a future EMU by forcing convergence before, rather than after, monetary unification, there is a strong likelihood that the 15 member states will continue to be buffeted by asymmetric shocks after the introduction of a single currency. In the presence of price and wage 'stickiness', the sacrifice of monetary sovereignty implied by EMU means that participating member states will have to give up an important 'shock absorber'. Since the EU is still far from being an optimum currency area and fiscal transfers between states at different stages in the economic cycle are negligible, there is no obvious substitute for the stabilizing role currently played by national monetary policies. While prices and wages eventually adjust following asymmetric shocks, the likelihood is that, after EMU, economic conditions within certain member states may be more unstable than at present. Those countries likely to be most adversely affected are those least integrated into the EU, notably Britain, Ireland, Portugal, Spain and Greece. This group of countries includes the three Southern states most heavily dependent on the hospitality industry for external earnings.

In addition to the likelihood that the price of eliminating intra-EU exchange rate uncertainty may be increased economic instability, the hospitality industry may also be adversely affected by the impact of the fiscal convergence criteria on the public finances of certain member states, notably the Southern Mediterranean countries. Greece, Spain, Portugal and Italy all rely particularly heavily on seigniorage profits to finance public expenditure, have budget deficits well in excess of the 3 per cent of GDP threshold, and are burdened with high public debt:GDP ratios. In order to meet the Maastricht criteria, all would have to reduce sharply both their budget deficits and public debt, by widening their tax base and curbing public expenditure. Both developments are likely to be of especial concern to the hospitality industry in these countries. Cuts in public spending are unlikely to spare the public infrastructure programmes upon which tourism depends - provision and expansion of airports, quality of motorways and public transport, etc. At the same time, governments forced to look for ways of widening the tax

Table 6.7 Convergence criteria and out-turns in 1994

Country	*Inflation rate 1994 (%)*	*Long-term interest rate 1994 (%)*	*Exchange rate criteria met?*	*Debt ratio 1994 (% GDP)*	*Budget balance 1994 (% GDP)*
1994 limits/criteria	*3.8*	*8.9*	*±15% EMS band/no devaluation*	*60.0*	*–3.0*
Belgium	2.6*	7.5*	Yes	142.6	–5.4
Britain	3.5*	8.2*	No	50.3*	–6.0
Denmark	2.0*	8.1*	Yes	82.2	–4.6
Germany	3.0*	6.3*	Yes	53.6*	–3.1
Greece	10.2	n/a	No	154.0	–17.9
Spain	4.8	8.8*	No	61.4	–7.2
France	1.8*	6.9*	Yes	48.1*	–5.6
Ireland	2.8*	7.9*	No	93.1	–2.5*
Italy	3.9	9.4	No	123.3	–9.5
Luxembourg	2.9*	6.4*	Yes	7.9*	–0.4*
Netherlands	2.3*	6.9*	Yes	82.2	–3.6
Portugal	5.6	10.0	No	70.2	–6.2

Note: * denotes convergence criteria met.
Source: European Economy.

base are likely to find foreign tourists and leisure activities, like eating out, an attractive target for additional taxes.

Overall, the balance of the costs and benefits of EMU for the member states of the EU in general, and the hospitality industry in particular, is difficult to gauge. Against the obvious benefits which should flow from eliminating exchange rate risk and transactions costs on intra-EU trade and travel, there are a number of costs which are more complex and multidimensional. What is clear, however, is that the scale of these costs depends upon:

- the flexibility of the member state's goods and labour markets;
- the extent to which the state is integrated into the rest of the EU;
- the extent to which the state is prone to country-specific shocks;
- the state's public finances (notably its budget deficit and outstanding public debt).

These costs are likely to be most pronounced in Britain and the Southern states. For the hospitality industry in these countries, therefore, it is quite possible that, in the short to medium term, the economic costs of EMU may outweigh the benefits.

CONCLUDING COMMENTS

EMU would involve the irrevocable locking of exchange rates and their subsequent replacement by a single EU currency, issued and managed by an EU central bank. The corollary of these changes would be the sacrifice of national monetary sovereignty, the acceptance of a common, EU-wide interest rate, and significant constraints on national public finances. The benefits for the hospitality industry in the EU would potentially be considerable. By eliminating exchange rate uncertainty and transactions costs within the EU, monetary unification would give a major fillip to the hotel and catering sectors by stimulating cross-border leisure and business travel. However, the loss of national monetary (and, to a lesser extent, fiscal) sovereignty could result in offsetting costs to the hospitality industry by increasing economic instability in certain member states. Given that the member states of the EU will continue to be peppered by asymmetric shocks for the foreseeable future, it is likely that certain states (such as Britain and the more inflation-prone Southern states) may suffer recurrent bouts of recession and unemployment, leading to destabilizing swings in the domestic demand for hospitality services in these countries. While the precise balance of the benefits and costs will vary from one state to another, what is certain is that, for the hospitality industry, EMU will not prove an unalloyed good.

REFERENCES

Alesina, A. (1989) 'Politics and Business Cycles in Industrial Democracies', *Economic Policy*, **8**, 55–98.

Alesina, A. and Grilli, V.U. (1991) *The European Central Bank: Reshaping Monetary Politics in Europe*. CEPR Discussion Paper Series, No. 563. London: Centre for

Economic Policy Research.
Artis, M. (1989) *The Call of a Common Currency*. Social Market Foundation, Paper No. 3.
Artus, J.R. and Young, J.H. (1979) 'Fixed and Flexible Exchange Rates: A Renewal of the Debate', *IMF Staff Papers*, **26**, 654–98.
Bank of England (1992) 'The Maastricht Agreement on Economic and Monetary Union', *Bank of England Quarterly Bulletin*, **32(1)**, 64–8.
Barrell, R. (1992) *Economic Convergence and Monetary Union in Europe*. London: Sage.
Barro, R.J. and Gordon, D.B. (1983), 'Rules, Discretion and Reputation in a Model of Monetary Policy', *Journal of Monetary Economics*, **12**, 101–21.
Bayoumi, T. and Eichengreen, B. (1992) *Shocking Aspects of European Monetary Unification*. CEPR Discussion Paper, No. 643. London: Centre for Economic Policy Research.
Begg, D. (1991) 'European Monetary Union – The Macro Issues' in *The Making of Monetary Union*. London: Centre for Economic Policy Research.
Brittan, L. (1991) 'European Monetary Union: What Money for Europe?', *TSB Forum*.
Cecchini, P. (1988) *The European Challenge – 1992: The Benefits of a Single Market*. Aldershot: Wildwood House.
CEPR (Centre for Economic Policy Research) (1991) *The Road to EMU: Managing the Transition to a Single Currency*. London.
Council of Ministers (1992) *Treaty on European Union*. Brussels.
de Grauwe, P. (1988) 'Exchange Rate Variability and the Slowdown in Growth of International Trade', *IMF Staff Papers*, **35**, 45–63.
——(1994) *The Economics of Monetary Integration*. Oxford: Oxford University Press.
de Grauwe, P. and Vanhaverbeke, W. (1991) *Is Europe an Optimum Currency Area? Evidence from Regional Data*. CEPR Discussion Paper, No. 555. London: Centre for Economic Policy Research.
Delors, J (1989) *Report on Economic and Monetary Union in the European Community*. Brussels: Committee for the study of Economic and Monetary Union, EC Commission.
Demopoulos, G., Katsimbris, G. and Miller, S. (1987) 'Monetary Policy and Central Bank Financing of Government Budget Deficits', *European Economic Review*, **31**, 33–49.
Drazen, A. (1989) 'Monetary Policy, Capital Controls and Seigniorage in an Open Economy', in De Cecco, M. and Giovannini, A. (eds) *A European Central Bank? Perspectives on Monetary Unification after Ten Years of the EMS*. Cambridge: Cambridge University Press.
Eichengreen, B. (1990) *Costs and Benefits of European Monetary Unification*, CEPR Discussion Paper, No. 435. London: Centre for Economic Policy Research.
Emerson, M. (1992) *One Market, One Money: An Evaluation of the Potential Benefits and Costs of Forming an Economic and Monetary Union*. Oxford: Oxford University Press.
European Commission (1990) 'One Market, One Money – An Evaluation of the Potential Benefits and Costs of Forming an Economic and Monetary Union', *European Economy*, **44**.
Feldstein, M. (1992) 'Europe's Monetary Union: The Case Against EMU', *Economist*, 13 June, 26.
Friedman, M. (1968) 'The Role of Monetary Policy', *American Economic Review*, **58**.
Goodhart, C.A.E. (1991) 'An Assessment of EMU', *Royal Bank of Scotland Review*, **171**, 3–25.

Grilli, V. (1989) 'Seigniorage in Europe', in De Cecco, M. and Giovannini A. (eds) *A European Central Bank? Perspectives on Monetary Unification after Ten Years of the EMS*. Cambridge: Cambridge University Press.
Harden, I. (1990) 'EuroFed or "Monster Bank"?', *National Westminster Bank Quarterly Review*, August, 2–13.
Healey, N.M. (1992a) 'From the Treaty of Rome to the Single Market', *Developments in Economics*, **8**, 1–28.
——(1992b) 'Designing a Central Bank for Europe: The Costs and Benefits of Central Bank Independence', *Banking Information Service Financial Review*, Summer, 1–11.
Healey, N.M. and Levine, P. (1992a) 'The Economics of European Monetary Union', *Economic Review*, **9(4)**, 2–7.
——(1992b) 'Unpleasant Monetarist Arithmetic Revisited: Central Bank Independence, Fiscal Policy and European Monetary Union', *National Westminster Bank Quarterly Review*, August, 23–37.
Jenkins, R. (1978) 'European Monetary Union', *Lloyds Bank Review*, **127**, 1–14.
Krugman, P. (1989) 'The Case for Stabilising Exchange Rates', *Oxford Review of Economic Policy*, **5(3)**, 61–72.
Kydland, F. and Prescott, E.C. (1977) 'Rules rather than Discretion: The Inconsistency of Optimal Plans', *Journal of Political Economy*, **85**, 473–92.
Levine, P. (1990) 'The European Road to Monetary Union', *European Research*, **1(6)**, 14–22.
Lomax, D.F. (1991) 'A European Central Bank and Economic and Monetary Union', *National Westminster Bank Quarterly Review*, May, 55–72.
MacDougall, D. (1977) *Public Finance in European Integration*. Brussels: EC Commission.
Minford, P. (1995) 'What Price European Monetary Union?', in Healey, N.M. (ed.), *The Economics of the New Europe: From Community to Union*. London: Routledge.
Minford, P. and Rastogi, A. (1990) 'The Price of EMU', in Dornbusch, R. and Layard, R. (eds) *Britain and EMU*. London: Centre for Economic Performance.
Mundell, R.A. (1961) 'A Theory of Optimum Currency Areas', *American Economic Review*, **51**, 657–65.
Temperton, P. (1993) *The European Currency Crisis: What Chance Now for a Single European Currency?* Cambridge: Probus Publishing.
van der Ploeg, F. (1989) *Monetary Interdependence under Alternative Exchange Rate Regimes: A European Perspective*. CEPR Discussion Paper, No. 358. London: Centre for Economic Policy Research.
Zis, G. (1995) 'Whither European Monetary Union?', in Healey, N.M. (ed.) *The Economics of the New Europe: From Community to Union*. London: Routledge.

SEVEN

Regional policy

Stephen Wanhill

INTRODUCTION

As discussed in Chapter 5, at any one time the European Union (EU) has a tourism programme containing a series of actionable measures which it sees as improving the quality and competitiveness of tourism services amongst member states. However, it is generally accepted that the most important impact of the EU on tourism arises not from specific tourism-related policies, but rather from mainstream policies and measures targeted at business in general. These include areas such as airline liberalization, environmental measures, competition policy, social legislation, consumer protection, unification of taxes and regional policy. It is the last aspect, which is the responsibility of Directorate General (DG) XVI, and how it affects tourism, that is the subject of this chapter.

One of the commitments of member states, fixed in the Treaty of Rome, is the unification of the economies of all member states by decreasing regional imbalances and promoting the development of the least favoured or disadvantaged areas. In the 1960s the European Commission drew attention to the fundamental contrasts between the regions in the Community. However, it was not until the 1970s that a Common Regional Policy (CRP) for the member states was implemented and financed. As Clout (1987) observes, the objectives of the CRP were to create a greater convergence between the economies of the member states and to ensure a better spread of the economic activities throughout its territory. In spite of many efforts, towards the end of the 1980s, in the run-up to the adoption of the Single European Act (SEA) (1987), there were still major disparities as measured by gross domestic product (GDP) per head, and shown in Table 7.1. As a result, a commitment to economic and social cohesion was formally written into the Act. This was to be achieved through:

- enlargement of the Structural Funds used for regional development;
- monitoring and co-ordinating the national economic policies of member states to promote pan-European development and ensure that individual government intervention does not distort competition;
- taking account of cohesion matters within the actual implementation of the single market programme.

Table 7.1 GDP per capita index in member states 1980–93[1]

Member state	*1980*	*1985*	*1990*	*1993*[2]
Belgium	107	104	104	106
Denmark	106	114	106	106
Germany	118	119	117	117[3]
Greece	52	51	47	49
Spain	72	70	75	76
France	113	112	111	109
Ireland	63	65	71	78
Italy	103	104	104	104
Luxembourg	116	120	127	132
Netherlands	108	104	102	101
Portugal	53	51	56	60
United Kingdom	98	101	101	99

Notes:
1 EU average equals 100.
2 1993 marks the end of the 1989–93 support programme following the reform of the Structural Funds (see text).
3 If East Germany is included (the new *Länder*) then this value falls to 104.

Source: Commission of the European Communities.

STRUCTURAL FUNDS

The EU has four Structural Funds:

- the European Regional Development Fund (ERDF), which is focused mainly on productive investment, infrastructure and small and medium-sized enterprise (SME) development in less favoured regions;
- the European Social Fund (ESF), which has the task of promoting jobs through vocational training and employment assistance;
- the European Agricultural Guidance and Guarantee Fund (EAGGF) guidance section, which promotes the adjustment of agricultural businesses and rural development measures;
- the Financial Instrument for Fisheries Guidance (FIFG), which was established in 1993 to promote structural measures in that sector.

The ERDF was created in 1975 as an instrument to help correct regional imbalances within the Community through participation in the development and structural adjustment of regions whose economies were lagging behind and in the conversion of declining industrial regions (Pearce, 1988). ERDF funds were granted originally on a quota basis, and different reforms of the ERDF were attempted in 1979, 1984 and 1988 (Yuill and Allen, 1990).

The first reform undertaken established a non-quota section to finance specific Community regional development measures. Although the non-quota section represented only 5 per cent of the total ERDF budget, the European Commission obtained some independence from the member states in the assignment of the regional development grants.

The second reform, that of 1984, resulted in a replacement of the quota system with a system of upper and lower limits for each member state (see Commission, 1984, for allocated percentages to member states). The lower limit was the minimum amount guaranteed for each member state if it submitted an adequate volume of aid applications to the Commission. The assistance above the minimum amount depended on the extent to which projects submitted for ERDF grants were considered of value to the Community (Pearce, 1988). Also, more stress was placed on programmes rather than on project financing, and ERDF became the principal instrument available to the Community for supporting development of the regions under Community programmes, national programmes of Community interest, investment projects and ERDF-related studies. In 1985, when the second reform was implemented, the total budget of the ERDF amounted to European currency units (ECU) 2290 million. For comparison, the start budget of ERDF in 1975 was ECU 258 million.

By the mid-1980s the objectives and implementation of the ERDF resources were increasingly overlapping with the ESF, with the EAGGF, and with other financial providers such as the European Investment Bank (EIB) or the European Coal and Steel Community (ECSC). Consequently, there was pressure for a more coherent approach towards social and regional development. Also, the enlargement of the EU with Spain and Portugal, which caused an increase in the number of disadvantaged regions, and the growing complexity of procedures and mechanisms for providing assistance, led to the need for a comprehensive reform of the Structural Funds.

STRUCTURAL FUNDS PROGRAMME 1989–93

In 1988 the new regulation on the activities of the ERDF was adopted in the reform of the Structural Funds (Commission, 1988, 1991a). The reform of the latter was based on three fundamental principles:

- transforming structural policy into an instrument with real economic impact by concentration on priority objectives;
- using a multiannual programming approach for expenditure planning to assure member states of the stability and predictability of EU support;
- implementing a partnership with all the parties actively participating in structural policy, especially the regional authorities.

From 1989 onwards, member states were required to co-ordinate, for the first time, the use of Structural Funds and draw together all forms of Community support, including lending by the EIB and ECSC. This also allowed the EU to adopt a greater degree of control over the use of funds within the sphere of integrated regional development programmes agreed between the Commission and member states. Through a decision of the European Council in February 1988, the resources available to the Funds were doubled in comparison with 1987, and the reform process specified that the Funds should be co-ordinated across five priority objectives, whether assigned jointly or separately. These are shown in Table 7.2: it is to be noted that Objective 5 has two parts and so it is possible to talk of six objectives. Objectives 1, 2 and 5b are regionally targeted, while Objectives 3, 4 and 5a are horizontal in character. This means that these objectives concern the entire EU. Since this chapter deals with regional development, attention is focused on Objectives 1, 2 and 5b.

Of the three Structural Funds, ERDF was designated by the Commission (1988) as the

Table 7.2 The five Structural Funds objectives

Objective	*Aim*	*Finance*
1	Promoting the development and adjustment of the regions whose development is lagging behind, that is where per capita GDP is less than, or close to, 75 per cent of the EU average	ERDF, ESF, EAGGF, EIB, ECSC
2	Converting the regions, frontier regions or parts of regions seriously affected by industrial decline	ERDF, ESF, EIB, ECSC
3	Combating long-term unemployment	ESF, EIB, ECSC
4	Facilitating the occupational integration of young people	ESF, EIB, ECSC
5	Adapting the structure of agriculture with a view to the reform of the Common Agricultural Policy	
5a	Adapting production, processing and marketing structures in agriculture and forestry	EAGGF
5b	Promoting the development of rural areas, including preservation of the countryside and the environment, rural and tourist infrastructures, and the development of forestry activities	EAGGF, ERDF, ESF

Source: Commission of the European Communities.

main instrument for meeting Objectives 1 and 2, with ESF in support. Objective 5b was to be assisted by all three funds. The budget of the Structural Funds for the period 1989–93 came to ECU 60,315 million, in 1989 prices. The following breakdown by objectives was fixed by the Commission:

Objective 1	ECU 38,300 million
Objective 2	ECU 7,205 million
Objectives 3 and 4	ECU 7,450 million
Objective 5(a)	ECU 3,415 million
Objective 5(b)	ECU 2,795 million
Transitional measures	ECU 1,150 million
Total	*ECU 60,315 million*

A new situation arose from the events in Central and Eastern Europe in general, and in East Germany in particular. German unification added another 16.4 million EU inhabitants. Generally, these new inhabitants were living in old industrial regions with very low productivity, or in agricultural regions with large and specialized, although low-productivity, farms. The service sector in the former East Germany was underdeveloped in comparison with the rest of Europe, and infrastructure was mostly obsolete and neglected. In order to assist the former East German economy and transform it from a centrally planned to a social market economy, the budgets of the Structural Funds were increased by ECU3,000 million. The urgent need is to arrest the unfolding process of deindustrialization since 1990, by improving the competitiveness of existing enterprises, support for the creation of new firms, and better use of the skills of the labour force.

Operational aspects

The reform of the Structural Funds aimed to simplify and rationalize the Community's structural actions by adopting uniform procedures for providing assistance and on-going assessment and monitoring of Community intervention. To the three principles of concentration, programming and partnership were added the following:

- Community assistance should be additional to the contributions of member states rather than reducing them.
- A higher authority may not and must not act if an objective can be achieved satisfactorily at a lower level. This principle of subsidiarity was enshrined in the Treaty of Maastricht, which came into force in 1993.

Finance from the Structural Funds is not usually used for individual projects proposed or selected by the Commission. The reform of the Funds introduced four stages in the bidding process (Commission, 1991b):

- Stage 1: Member states produce fully costed regional plans, setting out priorities for development and the use of all the Funds.
- Stage 2: Member states and the Commission, together with the local representatives and potential grant recipients, agree Community Support Frameworks (CSFs), which give priorities for funding the project categories to be supported and the level of resources to be made available.
- Stage 3: Member states, in partnership with the Commission, draw up a programme to implement the CSFs through the use of the appropriate forms of assistance.
- Stage 4: The implementation of the CSFs is monitored and assessed through projects being directed by Programme Monitoring Committees, which include representatives of all parties.

During 1989, the member states for the first time submitted multiannual plans under the five priority objectives. This approach was new for most of the member states, and completely different from the submission of the regional development programmes under the old ERDF rules. All the multiannual plans provided the Commission not only with an accurate, quantified and substantial overview of the objectives and the financial needs of the member states, but also with an estimate of their financial commitments. This gave rise to two considerations: first, the volume of funds requested was very large and exceeded the amount available, and second, the ERDF remained the fund most in demand.

Based on the needs formulated in the multiannual plans, the Community drew up the CSFs. In accordance with the principles of the reform, a CSF had to include:

- a statement of the priorities for action;
- an outline of the forms of assistance and a regional breakdown at the appropriate geographical level;
- an indicative cost plan specifying the financial allocations envisaged for the various forms of assistance and their duration;
- information on the means available for any studies or technical assistance necessary for the preparation and implementation of the measures concerned;
- indication of the procedures for implementing the CSF.

The negotiations on the CSFs led to meaningful exchanges between the Commission and its partners, particularly at the regional level. Finally, each CSF was adopted by a formal decision of the Commission in agreement with each member state. The geographical level of a CSF was normally the level proposed by the member states in their multiannual plans. An exception to this rule was possible if the Commission considered a more aggregated or a less aggregated geographical level to be appropriate. The duration of the CSFs depended on the plans submitted and was between three and five years.

The operation stage was the implementation of the CSFs with five different forms of assistance: operational programmes (OPs); global grants; individual applications for large-scale (development) projects; part-financing of national aid schemes; and financing through direct loans. The two most important forms of assistance were the OPs and global grants. The programmes were the predominant form of assistance. They were composed of multiannual measures covering two, three, four and five years and could receive assistance from one or more Structural Funds. The global grants were managed by an intermediary designated by the member states in agreement with the Commission. Generally the intermediary was a specialized body or agency other than the national or regional authorities.

Monitoring the programmes

The principle of subsidiarity governs the monitoring and evaluation of projects within a CSF. This is carried out by Programme Monitoring Committees, as mentioned above, which are normally made up of representatives of central and local government, public agencies and any other interested bodies. Targets are set for every project at approval stage, and managers must submit returns, indicating progress against targets, every quarter. Failure to do this may result in the suspension of grant payments.

Under EU regulations, the appropriate central government department responsible for administering CSFs is required to make site visits to examine specifications and project development. Since EU assistance is normally a matching payment, other public monies are usually involved, in which case it is customary for the government department concerned to undertake a post-evaluation study, via a questionnaire, to assess whether the project has lived up to its predicated performance. It is the member state's responsibility to see that funds are correctly spent and yield good value for money.

The Commission and the European Court of Auditors have powers of examination and verification to establish that projects are:

- eligible for funds as specified;
- managed in accordance with Community rules with regard to technical and financial controls;
- claiming grant against justifiable expenditure.

Verification is carried out by one or two visits every year, when a group of preselected projects is subject to detailed checking. Thus the Commission's involvement is normally to do with accounting and administrative procedures, rather than overall programme direction. This accords with the principle of subsidiarity stated earlier.

TOURISM WITHIN THE STRUCTURAL FUNDS

Europe is the world's largest tourist destination, with around 60 per cent of international arrivals, though Europe's share of global movements has been declining, reflecting a combination of economic growth and income distribution factors elsewhere in the world. Overall, tourism is estimated to provide over 6 per cent of total employment in member states and 5.5 per cent of GDP. Thus, the tourist industry plays a fundamental economic role in the EU and has particular regional significance in that it is of greater relative importance in the less-favoured member states: Spain, Portugal, Greece and Ireland. This contributes to the EU's goal of promoting greater cohesion amongst member states by narrowing income gaps through redistribution of expenditure. In another sense, tourism may foster cohesion through a better understanding of the culture, traditions and the various lifestyles of the populations of different member states.

The Community's regional policy for the tourism sector is directed towards two targets. First of all, the Community helps regions to develop their tourism potential by providing financial aid. Second, the EU directs its regional policy towards regions likely to become too dependent on tourists or on the seasonal character of the presence of tourists. Resources available to cope with these problems come from the Structural Funds. Efforts for solving the first problem contribute not only directly to the development of tourism projects such as marinas, conference infrastructure or tourist attractions, but also to investments yielding indirect benefits. Indirect interventions in the domain of transport infrastructure, telecommunications or environment also contribute to the development of tourism. Similarly, the improvement of accessibility of certain regions whose development is lagging behind creates the indispensable condition for the success of tourism initiatives in these regions. For regions becoming too dependent on tourism activities, funds are made available to solve problems in the environment, infrastructure, etc., on the one hand and to support efforts to diversify economic activities on the other.

A contributory reason for the fluctuating fortunes of many Southern European resorts in recent years is that insufficient attention was paid to environmental and social aspects at the development stage. Sustainability issues have led to an increased sensitivity to these matters and a tightening of regulations within the Community.

In essence, the Commission's policy for using tourism as an instrument of regional economic development is one of striking a balance between the positive and negative aspects. The positive ones are as follows:

- tourism is continuing to grow world-wide;
- disadvantaged regions often have a comparative advantage in natural tourism resources;
- tourism attracts spending from outside the regions;
- tourism has important spill-over benefits (multiplier effects) elsewhere in the regional economy;
- job creation within a relatively short period of time is an important aspect of tourism development.

Some of the adverse consequences that may arise include:

- negative impacts on cultural and natural resources and attractions;
- a predominance of unskilled and poorly paid jobs;
- supply being locked into those market segments which are highly volatile;
- internal linkages being weak, so that limited spill-over benefits may be realized;
- multinational firms squeezing out local enterprises and coming to dominate local markets;
- seasonal nature of demand leaving the region with a heavy burden of infrastructure costs.

The diversity of these issues and the differing nature of the tourist product within Europe leave the Community with little option but to assign the primary role of tourism policy to member states (Commission, 1995) and proceed with tourism projects only in close partnership with national and regional authorities, invoking the principle of subsidiarity.

Tourism assistance prior to the 1989 reforms

Since its start in 1975, the ERDF has participated in a number of important projects directly or indirectly linked to tourism. Grants have been awarded to a range of schemes: tourism infrastructure (marinas, development of coastal areas); infrastructure directly linked to the tourism sector (transport, energy and water supply); socio-cultural attractions (conference and exhibition facilities, sport and recreation complexes, museums, libraries, theatres); services in the tourism field (tourism animation, information, promotion) and tourist accommodation.

Although most Community interventions in the field of tourism were met by the ERDF, as indicated previously, the ESF and EAGGF have also contributed to initiatives in favour of employment and of the development of complementary tourism activities on farms. In mountain regions and in other unfavourable agricultural areas, EAGGF assistance ensured the necessary conditions for the success of rural tourism.

Between 1975 and 1985 the ERDF awarded in total ECU168 million of grants for projects directly and explicitly linked to tourism. This amount represented just over 1 per cent of the entire ERDF budget over that period. Between 1986 and 1988 ERDF allocated ECU 732 million for tourism, representing 5 per cent of the overall ERDF budget over this period.

Next to ERDF assistance, Community efforts that are particularly important in the tourism field have been realized by the Integrated Mediterranean Programmes (IMPs). By 1988, 29 programmes had been approved for Greece, France and Italy. About 13 per cent of the total budget of the IMPs (ECU3.2 billion) was reserved for financing the promotion of tourism activities and for the guidance of tourism policies in these countries.

Tourism assistance after the reform of the Structural Funds

When the CSFs were bring drawn up, a section on tourism was included among the priorities for assistance. Actions in the tourism field, which were given priority in the allocation of the resources available from the Structural Funds, were the improvement of tourism supply, the geographical equilibrium of tourism supply, the reduction of the seasonal character of tourism, the reappraisal of cultural heritage, the development of rural tourism, training for tourism careers and the protection of environment at tourism sites.

Structural Fund resources directly financing tourism activities in the Objective 1 regions, covering the period 1989–93, came to ECU 1,683.7 million. This amounted to 5.6 per cent of the total Community assistance under the CSFs for the period. The geographical distribution of this is shown in Tables 7.3 and 7.4.

For Objective 2 regions, the Structural Funds support included a spend of ECU 428.1 million for the period 1989–93 to favour tourism activity in a direct way. Objective 5b regions received ECU 194.1 million for the benefit of tourism initiatives in the period 1989–93, representing 7.5 per cent of total Community assistance under the CSFs. Of

Table 7.3 Structural Funds Community assistance to tourism 1989–93 (ECU million)

Country	*Objective 1*	*Objective 2*	*Objective 5b*
Belgium		12.9	4.4
Denmark		0.5	
Germany		5.7	
Greece	243.6		
Spain	182.0		17.7
France	34.3	44.1	105.6
Ireland	188.6		
Italy	786.0	24.7	51.2
Luxembourg			0.4
Netherlands		10.1	9.0
Portugal	203.0		
United Kingdom	46.2	173.9	5.8
Total	*1,683.7*	*271.9*[1]	*194.1*

Note:
[1] The disaggregated figures are only available for the period 1989–91; the total for the whole period 1989–93 is ECU 428.1m.
Source: Commission of the European Communities.

Table 7.4 Structural Funds Community assistance to tourism 1989–93 as a proportion of total assistance from the Funds (per cent)

Country	*Objective 1*	*Objective 2*	*Objective 5b*
Belgium		7.2	13.5
Denmark		1.6	
Germany		2.0	
Greece	4.5		
Spain	2.4		6.2
France	4.8	7.3	11.0
Ireland	6.6		
Italy	12.3	9.0	13.3
Luxembourg			16.0
Netherlands		13.0	20.5
Portugal	3.5		
United Kingdom	5.5	12.8	1.7
Total	*5.6*	*7.6*[1]	*7.5*

Note:
1 For the period 1989–91 only.
Source: Commission of the European Communities.

the total Structural Funds granted to the tourism sector, 86 per cent came from the ERDF, 5 per cent from the ESF and 9 per cent from the EAGGF (Commission, 1994a). Structural Funds' moneys were also boosted by EIB-subsidized loans. The Bank's actions in support of tourism over this period were almost exclusively allocated to regions benefiting from the Funds.

Community initiatives 1989–93

To help solve serious problems affecting the socio-economic situation in one or more regions, the Commission mounted a series of programmes on its own initiative in addition to the CSFs, but within the context of the five priority objectives laid down in the reform of the Structural Funds. These Community initiatives were negotiated between the member states and the Commission on the basis of regional or national development plans, with the general goal of encouraging more balanced economic and social development, thereby strengthening cohesion within the EU. Those initiatives of particular relevance to tourism were:

- Envireg
- Interreg
- Leader
- Resider
- Rechar
- Regis
- Prisma
- Stride
- Telematique.

Envireg

In 1990, the Commission decided to establish a Community initiative contributing to the protection of the environment. The aim was to help the least-favoured regions in the Community tackle their environmental problems. Eligible areas were coastal zones covered by Objective 1 and Mediterranean coastal locations covered by Objectives 2 and 5b, where environmental degradation was the result, amongst other things, of poor urban planning in both residential and tourist centres. The purpose was that, in future, tourism should be developed in a way which would not undermine efforts to protect the environment in these areas, and a sense of collective responsibility would be inculcated in tourists. Priority was given to areas experiencing rapid economic growth with serious environmental problems and areas subject to sharp seasonal fluctuations of the tourist population. Also included were schemes to protect biotypes while providing for the development of tourism.

Interreg

This was a Community initiative adopted in 1990, whose main purpose was to promote co-operation between border areas. The aims were to assist internal and external border areas of the Community in overcoming the special development problems arising from their relative isolation. Particular attention was given to creating alternative employment opportunities in areas where job losses might arise due to changes in customs and other border-related activities, as a consequence of the completion of the single market. Regions which were eligible for assistance included all Objective 1, 2 and 5b areas along the internal and external land borders of the EU. Areas of activity included the development of tourism, notably agriculturally based tourism, and the development and management for tourism purposes of natural parks straddling borders. The objective here was to diversify farmers' incomes through the development of general and farm-based tourism, in addition to income support through improving cross-border commercial networks and trade, as well as raising agricultural productivity.

Leader

Leader was an initiative established in 1991 to fund innovative and integrated rural development programmes led by community groups. It covered all regions eligible under Objectives 1 and 5b and involved a network of about 100 local rural development action groups, operating as part of an interactive network by using new communication technologies. In this way, the groups were helped to act as local intermediaries by linking up with database networks providing, among other things, studies of market potential, the establishment of relations with travel agencies, and sales and reservation systems for accommodation such as bed and breakfast.

Specific provision was made under this programme for rural tourism, in order to:

- improve knowledge of the demand for leisure in the countryside;
- develop both the quantity and quality of information provision, in the light of increasing demands of potential customers, in terms of the level of presentation and the diversity of tourist services;
- improve the organization of the supply of tourist services and match supply to demand in such areas as minimum standards, guaranteed quality of services, promotion of rural tourist products, reservation centres and so forth;
- encourage centres of rural tourism with basic equipment (swimming pools and tennis courts) and those offering cultural facilities and opportunities for themed holidays, such as arts and crafts or environmental discovery breaks;
- develop more broadly based rural tourism, particularly farm tourism centred on individual investment.

Global grants were used to finance collective programmes. Funds were also available for the adaptation of infrastructure to meet needs arising from the supply of tourist services: the listing, restoration and development of buildings and rural sites of tourist interest were financed under Leader, as were promotional activities, market studies, and measures to extend the tourist season, such as the promotion of additional holidays in the form of short breaks and weekend tourism.

Resider and Rechar

These initiatives were brought forward in 1988 and 1989 respectively, in order to support the economic and social conversion of declining heavy industry locations, namely steel-producing and coal-mining areas. Tourism was listed amongst the eligible measures, particularly in respect of projects based on the industrial heritage of the area.

Regis

Adopted in 1992, this initiative was set up to assist the most remote regions of the EU: the overseas departments of France, Madeira, the Azores and the Canary Islands. The aim was to strengthen ties with the rest of the Community and to improve co-operation with neighbouring non-member countries. Measures included the diversification of agricultural, industrial and tourism investment, aid for trade, and tourism and technology exchanges with neighbouring non-member countries.

Prisma, Stride and Telematique

These three initiatives were developed between 1990 and 1993, with the objective of contributing to the modernization of small to medium-sized businesses in general. Their specific roles were:

- Prisma: improving business services;
- Stride: strengthening technology in less-favoured regions;
- Telematique: promoting the case for advanced telecommunications services.

ECONOMICS OF STRUCTURAL ASSISTANCE

As the ERDF is the principal instrument for regional intervention, the nature of Community assistance may best be understood by considering ERDF project support (Wanhill, 1993). The Fund may be used for:

- infrastructure improvement and modernization;
- productive (revenue earning) investments;
- measures to exploit the potential for internally generated development of regions, such as financing the transfer of technology, consulting advice, sector studies, and assistance to organizations concerned with the promotion of tourism and the co-ordination management of accommodation.

CSFs provide for different rates of project assistance: the limit rate is normally 50 per cent, but can be up to 55 per cent in the case of projects of particular importance to the development of the region or areas in which they are located. The majority of projects no longer receive support at the limit rate.

Since ERDF grants are, in essence, drawn from public funds, their use by the private sector has been strictly limited. This is because they are controlled by the 'Solima' principle (named after the originating Commissioner) that shareholders should not benefit directly from such grants. In the main, grants are awarded to public authorities, public/private sector partnerships, quasi-public bodies and agencies, development corporations, charities and a variety of voluntary organizations. The argument supporting this is based on the principle that public sector projects benefit the private sector and on the fact that the EU budget comes from public funds, so it is only fitting that moneys coming back should be used for public expenditure; though the matter is debatable at a time when governments are increasingly trying to involve the private sector in their activities. A consequence of this public orientation has been that, on a Europe-wide basis, considerable sums have gone into the development of tourist attractions and amenities because so many of them lie within the public domain.

Although ERDF moneys for CSFs are ultimately limited by overall budget allocations, their impact at the bidding level of a regional authority is one of a conditional matching grant with an open-ended commitment. An analysis of this situation is shown in Figure 7.1. In the initial situation, the authority has a budget constraint

$$T_1 + O_1 = Y_1 \tag{7.1}$$

where T_1 is expenditure on tourism, O_1 expenditure on other public services, and Y_1 the level of the authority's income.

The regional authority is now invited to bid for ERDF funds for tourism development. How much assistance is given depends on the projects put forward by the authority and the agreement reached concerning the CSF. The effect of ERDF funding is to rotate the authority's income line from Y_1Y_1 to Y_1Y_4, so that if there is no eligible tourist spending there will be no grant, as occurs at point Y_1 on the axis for 'Other expenditure'.

Suppose that agreement is reached to settle at point D. At this point expenditure on tourism is T_2 and other public services, O_2. The amount of grant payable will depend on the appropriate rate (r) for tourism in the CSF and the amount of eligible expenditure within T_2, say eT_2, where e is the fraction that is eligible. The budget is now

$$\begin{aligned} T_2 + O_2 &= Y_1 + reT_2 \\ (1 - re)T_2 + O_2 &= Y_1 \end{aligned} \tag{7.2}$$

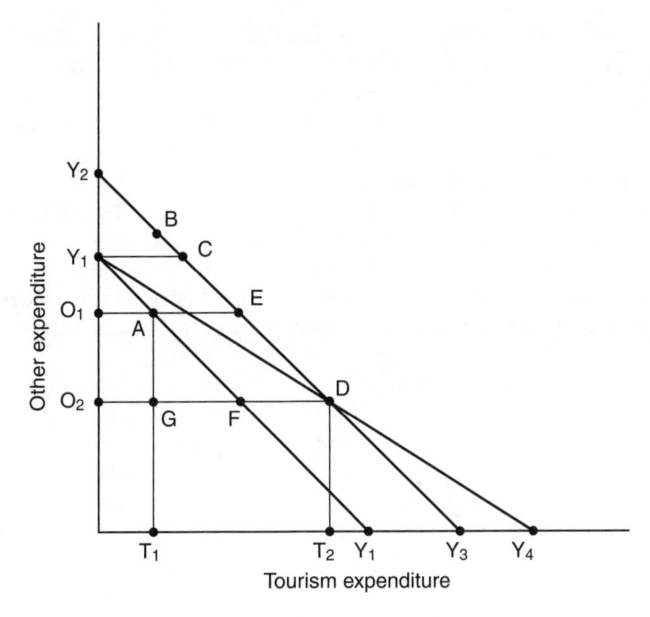

Figure 7.1 Economics of grant aid

where the first term on the left-hand side of equation (7.2) is the amount the regional authority has to devote to tourism expenditure to gain the required ERDF funds.

Subtracting equation (7.1) from equation (7.2) gives

$$(1 - re)\ T_2 - T_1 = -(O_2 - O_1) \tag{7.3}$$

Thus, any increase in regional authority spending on tourism to earn ERDF moneys is matched by a reduction in spending on other public services. This is shown in Figure 7.1: by increasing expenditure to T_2 the authority receives an ERDF grant of *DF* and spends an extra *FG* of its own resources on tourism by diverting O_2O_1 expenditure from other public services. The ability of the authority to do this depends on the amount of discretionary spending it has in comparison to its statutory requirements.

The extent to which the application of the ERDF mechanism constrains local development policies may be examined by considering alternative grant mechanisms. A lump-sum grant, without any conditions as to its use, that is equivalent to *DF* in Figure 7.1 will give the authority a budget line Y_2Y_3. A conditional grant (to be spent on tourism projects) but non-matching will present the authority with a budget line Y_1CY_3. The ERDF grant criteria constrain the authority to a budget line Y_1DY_3, once the CSF has been agreed. Consequently, any points on the line Y_2D are unobtainable by the regional authority under ERDF.

Consider the case of an unconditional grant: the authority's desired policy may be to position its expenditure at point *B*, using part of the grant to maintain tourism spending as before and switching the rest, plus own resources, to increase expenditure on other public services. Hence *D* is sub-optimal and the ERDF mechanism is distorting planned expenditure. Experience has shown that this situation is unlikely, because receiving authorities are normally quite willing to spend some of their own resources on grant-aided sectors. In fact, the availability of grant-in-aid often stimulates a change in political preferences, enabling regional government officers to rally support and obtain political commitment to bring forward or maintain tourism spending programmes.

The more likely situation is the case of the conditional lump-sum grant represented by the budget line Y_1CY_3. Under this regime the authority may position itself anywhere along the line CY_3, of which *CD* is unobtainable under ERDF. It is not very probable that the authority will position itself at *C* for the reasons given above, but *E* is the critical point, for beyond *E* the authority has to switch expenditure from other public services to meet its ERDF commitments. Since *E* cannot be reached under the conditional matching rules of ERDF without regional authorities raising additional funds from elsewhere, then clearly a conditional non-matching grant system would be preferable from the perspective of the authority in terms of freedom of action, but not necessarily from the perspective of the Community, which is specifically trying to lever in a certain percentage of other funds to match its own contribution to the tourism projects in question.

Prior to 1992, when the additionality principle was adopted, some member states were using ERDF grants as a substitute for their own contributions. On Figure 7.1, this practice had the effect of moving Y_1DY_3 to the left so that points *D* and *F* coincided, leaving the regional authority no better off in terms of income, but with reorganized expenditure. This was against the spirit of ERDF, and from 1993 onwards it was agreed that European moneys would be truly additional. However, in an era when member states have been trying to limit public expenditure, many authorities have complained that they have not been able to take full advantage of ERDF because they have been unable to switch commitments from elsewhere. The facts that grant payments are retrospective and 5 per cent is held back until the project is physically and financially complete also mean that regional authorities have to earmark total project costs in their budget allocations.

PROJECT EVALUATION

The principles governing the bidding process for ERDF grants for productive investment are as follows:

- An indication of the market outlook in the sector concerned should be given.
- The effects on employment should be examined.
- An analysis of the expected profitability of the project should be undertaken.

In practice, local income and employment generation are the most significant factors affecting project acceptability, since the primary use of Structural Funds is to correct for regional imbalances. In terms of profitability, project feasibility is the main consideration: the scheme must have the capacity to generate revenues above operating costs so that it can support its own running arrangements. Project viability, which relates to the return on capital employed, is not so significant, because the objective of ERDF is to make up for shortfalls in finance to ensure that the investment will go ahead, and that the project has the means to service the cost of debt out of its operating surplus. Tourism and hospitality projects are normally well suited to this type of funding because they usually have a high operating leverage; that is, a relatively low level of operating costs and a high level of fixed costs caused by prior capital spending. Once the financing of the capital has been adequately taken care of, the project usually runs into surplus after three years and can maintain itself thereafter.

It is clear that a project cannot stand alone: its wider relevance and impact within a

CSF must be demonstrated, and it must be ensured that it meets one or more of the overall regional objectives laid down by the Community. As noted earlier, tourism projects in this category tend to be public sector led, and the principal aspects that should be addressed are as follows:

- The use of the project should be 50 per cent non-local.
- The project should result in an increase in overnight stays.
- The project should result in an increase in employment opportunities.
- The economic position of the project within the local area should be examined.
- The project should form part of a tourism strategy for the local area.
- National/regional tourist authority support will give weight to the application.

The important aspects to consider in respect of applications for ERDF support are the impacts of on-site and off-site tourist expenditure generated by the project. To derive the appropriate methodology, suppose there exists a tourist destination with a hotel and a seaside. It is proposed that an attraction should be established, with the use of public funds, to develop the destination. Visitors are surveyed at the hotel and on the beach to ascertain what motivated them to come to the area and the potential drawing power of an attraction.

Total spending at the destination (T), including the hotel, is expected to be made up of expenditure at the attraction (T_a) plus expenditure at the hotel (T_h) and all remaining expenditure (T_r). The pull factor (reason for visit) for the hotel is y; that for the attraction is estimated at x, leaving $1 - x - y$ as the significance of the seaside. It follows, therefore, that the attributable tourist expenditure by drawing power is:

$$
\begin{aligned}
\text{Attraction} &= xT_a + xT_h + xT_r \\
\text{Hotel} &= yT_a + yT_h + yT_r \\
\text{Seaside} &= (1 - x - y)\,(T_a + T_h + T_r) \\
T &= T_a + T_h + T_r
\end{aligned}
$$

The benefits (B) of developing the attraction are the difference between with (T) and without (T_w) the project. The without situation is:

$$
\begin{aligned}
\text{Attraction} &= 0 \\
\text{Hotel} &= yT_h + yT_r \\
\text{Seaside} &= (1 - x - y)\,(T_h + T_r) \\
T_w &= (1 - x)\,(T_h + T_r)
\end{aligned}
$$

Hence

$$
\begin{aligned}
B &= T - T_w \\
&= T_a + x(T_h + T_r) \qquad (7.4)
\end{aligned}
$$

The benefits are in two parts: the first term on the right-hand side of equation (7.4) is the amount of on-site expenditure, and the second term is the off-site expenditure. The amount of off-site expenditure attributable to the attraction depends on its ability to generate additional visitors. Hence, this may be termed the 'visitor additionality factor'. The application of employment multipliers per unit of tourist spending to equation (7.4), either on a full-time equivalent (FTE) or an employment head-count basis, will give the gross employment (E) generated by the project. These multipliers are calculated so as to encompass the direct employment effects of the project, the indirect effects arising out of intermediate purchases made by the project, and the induced effects on the local economy as a result of the re-spending of local incomes derived from the project, and similarly for off-site expenditure. Thus:

$$E = T_a e_a + xOe_o \qquad (7.5)$$

where e_a is the employment multiplier appropriate to the attraction, O is the sum of off-site expenditure ($T_h + T_r$), and e_o is the required job multiplier. However, equation (7.5) ignores any demand diversion from elsewhere in the area. This is termed 'displacement', which, in turn, depends upon the boundary agreed for the project. The greater the area, the more likely is it that the project will displace business from elsewhere.

From the ERDF standpoint, the boundary is the limit defined by the CSF. Thus, if the project draws visitors in part from the local CSF area or an alternative assisted region, then their spending is counted as displacement for evaluation purposes. The ideal development is one that brings in tourists from the richer parts of the country that are not eligible for regional assistance or from abroad. This is a rather strong ruling with regard to displacement, for some local demand generated by the project may be additional. More generally, if d is the proportion of locally diverted demand (or demand diverted from other assisted projects) in equation (7.4), then from equation (7.5) net employment (N) is:

$$\begin{aligned} N &= E - dE \\ &= (1 - d)\,(T_a e_a + xOe_o) \qquad (7.6) \end{aligned}$$

Equation (7.6) forms the core of the basic evaluation model that can be used to judge in employment terms the return to capital invested. In ERDF terms, equation (7.6) may be used to evaluate the worthiness of the project for grant support and, therefore, inclusion within a CSF.

As an example of the workings of equation (7.6), consider the data in Table 7.5.

Table 7.5 Employment impact of an attraction

	On-site expenditure	*Off-site expenditure*
Market segments:		
Stay visitors	ECU 789,000	ECU 4,614,000
Day visitors	ECU 880,000	ECU 785,000
Local residents	ECU 1,366,000	ECU 510,000
Total	*ECU 3,035,000*	*ECU 5,909,000*
Visitor additionality:		
Stay visitors	n/a	15%
Day visitors	n/a	90%
Local residents	n/a	100%
Displacement:		
Stay visitors	0%	0%
Day visitors	30%	30%
Local residents	100%	100%
FTE multipliers per ECU 10,000 of visitor spending:		
Direct	0.0995	0.0816
Indirect	0.0535	0.0508
Induced	0.0077	0.0077
Total	*0.1607*	*0.1401*

The total expected on-site and off-site expenditure arising from the project is ECU 8,944,000. Visitor surveys have shown that only 15 per cent of staying visitors are likely to come to the destination because of the existence of the attraction. This percentage is expected to be much greater for day visitors and local residents. From equation (7.4):

$$B = \text{ECU } 3{,}035{,}000 + (0.15 \times \text{ECU } 4{,}614{,}000) + (0.9 \times \text{ECU } 785{,}000) + (1.0 \times \text{ECU } 510{,}000)$$
$$= \text{ECU } 4{,}943{,}600$$

It is anticipated that the attraction will create 44.5 FTEs directly on-site, and so the required additions to this number will be the expected indirect and induced employment generated from on-site spending. Using the appropriate FTE multipliers shown in Table 7.5, this figure comes to (0.0535 + 0.0077) × ECU3,035,000/10,000 = 18.6. Off-site jobs amount to 0.1401 × ECU1,908,600/10,000 = 26.7. Hence, the number of FTEs expected in accordance with equation (7.5) is:

$$E = 44.5 + 18.6 + 26.7$$
$$= 89.8 \text{ FTEs}$$

So far the analysis has only measured gross FTEs likely to be generated by the attraction. The net figures have to account for the displacement factors shown in Table 7.5. It is estimated that there will be zero per cent of staying visitors taken from competitors, 30 per cent of day visitors and 100 per cent of local residents. Weighting these factors by the different categories of visitor spending gives an overall displacement value of 0.4329; hence the solution to equation (7.6) is:

$$N = 89.8 - 0.4329 \times 89.8 = 50.9 \text{ FTEs}$$

It is this number of FTEs that should be used to evaluate the project's worth for grant assessment.

The core model given by equation (7.6) is capable of further adjustment to take into account factors such as project additionality, business displacement, differential impacts on the local labour market, and externalities. The assessment of the additionality position involves considerable subjective judgement about the likely future behaviour of the investor. British practice requires the investor to sign a document to the effect that the funds are a necessary condition for the project to go ahead. In reality, there are degrees of project additionality. The investment could go ahead at a later date, on a smaller scale, or at a lower quality. If a numerical value can be placed upon such assessments, then they can be included in the model. Similarly, business displacement may arise in several ways: the funded project crowds out a competing investment opportunity; the investment replaces an existing business on the same site; or the project may result in a property move to a new site, leaving the old site vacant.

Replacement of an existing business may have a beneficial effect if a quality and cost improvement results in an improvement of long-term viability. Many assisted tourist projects have been built on derelict sites and have therefore resulted in a net improvement. Differential impacts on the labour market relate to the use of unemployed as opposed to employed people; improving the skills of the workforce; full-time, part-time and seasonal jobs; the male–female ratio; and local people versus outsiders. Externalities would account for the agglomeration benefits arising by virtue of the synergy of one project with another and its linkages with the rest of the economy. The art in tourism development is to ensure a balanced growth of facilities to meet the many and changing needs of visitors.

FUTURE POLICIES 1994–9

In assessing regional progress over the 1989–93 period, the Commission (1994b) concluded that the weaker regions had made some movement towards converging in real terms with the rest of the EU. However, the evidence indicated that structural change is a slow process, and during 1993 adjustments were made to the regulations governing the Structural Funds prior to the new phase commencing in 1994 and running through to the end of 1999. From a strategic perspective, the principles and direction underlying the Community's structural measures in the new programme follow on closely from what went before. The adjustments are largely tactical, through not only deepening, by raising the budgetary resources available to around ECU 150 billion at 1994 prices (the comparable amount for the 1989–93 programme was about ECU 85 billion), but also widening, by adding to the objectives and introducing a further instrument, the Cohesion Fund.

Objectives

The revised objectives for the new programme are listed in Table 7.6.

Table 7.6 Revised Structural Funds objectives

Objective	*Aim*
1	The economic adjustment of regions whose development is lagging behind
2	The economic conversion of declining industrial areas
3	Combating long-term unemployment, integrating into working life both young people and those threatened with exclusion from the labour market
4	The adaptation of workers to changes in industry and systems of production through measures to prevent unemployment
5a	The adaptation of the structures in the sectors of agriculture and fisheries in line with reform of the Common Agricultural Policy
5b	The economic diversification of fragile rural areas
6	Meeting the special problems of the very thinly populated regions of the Nordic countries

Source: Commission of the European Communities.

The previous Objectives 3 and 4 have been combined in a new Objective 3, and a new Objective 4 has been designated to help workers adapt to economic changes by incorporating measures to anticipate and impart new skill requirements to the labour force. Changes have also been brought about by a broadening of the detail of Objective 1 to include education and health, and, as Table 7.6 indicates, fisheries and fishing have been integrated into Objective 5a.

Negotiations over the enlargement of the EU by including the four European Free Trade Association (EFTA) countries also had on the agenda the matter of Structural Funds' assistance. It was anticipated that the four candidate countries (Austria, Norway, Sweden and Finland) would join on 1 January 1995, but the referendum in Norway went against membership of the EU, somewhat to the disappointment of the government, and only Sweden and Finland joined Denmark to increase the number of Nordic countries in the Community. To strengthen Objective 1, a new Objective 6 was created to account for the special conditions in the underpopulated peripheral areas of the Nordic candidate countries.

The widening of the regional objectives (Objectives 1, 2 and 5b) meant that for the original 12 member states the population covered has risen from 43 per cent for the 1989–93 programme to just under 52 per cent for the 1994–9 period. However, half of this increase relates to the unification of Germany. In 1989 the population covered by the regional objectives was 140.3 million; in 1994 this figure had risen to 178.6 million, of which 16.4 million is the population of the former East Germany. It is expected that, when the details are fully worked out, the new member states will add a further six million or more people to those eligible for regional assistance under the Structural Funds.

Accompanying the revised objectives are some changes in emphasis on the underlying principles and procedures. By devoting a higher share of resources to Objective 1, greater weight is being given to the principle of concentration to smooth the path of the most vulnerable areas towards European monetary union (EMU). From a procedural standpoint, there are now two ways in which member states may initiate development programmes (Commission, 1994c). The first is the same as before: acting in conjunction with regional authorities, the member state submits a development plan setting out priorities for action. CSFs are then agreed between the Commission and the member state, and from these a series of programmes is derived. This is most appropriate for new regions. The alternative is for the member state to submit single programming documents (SPDs), which combine priorities and programmes from the outset and become operational as soon as they have the Commission's approval.

The latter has become the most common method of submitting development programmes, since most of the eligible regions established a track record during the 1989–93 phase of the Structural Funds. In implementing the SPDs, the Commission is strengthening procedures to verify additionality and giving more emphasis to evaluation, appraisal and the formulation of quantitative intermediate objectives.

Cohesion Fund

In order to accelerate convergence, the Cohesion Fund has been created to provide additional aid for the poorest member states (Ireland, Greece, Portugal and Spain), where per capita GDP is less than 90 per cent of the Community average. As shown in Table 7.7, which presents the financial arrangements for the regional objectives and the Cohesion Fund, the latter will add considerably to the support given to regional development by the Structural Funds. Given the importance of tourism in the poorest member states, it is clear that this sector will be a major beneficiary of the Cohesion Fund.

Table 7.7 Structural Funds and the Cohesion Fund 1994–9 (ECU million, 1994 prices)

Country	*Objective 1*	*Objective 2*	*Objective 5b*	*Cohesion Fund*
Belgium	817	380	87	
Denmark		132	59	
Germany	14,686	1,765	1,359	
Greece	15,141			2,600
Spain	28,447	2,578	702	8,020
France	2,604	4,099	2,431	
Ireland	6,033			1,230
Italy	16,098	1,590	979	
Luxembourg		19	8	
Netherlands	158	694	161	
Portugal	15,489			2,600
United Kingdom	2,557	4,963	881	
Total	*102,030*	*16,220*	*6,667*	*14,450*

Source: Commission of the European Communities.

Table 7.8 Planned allocation for Community initiatives 1994–9 (ECU million, 1994 prices)

Initiative	*Allocation*
Interreg II	2,900
Leader II	1,400
Regis II	600
Employment	1,400
Adapt	1,400
Rechar II	400
Resider II	500
Konver	500
Retex	500
Portuguese textile industry	400
SMEs	1,000
Urban	600
Pesca	250
Reserve Fund	1,600
Total	*13,450*

Source: Commission of the European Communities.

Community initiatives

Amendments to the regulations governing the Structural Funds in July 1993 drew in the Community initiatives by allowing 9 per cent of the Funds to be devoted to these instruments (Commission, 1994d). The planned allocations for 1994–9 are shown in Table 7.8. Complementarity with the CSFs and SPDs is assured in the provision that at least ECU 8,150 million must go to Objective 1 regions. Furthermore, at least ECU 5,200 million should go to Ireland, Greece, Portugal and Spain.

Of the 13 initiatives shown in Table 7.8, six are continuations from previous programmes, namely: Interreg, Leader, Regis, Rechar, Resider and Retex; the last originating in 1992 to assist areas highly dependent on the textile and clothing industry. Some are reformulations of what went before: Employment, Konver, SMEs; while others are largely new: Adapt, Urban, Pesca and the special support for the textile and clothing industry in Portugal. Employment combines a new scheme, Youthstart (integration into the labour market of young people without qualifications), with initiatives launched in 1990, namely Now (for women) and Horizon (for disadvantaged and handicapped persons). Konver brings together special measures which had hastily been implemented to support regions weakened by the decline of defence industries and installations. The SME initiative covers the aspects that previously belonged to Stride, Prisma and Telematique. Adapt is a new initiative designed to complement Objective 4 of the Structural Funds (Table 7.6), while Urban is a measure to extend and improve co-ordination of urban policies supported through CSFs. The aim of Pesca is to help the fishing industry cope with the major structural changes that are currently taking place due to a surplus of capacity and over-fishing.

ISSUES FOR TOURISM

It is not difficult to appreciate that as leisure time increases and more people cross the income threshold for international travel, and there is increased segmentation of the market, tourism projects will achieve greater importance in the EU through meeting:

- the regional objectives of the Structural Funds;
- developments originating from the Cohesion Fund, given the continued dominance of sun, sand and sea destinations;
- priorities set by the Community initiatives in terms of structural adjustments: SME development, helping rural and remote areas, employment creation and the fostering of cross-border networks.

As a consequence it is expected that tourism will not only substantially increase the amount of regional aid it receives over the 1994–9 programme, but also increase its share of moneys coming from the various regional funds. Many of the newly eligible areas included in the 1994–9 programme have either an established tourism sector or the potential for developing tourism. It should not be thought, however, that new developments will be confined to the periphery, for tourism is known to thrive in run-down urban areas, such as redundant docks, old industrial complexes and obsolete market halls, where it may also act as a catalyst by attracting other investment. At the same time, it would be naïve to suppose that tourism development will be effective in every region or locality. Increasing market segmentation will generate niche markets for some areas, but the cost of supplying these markets could be prohibitive.

There are trends within the EU, which are recognized by the Commission and member states, that run counter to the policy of convergence. These will lead the Community into a policy of further compensating the less-favoured regions; this is the purpose of the Cohesion Fund. For example, the road to EMU will increasingly draw resources into the centre of Europe at the expense of the peripheral areas. This is the cumulative causation aspect of regional growth – the attractiveness of advanced regions has a cumulative effect in sucking in labour, capital and materials. Harmonization of travel arrangements with the completion of the internal market will encourage both outflows and inflows in respect of Objective 1 areas. It has already been estimated (Commission, 1994d) that there are important spill-over effects gained by the advanced member states from the contributions they make to those less favoured through the Structural Funds: of every ECU 100 invested in this manner, ECU 22–33 comes back in payment for capital goods and technology provided by the most developed regions.

The importance of tourism as an agent of regional development within the Community raises the question as to whether tourism should be designated directly as an instrument of the Structural Funds, or treated as such implicitly on a project-by-project basis within the CSFs or SPDs, as is current practice. In 1991 the European Parliament (EP) concluded that the regional development role of tourism was not given sufficient direct emphasis in EU policies. As noted at the beginning of this chapter, tourism interventions by the Community are spread across a wide range of activities and, in consequence, a number of DGs within the Commission, although there is a Tourism Unit within Directorate General XXIII (Enterprise Policy, Distributive Trades, Tourism and Co-operatives). Until the establishment of this DG in 1989, the Tourism Unit was in DGVII (Transport). In view of the dispersed nature of tourism interests, the EP recommended a specific Community initiative for tourism, which would imply earmarking a portion of the Structural Funds to support it. The range of areas that such an initiative would cover included:

- networking for SMEs (to include hotels, travel agencies and tour operators);
- training for local and national government officials on the role of tourism in development and the planning process;
- best practice transfers of knowledge and skills between regions and member states;

- assistance for the provision of business services, such as marketing, financial advice and information technology.

A report published by DGXII (Research), after considering the many arguments for and against, recommended against a separate Community initiative for tourism (Fitzpatrick Associates, 1993), on the grounds that any programmes for developing tourism within Objective 1 regions would need to cover a comprehensive range of tourism-related issues and also require close integration with the broader economic and development aspects of a region that are handled within CSFs or SPDs. Instead, the report proposed:

- a new Tourism Policy Division in the Commission, with enhanced powers to co-ordinate tourism actions across the DGs;
- a Tourism Action Programme, incorporating a variety of measures based on the establishment of Advice Centres for Tourism in Objective 1 regions;
- stronger tourism policy input and actions regarding decisions relating to the Structural Funds.

Clearly, these are medium- to long-term proposals, which do not have to be fully implemented.

One issue that is the subject of some debate and remains to be completely resolved is the role of the private sector and the position of the 'Solima' principle. This stems from changes in macro-economic policy during the 1980s, with a shift from demand to supply-side management and the emphasis on restricting (or reducing) public expenditure in the Northern member states. This led to the abandonment of automatic regional incentives and direction of industry in favour of selective assistance. By contrast, the Southern member states generally maintained or increased expenditure on regional policy, aided by support from the Structural Funds. Supply-side policies saw a move away from the reliance on subsidies for attracting regional investment and generating employment, and towards improving competitiveness and the regional business environment as a means of stimulating private sector projects. This is mirrored in the Structural Funds, which focus on the restructuring of regional production systems. Privatization of traditional state activities, particularly in the UK, and the move to attract private capital for public sector projects have altered the nature of public finance.

In view of this, it has been agreed with the Commission that private sector contributions should be included as part of the overall funding package for the assessment of matching grants from the Funds. It remains to be seen whether the 'Solima' principle will be overturned so that the Funds will be used directly in support of private sector projects.

ACKNOWLEDGEMENTS

The author is grateful for comments and assistance given by Tim Beddoe of the Wales Tourist Board, Alan Landsdown of the Welsh Office, Claire Warner of the European Commission, and Els Lowyck, a colleague who previously worked on this subject area with the author. However, the views and conclusions expressed in this chapter are the responsibility of the author.

REFERENCES

Clout, H. (1987) *Regional Development in Western Europe*. London: David Fulton.

Commission (Commission of the European Communities) (1984) 'Council Regulation No. 1787/84'. *Official Journal of the European Communities*, **169**, 1–16.

——(1988) 'Council Regulation No. 2052/85'. *Official Journal of the European Communities*, **185**, 9–20.

——(1991a) *Annual Report on the Implementation of the Reform of the Structural Funds*. Luxembourg: OOPEC.

——(1991b) *Guide to the Reform of the Community's Structural Funds*. Luxembourg: OOPEC.

——(1994a) *Community Measures Affecting Tourism*. Luxembourg: OOPEC.

——(1994b) *Competitiveness and Cohesion: Trends in the Regions*. Luxembourg: OOPEC.

——(1994c) *Europe at the Service of Regional Development*. Luxembourg: OOPEC.

——(1994d) *Guide to the Community Initiatives*. Luxembourg: OOPEC.

——(1995) *The Role of the Union in the Field of Tourism*. Commission Green Paper, Luxembourg: OOPEC.

Fitzpatrick Associates (1993) *The Role of the EC in Regard to Tourism and Regional Development*. Regional Policy Series E1. Brussels: Directorate General for Research.

Lowyck, E. and Wanhill, S. (1992) 'Regional Development and Tourism within the European Community', *Progress in Tourism, Recreation and Hospitality Management*, **4**, 227–44.

Pearce, D. (1988) 'Tourism and Regional Development in the European Community', *Tourism Management*, **9**, 13–22.

Wanhill, S. (1993) 'European Regional Development Funds for the Hospitality and Tourism Industries', *International Journal of Hospitality Management*, **12**, 67–76.

Yuill, D. and Allen, K. (1990) *European Regional Incentives*. London: Bowker-Saur.

APPENDIX

This appendix provides an explanation of the various acronyms used by the European Union to refer to the range of Community initiatives and action programmes mentioned in this chapter. Note that not all the acronyms are direct abbreviations of the Community's descriptions of the initiatives or action programmes.

Adapt	Community initiative for the adaptation of workers to changes in industry and production systems
Employment	Combines Horizon, Now and Youthstart
Envireg	Regional environment
Horizon	Community initiative concerning handicapped persons and certain other disadvantaged groups
Interreg	Community initiative concerning border areas
Konver	Conversion of regions whose economies depend on defence industries and military bases

Leader	Links between actions for the development of the rural economy
Now	New opportunities for women
Pesca	Community initiative for the structural adjustment of the fishing industry
Prisma	Preparation of businesses for the single market
Rechar	Reconversion of coal basins
Regis	Isolated regions
Resider	Reconversion of steel areas
Retex	Restructuring of the textile and clothing industry
SME	Combines Prisma, Stride and Telematique
Stride	Science and technology for regional innovation and development in Europe.
Telematique	Community initiative for regional development concerning services and networks related to data communication
Urban	Community initiative to extend and improve the co-ordination of urban policies
Youthstart	Community initiative to help young people without qualifications obtain a start in the labour market

EIGHT

Enterprise policy

Rhodri Thomas

INTRODUCTION

The European hospitality industry is characterized by fragmentation. However, several commentators have suggested that the market conditions which currently obtain are likely to lead to increased concentration, with multinational corporations expanding at the expense of smaller hospitality operators (Litteljohn, 1993; Crawford-Welch and Tse, 1990). It has been argued, moreover, that smaller firms will increasingly be forced to compete in marginal or low-profit locations, as the larger companies exploit the most lucrative markets (Viceriat, 1993).

These observations are neither new – the Pickering Report noted similar trends in the context of the UK almost 25 years ago (Pickering *et al.*, 1971) – nor unique to the hospitality industry. Indeed, one of the anticipated benefits of the single European market (SEM) was that larger European companies would emerge to compete successfully in global markets (Cecchini, 1988).

This notwithstanding, the European Commission has through its enterprise policy sought to support the development of small and medium-sized enterprises (SMEs).[1] This chapter reviews the measures which have been taken in this respect, examines their rationale and evaluates their implications for the hospitality industry in the light of available empirical evidence. Unfortunately, few researchers have analysed the impact of public policy on small hospitality firms.[2] Consequently, this chapter draws heavily upon the burgeoning small-firms literature, particularly where research has been undertaken in the context of other comparable services. It begins by providing an overview of enterprise policy, followed by a more detailed assessment of its three main themes: the creation of a favourable business environment, Europeanization, and the provision of business information and support.

ENTERPRISE POLICY IN EUROPE: AN OVERVIEW

Early official activity in support of SMEs included the dedication of 1983 as European Year for Small and Medium-sized Enterprises and Craft Industry. This was followed by the creation in 1986 of Task Force SME, which spawned an action programme that was adopted in principle by the Council of Ministers in November of that year (Council, 1986). Although this is significant in terms of highlighting official perceptions and, indeed, can be seen as the foundation of enterprise policy, it was in 1989 that the position became more formalized. In addition to the creation of Directorate General XXIII with specific responsibility for enterprise policy (and tourism), a Council decision taken on 28 July laid down the three central features of enterprise policy (Council, 1989). First was an attempt to create a favourable environment in which SMEs could flourish. The focus here was on the removal of what were seen as unnecessary and costly administrative, fiscal and legal burdens, which would have a disproportionate impact on smaller businesses. The second major plank of policy related to cross-border co-operation between enterprises, or Europeanization. The Commission established a number of initiatives to support this objective, notably the Business Co-operation Network (BC-Net). Finally, the decision made a commitment to the provision of business information; the main instrument developed to achieve this was the creation of European Information Centres (EICs).

There has subsequently been a series of Commission reports and Council decisions which have strengthened the framework by enhancing the number of policy instruments and increasing the level of funding.[3] Moreover, it is noteworthy that Article 130 of the Treaty on European Union (TEU) further elevates the status of SMEs in policy terms (Council and Commission, 1993). However, the principles established during the 1980s have remained largely unchanged. Thus, the Council decision taken in June 1993, which set out the action programme for the period of July 1993–December 1996, noted that:

> this policy primarily involves the improvement of the administrative, legal and fiscal environment of enterprises, the intensification and wider distribution of Community information for enterprises, the stimulation of cooperation between enterprises, and the promotion and coordination of Community instruments to assist enterprises, particularly SMEs. (Council, 1993, p. 69)

Table 8.1 summarizes the main themes and instruments of the three major areas of policy. The table is intended to be indicative and readers should consult the sources cited for details of the various programmes (some are discussed later in the chapter). It should be noted that although the instruments and declarations listed apply to SMEs, several are more centrally concerned with other policy areas and do not necessarily apply to all SMEs. For example, EUROPARTENARIAT is a business co-operation programme with a particular emphasis on firms in less-favoured regions, and to that extent can be seen primarily as part of regional policy. Nevertheless, the table is a useful indicator of the range of measures which apply to the development of SMEs.

Recent political concern at increasing levels of unemployment has prompted the Commission to concentrate its efforts more overtly on employment creation. The wide-ranging White Paper *Growth, Competitiveness, Employment* (Commission, 1993b) recognized the role that SMEs had to play in this respect and called for greater policy co-ordination. This precipitated the *Integrated Programme in Favour of SMEs and the*

Table 8.1 Major themes and policy instruments to support SMEs

Improving the business environment:
Administrative simplification/impact assessment
Improving the fiscal environment
Increasing access to public procurement
Encouraging Europeanization:
BC-Net
Bureau de Rapprochement des Enterprises (BRE)/Business Co-operation Centres
EUROPARTENARIAT
INTERPRISE
SPRINT
SIMAP
European Economic Interest Groupings (EEIGs)
Subcontracting
Information and support:
EICs
Forums to consider 'best practice'
Improving management quality: EUROMANAGEMENT, ADAPT
European Business and Innovation Centres
Increasing access to finance and credit

Notes:
Some measures apply to all enterprises and not only to SMEs.
Some of the instruments are under the jurisdiction of directorates general (DGs) other than DGXXIII.

Sources: Council (1993), Commission (1993a, 1994a).

Craft Sector (Commission, 1994a). The programme, which covers the period 1994–9, retains the central features of the policy agenda discussed above but shifts the emphasis from growth to employment.[4] It is noteworthy that the document singles out tourism as one of the sectors which has significant employment creation potential. Before examining the rationale and assessing the implications of enterprise policy for the development of the hospitality industry, it is appropriate, as far as possible, to comment on the position in the various member countries.

The varying institutional, political and cultural frameworks which exist in Europe make comparison of SME policies difficult and perhaps explain the shortage of academic contributions in this area. Some of the problems of analysis are illustrated clearly by the non-comparability of official statistics. For example, a comparison between Germany and the UK of the creation and cessation of hospitality firms based on VAT registrations (a commonly used if not entirely satisfactory indicator) would have to deal with significant differences in industrial classification systems and variations in VAT thresholds (Bannock and Albach, 1991). It is perhaps not surprising that a call for further research is a unifying feature of much of the literature which addresses issues associated with SME development in Europe (see for example Keeble and Wever, 1986; Korte, 1986; Storey, 1988).

One of the few studies to explore SME policies across the member states (reviewed by Anderson, 1993) demonstrates that there is no uniformity in terms of the number of instruments used to pursue particular objectives (see Table 8.2). For example, all countries have means of promoting start-up (some have one or two programmes while others have five or more), whereas environmental initiatives are confined to only five member countries.

Although useful as a starting point, taken alone the data in Table 8.2 has severe limitations. It gives no indication of the resources invested or of effectiveness; it is possible, of course, that a few effective instruments achieve more than many ineffective ones. Further, the polices may be geared to certain sectors (and serve them well) but not to others, or be of differing utility for businesses at varying stages of development.

Although a few rigorous comparative studies have been undertaken which have examined particular types of policy,[5] the paucity of published work suggests that any evaluation offered here would be partial. The Commission's intention to initiate Europe-wide panels to explore 'best practice' may begin to redress this situation, or at least stimulate further research. The remainder of this chapter seeks to assess in turn the three dimensions of enterprise policy referred to earlier.

IMPROVING THE BUSINESS ENVIRONMENT

As has been discussed in Chapter 3, the impetus for the creation of the SEM was to remove the physical, technical and fiscal barriers to trade within the Community. In large measure, this was seen as the basis for creating the appropriate environment to encourage increased competitiveness amongst European firms. Enterprise policy is an attempt to extend this; improvement of the business environment via administrative simplification (or deregulation) is a dominant theme. As the Commission's report on community measures affecting tourism (Commission, 1994b, p. 50) notes:

> To provide a favourable environment for firms, especially small and medium-sized businesses, Community policy acknowledges the need to simplify legislation and reduce the constraints which it imposes on them ... like firms in other sectors, tourist enterprises, which are overwhelmingly of small or medium size, benefit from this rationalization of administrative procedures, which is designed to avoid any unwarranted burden being placed on them.

This concern has resulted in the adoption of a formal impact assessment procedure for new legislative proposals and a review of existing regulation (Council, 1988, 1992a). During the assessment, the following questions are posed:

- Taking account of the principle of subsidiarity, why is Community legislation necessary in this area and what are its main aims?
- Who will be affected by the proposal?
- What will businesses have to do to comply with the proposal?
- Does the proposal contain measures to take account of the specific situation of small- and medium-sized firms (reduced or different requirements etc.)?

(Commission, 1992e, p. 44)

As part of this process it is incumbent upon the Commission to canvass the views of representative associations in the member states. Thus, for measures likely to affect tourism, DGXXIII has a list of 31 organizations which may be consulted, such as the Confederation of National Hotel and Restaurant Associations in the EC (HOTREC) and the European Tour Operators Association (ETOA). In many cases these bodies have a federal structure, drawing their membership from national trade or professional associations. The extent to which 'representative' organizations are in reality representative has been questioned by some commentators (Storey, 1994). Certainly in the UK it might be argued that although the British Hospitality Association (BHA), which is affiliated to HOTREC, has some 22,000 members, it may well be subject to the influence of large corporate donors and not always reflect the interests of small or medium-sized firms

Table 8.2 Policy instruments of 12 member states

Policy field	*B*	*DK*	*F*	*G*	*GR*	*IRL*	*I*	*L*	*NL*	*P*	*SP*	*UK*
General tax facility	**	–	*	**	*	*	–	*	**	–	*	**
Regional development	*	*	**	**	**	***	**	–	*	*	*	**
Technology and research and development	**	**	***	***	***	***	**	*	**	**	**	**
Supply and subcontracting	*	–	*	*	*	*	–	–	*	*	*	*
Export	**	**	**	**	**	***	**	*	**	*	*	**
Employment	**	*	–	*	*	**	*	–	*	*	**	**
Start-ups	*	**	***	**	**	**	*	*	**	**	**	***
Information and counselling	**	**	***	**	*	**	**	*	*	*	*	**
Financing	**	*	**	***	***	***	**	**	*	**	**	*
Training	**	*	***	*	*	***	**	*	**	*	*	***
Business licence	**	*	*	***	–	–	*	***	**	*	–	–
Administrative simplification	*	–	*	*	*	*	*	–	*	–	**	*
Co-operation	–	*	*	*	*	*	*	–	–	*	**	**
Environmental/energy	–	–	–	***	–	***	–	–	**	*	**	–

Key:
– No instruments
* 1 or 2
** 3 to 5
*** more than 5

Source: 'SME – Policy of the European Community', Economisch Instituut voor het Midden-en Kleinbedruf, Zoetermeer, the Netherlands, 1992, in Anderson (1993, p. 21).

within the sector. If this proposition has any validity, the implication is that the Commission should devise alternative means of garnering the views of SMEs within the industry.

A report from the Commission in 1992 expressed disappointment with progress towards deregulation, noting that SMEs continue to pay heavy administrative costs (Commission, 1992f). Although the sentiment remains, the Commission is also shifting the emphasis to the role member states should play in reviewing domestic legislation. Thus, it points out that Belgium, France, Germany and the UK are all seriously addressing this question, while others are not (Commission, 1994a).[6]

There has, nevertheless, been some modest 'success'. For example, Anderson (1993) provides clear illustrations of how these concerns have resulted in less rigorous accounting procedures for SMEs, and the administrative requirements on small firms entering exclusive contracts have been eased (Commission, 1993c, p. 10). That the Commission is now turning its attention to the simplification of public procurement procedures (to encourage SME participation), strengthening its internal evaluation mechanisms for proposals, easing transfer (of ownership) problems, and, as noted, extolling the virtues of deregulation to member states, is unlikely to appease critics. For example, Ann Robinson of the Institute of Directors recently commented:

> During its life some of the most burdensome regulations for small firms have passed through the Council of Ministers without so much as a peep from DG23 ... The [Institute of Directors] believes that the EC should focus more closely on the real problems that SMEs face in doing their day-to-day business and on the impact of taxation on those firms ... Action to reduce 'red tape' should be given a much higher priority by DG23. (quoted in Storey, 1994, p. 267)

Mulhern (1994) offers a similar, if less scathing, assessment, arguing that the rhetoric has not been matched by action.

In spite of the number of documents which contain the theme, there is little official justification for administrative simplification. Instead, it is taken as almost axiomatic that smaller firms face an unreasonable regulatory burden which, crucially, stifles enterprise; easing that 'burden' will result in increased growth and employment, as owners and managers will have more time to devote to their businesses and become less risk-averse, since the consequences of breaching regulations will be more readily understood (and less severe).

Where justification is offered it is often nebulous. For example, the *Integrated Programme* talks of the 'many studies and research projects [which] demonstrate the vital importance to operators making employment decisions of a reduction in the legal, administrative and fiscal burdens on enterprises' (Commission, 1994a, p. 6). This is perhaps not as surprising as it first appears, since many have pointed out (such as Collins, 1994) that the whole movement towards economic integration in Europe and elsewhere is primarily politically motivated rather than the result of considered economic analysis.

Bannock and Peacock (1989) are amongst the few academics who present a systematic case in favour of deregulation. Two main arguments emerge from their international review of empirical studies. First, they cite survey evidence which highlights a general concern amongst firms relating to government regulation. Second, and more importantly, they point to studies which estimate that compliance costs amount to some 3–4 per cent of gross national product (GNP); resources which could more productively be used by businesses. Moreover, they point out that compliance costs are regressive, falling disproportionately on smaller firms. For example, in a study conducted in Britain and Germany, compliance costs as a percentage of turnover were 2.5 per cent and 7.8 per cent respectively for the smallest firms in the sample, but declined to 0.07 and 0.02 per cent for slightly larger firms.

Advocates of deregulation in the context of the hospitality industry might point to the closure of many small establishments in the UK during the 1970s, following the introduction of more stringent fire regulations. More recently, one survey of small businesses in Cornwall, which included a high proportion of hospitality and tourism firms, noted that in 'almost all cases firms complained about unnecessary rules and regulations' (Restormel Economic Development Service, 1994, p. 17). In addition, even casual observers of the trade press will not have missed such arguments being applied in reaction to the perceived threats arising from proposed social policy measures.[7] Indeed, the BHA's enthusiasm for deregulation has extended to conducting a project which attempts to establish the compliance costs associated with new health and safety regulations (BHA, 1994).

Thorough evaluation of the impact of state regulation is, however, extremely complex. As Storey (1994) has made clear, any analysis must consider the purpose of each regulation. Thus, measures designed to improve the environment, to encourage job security or to protect consumers may well provide benefits to society which outweigh the private costs to firms. Clearly there are difficulties in excluding smaller operators from many of these requirements. Crudely, it would seem unacceptable that those visiting small cafés were more at risk of food poisoning, as a result of the cafés not having to comply with hygiene regulations, than consumers in an establishment owned by a multinational corporation.

Stanworth and Gray (1991) offer a robust theoretical critique of deregulation. They present three interrelated arguments. First, they anticipate that any preferential treatment of smaller firms in relation to labour market regulations may initially reduce costs but are likely in the longer term to lower wages and other conditions of employment. Consequently, the competitive position of these firms may in fact be reduced as high-calibre employees became more difficult to attract. Second, they suggest that the immediate benefits associated with deregulation may in the longer term lead to complacency among smaller operators. The removal of the necessity to compete on innovation and market development, replaced by the possibility of competing on price, may not ultimately result in enhanced performance by these firms. Finally, significantly different cost structures between smaller and larger firms may simply cause increased subcontracting. Although this is potentially beneficial to small firms, there may be no net gains in terms of overall economic activity or, in this case, the development of the sector.

Arguably many of their criticisms do not apply as forcefully to an industry which does not generally require skilled personnel and is not predominantly technologically driven. However, the possibility of increased subcontracting if smaller firms become increasingly exempt from compliance with regulations is more persuasive. There is evidence that the cost-cutting strategies of some hospitality firms incorporate subcontracting of certain functions, including the use by large city-centre hotels of smaller firms operating in the informal economy (Thomas and Thomas, 1994; Williams and Thomas, 1996). Naturally, the latter is circumscribed by factors such as potentially adverse publicity or poor quality. With the legitimacy afforded by deregulation, however, smaller businesses may flourish, but at the expense of large firm activity, resulting in no net benefits to the sector.

Available empirical evidence of the impact of state regulation is equivocal. Surveys often appear to support official assertions, but the picture is not uniform. For example, almost two-thirds of Curran *et al.*'s (1993) sample did not consider that employment legislation made a major impact on their business. It is interesting that there appeared to be greater concern amongst hospitality firms, but their perceptions were often based on ignorance of the law, implying that a programme of education would be more appropriate than further deregulation.

In a detailed critique of five surveys which also focused on the impact of employment law, it is significant that Westrip (1986) found considerable variation in their methodological rigour, which, she argues, goes some way to explaining apparently contradictory findings. Nevertheless, there does appear to be some consensus that small firms tend to be hostile to government intervention in the employment process. Often, commentators part company when attention is turned to the likely effect of removal of particular regulations; naturally, if asked, it is not surprising that small employers do not generally see regulation as helpful to the development of their businesses, but there may be a sharp contrast between general dispositions and consequent actions. Westrip's (1986) analysis suggests that current survey evidence in the UK provides little support for the notion that deregulation in this sphere would stimulate greater employment. There are no *a priori* reasons to suppose that this would be different in other European Union (EU) member states.

A similar observation may be made in relation to the taxation of small enterprises. For example, part of the British government's rationale for reducing direct taxation following their election in 1979 was to offer incentives whereby entrepreneurs would invest and expand their businesses. Yet, as Rees and Shah's (1994) research has revealed, the self-employed tended to work fewer hours during the 1980s, suggesting that the removal of an unpopular 'burden' need not necessarily lead to the development of business activity.

In the context of the hospitality industry, Thomas and Thomas (1992) have examined the impact of planning regulation on hot food take-aways. The evidence from that study indicated that in spite of moves to deregulate and simplify the planning process, small firms in that sector tended to be confused by the deliberative process of planning authorities (though many had not read the available notes of guidance) and faced geographical variation in how regulations were implemented. The main recommendation was not further deregulation, but rather clarification of the criteria used and an encouragement to greater consistency of decision making.

Finally, Goss (1991) questions the appropriateness of deregulation in relation to health and safety at work. He argues that moves to reduce the requirements on smaller firms to comply with legislation and the encouragement of inspectors to be more sympathetic to small firms sits uncomfortably with the varied evidence he provides that smaller firms are more prone to industrial injuries than larger ones. Although not considered specifically from the perspective of the hospitality industry, this nevertheless highlights another legitimate concern, which cautions against a bifurcated approach to state regulation.

It should be clear that what is being argued here is not a defence of regulation *per se*. Clearly, the Commission and Council *should* consider the implications of regulations for the development of smaller firms. Equally, it is desirable that proposals should be amended where the aims can be achieved without imposing significant compliance costs. What is at issue is the veracity of assertions that smaller firms currently face an unreasonable burden, the removal of which would encourage enterprise; available evidence suggests that a degree of ambivalence is appropriate in evaluating such a claim.

EUROPEANIZATION

The Commission's aspirations to create a *de facto* unified European market, the second main strand of enterprise policy, has led to a number of initiatives designed to increase cross-border co-operation between enterprises. Indeed, some 20 per cent of enterprise policy funding has been allocated to finance measures for this purpose (Commission, 1994b, p. 51). Table 8.1 above illustrates the main instruments of policy.

As has already been noted, the operation and orientation of individual initiatives vary. Their common feature is that they represent attempts by the Commission to provide channels whereby firms can identify potential collaborative partners in different member states.

BC-Net is undoubtedly the flagship of this dimension of policy. Briefly, it is a computerized network of consultants (including EICs, discussed later in the chapter) both within and outside the EU. The consultant draws up a confidential co-operation profile (CP) on behalf of organizations, which contains details of the company and the nature of the partnership it is seeking. The Central Unit in Brussels then attempts to match the profile with CPs submitted from other locations. Where appropriate, the companies are then introduced to each other. Criticisms that potential partnerships may flounder at this stage have led the Commission to propose extending the support available until formal contractual arrangements are made (Commission, 1994a, pp. 30–1).

It is difficult to find extensive justification for activity in this area. As is often the case, commentaries concentrate more on describing the details of the initiative than on providing clear policy aims or a rationale. Thus a background report on BC-Net notes only that:

> the project was established to encourage and assist co-operation between small and medium-sized companies (SMEs). Many of these companies need assistance to face the increased competition and to take advantage of the opportunities created by the opening of the Single European Market. (Commission, 1992b, p. 1)

Evaluation of this type of policy instrument is also difficult because of the lack of published research. Official comment, which tends to focus primarily on usage statistics, is sanguine. For example, the Commission (1992b) points out that between BC-Net's inception in 1988 and mid-1992, there were almost 58,000 partnership offers or requests. Moreover, as far as tourism is concerned, during the period to 1994 there had been 823 requests for co-operation using the network, of which more than half related to the hotel sector (Commission, 1994b, p. 51). What is conspicuously absent is any indication of how many of these requests were translated into successful partnerships. Official publications are also silent on the nature of the co-operation that might be encouraged in this sector, which is in sharp contrast to other industries, notably manufacturing. This clearly implies that either less effort is made to promote the service to firms in the hospitality and tourism industries or, indeed, the network has little to offer.

One small study of a non-confidential partnership search scheme, Eurokom (which utilized the BRE network), found no hospitality-sector-specific requests for co-operation or partnership during a two-month period in 1992 (Thomas, 1993). Although official statistics point to higher usage than implied by that project, with 273 tourism-related BRE partnership searches during 1993, the Commission's (1994b, p. 51) bold claim that this demonstrates the effectiveness of the system is inappropriate. The illustration provided by Figure 8.1 (which was received by Mid Yorkshire EIC on 13 September

1994) may suggest that the networks have a high potential value, but the lack of information available, even to the Commission, regarding the outcome of such searches makes thorough evaluation impossible.

The Commission has also encouraged Europeanization by the creation of EEIGs. Introduced in July 1989, these are associations of firms that wish to co-operate on certain aspects of their activity. Although they have full independent 'legal personality' and, notably, operate within a European rather than a national legal framework, they should not be considered as similar to holding companies. They may not, for example, be established with the main aim of making profits for themselves. The intention is that by being granted legal status an EEIG may overcome fragmentation and effectively take action to promote its aims (Commission, 1991, pp. 90–1).

A survey of EEIGs carried out by the Commission (1993d) shows that membership of the 310 groupings established by March 1992 was drawn predominantly from the private service sector, with a tendency to bring together members in the same type of occupational activity. The extent to which tourism-related EEIGs have been formed is not clear but, on the basis of existing schemes, the report usefully highlights the potential of these arrangements in promoting particular destinations and shared facilities (such as training) within them. Currently most EEIGs are registered in France, Belgium and the Netherlands, followed by Germany and the UK.

BUSINESS INFORMATION AND SUPPORT

The provision of business information and support is the third major component of enterprise policy. As in the case of 'improvements' to the business environment and Europeanization, this feature of policy has also resulted in the creation of a range of instruments and programmes. In budgetary terms, the EIC network is the most significant, accounting for some 40 per cent of DGXXIII's budget (Commission, 1994b, p. 51). The Commission has, however, increasingly promoted support mechanisms which are designed to overcome what it sees as specific disadvantages faced by SMEs compared with larger organizations, notably in relation to management development and the availability of finance.

Heinrich von Moltke, Director General of DGXXIII, summarized the role of EICs as follows:

> [a small firm] may not have the time or resources needed to study the wide range of opportunities that are available. The European Information Centres open these doors – doors to local, national and European markets, doors to partnerships across borders, doors to public procurement contracts, to calls for tender, to all manner of opportunities ... the services that EICs provide are essential for SMEs if they are to compete on a level playing field ... in the internal market. (Von Moltke, 1993, p. 93)

As is clear from the above, the Commission's rationale rests on a perceived market failure for business information which necessitates public sector involvement. The argument is that small firms are not likely to have the resources and internal structures to gather and process information as effectively as their larger counterparts. The creation of public sector mechanisms which generate appropriate business information and assist firms in the development of suitable strategies (perhaps as a result of advice, training or

Company name:	Deleted
Activity:	Self-catering holiday houses and management
Creation:	1991
Turnover:	£200,000
Staff:	4
International experience:	England, Spain

Description of co-operation seeking:
A financial partner possibly with a background in building development or connections in holiday and tourism business.

Objective:
To develop a three phase project on the outskirts of Essaouira (Moroccan leisure resort on the Atlantic). Land surface of 31 acres.

Contact: A. Taadi, Information Officer, EIC MA1741, Morocco

Source: Mid Yorkshire EIC (September 1994).

Figure 8.1 Example of a non-confidential request for co-operation or partnership

access to funding) should ensure that smaller organizations can prosper in an increasingly competitive environment.

The rationale certainly has an intuitive appeal, and varied evidence might be drawn upon in its support. For example, there is widespread acceptance that organizations need business information to operate effectively, with some commentators pointing to increasing empirical evidence which links environmental scanning with enhanced business performance (Zhao and Merna, 1992). Moreover, the few studies which specifically address information gathering and processing in small businesses point to great areas of uncertainty in their approach (Sharkey, 1992). However, taken alone these factors do not represent an endorsement of the Commission's actions; more substantial evidence is required before it can be supposed that the public provision of information and advice will lead to the development of the small firms' sector in general and the hospitality industry in particular.

The Commission's justification for its actions and the evaluative criteria applied to monitor the effectiveness of policy instruments are, typically, implied rather than explicit. Careful reading of official publications is required to identify the kind of evidence which is used to inform decisions. The following extract is one of a few instances where the Commission is unambiguous:

> it is a fact that good support measures for enterprises greatly increase their chances of surviving and expanding. For example, it is acknowledged that the level and type of initial training for the creator of an enterprise, and the existence or otherwise of external advisory services, greatly influence the possibility of an enterprise closing down or surviving. According to a 1990 survey of 16,000 French enterprises created in 1984/5, the closure rate within five years was 59% in the case of new enterprises which had not used advisory services, compared with 19% for those who had consulted experts. (Commission, 1994a, p. 17)

Elsewhere in the same document, the perceived effectiveness of Business Innovation Centres (BICs) is highlighted by noting that between 1984 and 1993 they were responsible for the creation of 2726 firms employing 15,953 people. In addition, the seed capital project has since its inception in 1989 apparently resulted in 187 new organizations and over 1700 jobs (Commission, 1994a, pp. 7–10).

As far as EICs are concerned, it is clear that the Commission's primary indicator of success is the number of queries handled by the network. On this measure their performance is, indeed, impressive. Official estimates for the network as a whole suggest that the number of enquiries grew from approximately 12,000 in 1987/8 to 120,000 by 1991, with the majority coming from firms employing fewer than 20 people. Not surprisingly, then, the Commission can claim that it is achieving its objective of reaching SMEs (Commission, 1993e). Indeed, it is likely to be equally positive about its record of encouraging participation from a wide range of sectors; Table 8.3 suggests usage across most industries. Of particular interest for the purposes of this chapter is Nomenclature des Activités de la Communautée Européenne (NACE) classification 6, 'Distribution and catering', which accounted in 1991 for 7.5 per cent of total enquiries. As with all aggregated figures there is a danger of obfuscation; what is not clear, for example, is usage levels by hospitality firms.

Table 8.3 EIC use by industrial sector 1991

NACE sector		*Usage (%)*
0	Agriculture	8.8
1	Energy, water	2.0
2	Energy, processing of non-energy minerals, chemicals	4.0
3	Metal manufacture, mechanical, electrical engineering	13.0
4	Other manufacture	15.0
5	Building and civil engineering	5.5
6	Distribution, catering	7.5
7	Transport, communication	4.5
8	Banking, financial and business services	13.0
9	Other services	27.0

Source: Cooper (1993, p. 20).

The disaggregated statistics contained in the Commission's report on initiatives affecting tourism (Commission, 1994b, p. 51) suggest significantly lower contact with the sector. The report notes that between 1991 and November 1993 only 136 requests for information and support related to the industry; it somewhat optimistically adds 'to these should be added the hundreds of oral questions to which a direct answer was given by the various members to the network'.

Thomas's (1994) study of UK and Irish EICs also found low usage amongst hospitality firms. Moreover, the promotional methods used by centres and the evidently low sector-specific knowledge of EIC personnel revealed by that work suggest that contact between small hospitality firms and EICs is unlikely to increase in the foreseeable future unless there are significant organizational changes. A policy shift, whereby EICs concentrate their activities on particular groups of industries which share common features might encourage increased usage and result in greater responsiveness to the needs of hospitality businesses. Clearly, such a move would make the appropriate EIC geographically remote for numerous organizations but, as has been argued elsewhere, many EIC services may be accessed easily by telephone (Thomas, 1994).

It should be noted that official monitoring of EIC performance has also included two generally favourable quality control reports and there are plans to introduce biannual reports in the future. However, these exercises have been based largely on reports completed by EICs themselves and did not include sectoral considerations (Commission, 1992c, 1992d). Again, it could well be that centres perform a vital function for some industries but not others.

At this stage it is instructive to consider Haughton's (1993) review of studies which have examined the value of information and support services because many incorporate clients' perspectives. He notes that participation rates are generally low and that the perceptions of users vary significantly; in some studies up to 65 per cent of the sample considered the support available to be very useful or crucial to the development of their businesses, whereas others reveal predominantly negative attitudes. Perhaps the variation is not surprising, since the agencies studied had differing aims and objectives. Generally, it appears that there is some consensus in the literature that greater co-ordination of activity at a local level and careful targeting would improve the effectiveness of support agencies. Indeed, some go further, arguing that sector-specific initiatives are more likely to yield positive benefits (Curran, 1993).

The main weakness of much of the research cited above, including that referred to by the Commission, however, is its failure to address fundamental but methodologically more complex questions: to what extent do smaller firms that *do* utilize the support services on offer (EICs or otherwise) perform better (or worse) than those that do not? Are they, for example, less likely to fail? Clearly, evaluation of policy must move beyond participation rates and user perceptions and consider possible 'displacement' (the failure of some firms precipitated by the creation of new assisted enterprises), 'additionality' and 'deadweight' (consideration of what would have happened anyway in the absence of the policy). Some of these issues may be particularly pertinent for a sector which has low entry barriers and, therefore, attracts many new firm formations and numerous cessations.

It is important to recognize that the inferences made by the Commission and studies reviewed by Haughton (1993) are not borne out conclusively by the literature which seeks to identify determinants of small-firm success or failure. Although a major econometric analysis of small firms in the UK found some positive association between support agency activity and business performance (Keeble and Walker, 1993), Storey's (1994) extensive and highly regarded review suggests that the influence of this variable is relatively minor when compared with factors such as size, age and the previous growth patterns of small firms. Clearly, further research is required, some of which should pay particular attention to the structural features of the European hospitality industry.

CONCLUDING COMMENTS

The lack of available data makes it difficult to draw firm conclusions about the impact that enterprise policy is likely to have on the hospitality industry. Indeed, the only observation that can be made with any degree of certainty is that any positive benefits which may accrue to firms in the sector will have more to do with serendipity than with careful judgement on the part of the Commission. It appears that Storey *et al.*'s (1987, p. 2) comments, made almost a decade ago, remain as pertinent now as they were then: 'public policies to promote the development and growth of small firms have been developed, particularly in Western Europe, rather faster than our knowledge about small firms'.

As far as the first feature of enterprise policy is concerned, that of improving the business environment, the available evidence suggests that there are dangers of extending the bifurcated approach adopted in some spheres. Although the compliance costs of state regulation are undoubtedly regressive, there is little hard evidence to support the notion that current requirements stifle enterprising small firms in this industry. Some regulations may be unpopular, but their removal will not necessarily counter trends towards concentration. Moreover, since one agent's regulation is another's protection, there are potentially significant costs. As has been argued earlier, this is not to suggest that the Commission should not be mindful of the interests of SMEs when drafting regulations; if their aims can be achieved with minimum impact upon the sector then that is clearly desirable.

Examination of measures designed to encourage the Europeanization of businesses, the second major component of enterprise policy, reveals some relatively isolated uses of instruments by firms in the hospitality industry. Although consideration of these is interesting, because they offer the possibility of illustrating their potential value to other firms within the sector, it is not possible at this stage to assess their significance effectively. Lack of participation by hospitality firms may signal weaknesses in the promotion of these instruments, but equally, and probably more plausibly, it could be a reflection of the fact that the benefits on offer are minimal. A detailed assessment of any advantages accruing to participating firms is required before any valid judgement can be made.

The third element of enterprise policy rests on the premise that there is a market failure for business information and support, which necessitates public sector involvement at a European level. The Commission's most celebrated innovation is the creation of EICs. As has been discussed, the Commission's evaluation is positive. However, careful examination of usage statistics, coupled with the results of independent studies, suggests that hospitality firms do not use the services on offer to the extent implied by the aggregated usage statistics which are often quoted. In addition, current organizational arrangements, the manner in which services are promoted, and the lack of sector-specific knowledge amongst EIC personnel undermine official optimism. Although it has been tentatively suggested that some of the information and support available is potentially valuable to firms in this industry, there are reasons for questioning the validity of research which examines the value of public sector support mechanisms on the basis of usage statistics and users' perceptions of utility. This form of business support appears not to be a key feature of many multivariate analyses which focus upon the reasons for the creation, growth or cessation of small businesses.

Perhaps above all, this chapter has highlighted lamentable deficiencies in hospitality management research. Notwithstanding the fact that much of the industry is still dominated by small firms, little energy has been expended by researchers attempting to understand their dynamics or how public policy designed to support their development impacts upon them. A new research agenda is required, which informs the deliberations of policy makers and enables those engaged in supporting the management of small firms to be effective in that role.

ACKNOWLEDGEMENTS

I am grateful to Heather Smith and Paul Vance who helped gather the official documents referred to in this chapter, and to staff members at DGXXIII, who provided papers which are not available through European Documentation Centres (EDCs).

NOTES

1. The Commission has recently adopted a new common definition of SMEs as follows: 'micro' or 'very small enterprises' employ fewer than 10 people, 'small enterprises' employ between 10 and 49 pcople, 'medium-sized enterprises' employ more than 50 but fewer than 250 people. There are also criteria relating to turnover and balance sheet totals and degree of independence (see Commission, 1996a).
2. For a review of public policy and small hospitality firms in the UK, see Thomas (1995).
3. Those interested in examining the development of policy in more detail should consult Commission (1990, 1993e) and Council (1989, 1991, 1992b).
4. Although the 'integrated programme' provides the framework for EU enterprise policy, it is important to recognize that key specific measures are contained in the 'multiannual programmes for SMEs'. The Commission has recently published proposals for a third multiannual programme for the period 1997–2000 (see Commission, 1996b).
5. For example Meager (1993), Lauder *et al.* (1994), Bannock and Albach (1991), and de Koning and Snijders (1992). Two Commission reports (1989, 1992e) offer an overview of measures taken at member-state level which are consistent with enterprise policy, but they tend to describe initiatives rather than evaluate their effectiveness.
6. In at least some cases, however, the measures resulting from apparently radical official declarations have been diluted forms of what were initially anticipated (see for example Stanworth and Gray, 1991).
7. See for example BHA (1993a, 1993b, 1995) for more general statements in favour of deregulation.

REFERENCES

Anderson, C. (1993) *Getting European Community Help for Your Company*. London: Kogan Page.

Bannock, G. and Albach, H. (1991) *Small Business Policy in Europe: Britain, Germany and the European Commission*. London: Anglo-German Foundation for the Study of Industrial Society.

Bannock, G. and Peacock, A. (1989) *Government and Small Business*. London: Paul Chapman.

BHA (British Hospitality Association) (1993a) 'Social Policy in Europe', *Voice* **2(2)**, 22–3.

——(1993b) 'EC Tourism Policy – Wanted: A Real Action Plan and Cuts in Red Tape', *Voice* **2(4)**, 14–15.

——(1994) 'Deregulation Remains a Live Issue', *Voice* **3(8)**, 9.

——(1995) 'Europe Presses De-reg Button', *Voice* **4(2)** 24–5.

Cecchini, P. (1988) *The European Challenge – 1992: The Benefits of a Single Market*. Aldershot: Wildwood House.

Collins, C.D.E. (1994) 'History and Institutions of the EC' in El-Agraa, A.M. (ed.) *The*

Economics of the European Community, 4th edition. Hemel Hempstead: Harvester Wheatsheaf.

Commission (Commission of the European Communities) (1989) *Report by the Commission on Measures Taken by Member States on Behalf of Enterprises in the Community with Regard to Administrative Simplification*, SEC (189) 726 Final.

—— (1990) *Enterprise Policy: A New Dimension for Small and Medium-sized Enterprises*, COM (90) 528 Final.

—— (1991) *Operations of the European Community Concerning Small and Medium-sized Enterprises*. Brussels: DGXXIII.

—— (1992a) *Report from the Commission to the Council on the Definitions of Small and Medium-sized Enterprises (SMEs) used in the Context of Community Activities*. SEC (92) 351 Final.

—— (1992b) *BC-Net (the Business Co-operation Network)*, Background Report, ISEC/B24/92.

—— (1992c) *Balance and Perspectives of EIC Activity*. Brussels: DGXXIII.

—— (1992d) *Euro Info Centres – Annual Report 1991–92*. Luxembourg: OOPEC.

—— (1992e) *Report by the Commission on Administrative Simplification Work in the Community in Favour of Enterprises, in Particular SMEs*, SEC (92) 1867 Final.

—— (1992f) *Evaluation of the Community's Enterprise Policy*, SEC (92) 1999 Final.

—— (1993a) *Guidelines for Small and Medium-sized Enterprises*. London: Commission of the European Communities.

—— (1993b) *Growth, Competitiveness, Employment: The Challenges and Ways Forward into the 21st Century*. Luxembourg: OOPEC.

—— (1993c) *Third Report on the Application of the Council Decision of 28th July 1989*, COM (93) 365 Final.

—— (1993d) *EEIG: The Emergence of a New Form of European Cooperation – Review of Three Years' Experience*. Luxembourg: OOPEC.

—— (1993e) *The Enterprise Dimension Essential to Community Growth*, COM (92) 470 Final.

—— (1994a) *Integrated Programme in Favour of SMEs and the Craft Sector*, COM (94) 207 Final.

—— (1994b) *Report from the Commission to the Council, the European Parliament and the Economic and Social Committee on Community Measures Affecting Tourism*, COM (94) 74 Final.

—— (1996a) 'Commission Recommendation of 3 April 1996 concerning the definition of small and medium-sized enterprises', *Official Journal* L107/4 of 30.4.96.

—— (1996b) *Maximizing European SMEs' Full Potential for Employment, Growth and Competitiveness*, COM (96) 98 Final.

Cooper, M. (1993) 'EICs: Use and Users – A Statistical Review', *EIA Review*, **1**, 19–23.

Council (Council of the European Communities) (1986) 'Council Resolution 86/C 287/01', *Official Journal*, C 287/1 of 14.11.86.

—— (1988) 'Council Resolution 88/C 197/04', *Official Journal*, C197/6 of 27.7.88.

—— (1989) 'Council Decision 89/490/EEC', *Official Journal*, L239/33 of 16.8.89.

—— (1991) 'Council Decision 91/319/EEC', *Official Journal*, L175/32 of 4.7.91.

—— (1992a) 'Council Resolution 92/C 331/02', *Official Journal*, C331/3 of 16.12.92.

—— (1992b) 'Council Resolution 92/C 178/04', *Official Journal*, C178/8 of 15.7.92.

—— (1993) 'Council Decision 93/379/EEC', *Official Journal*, L161/68 of 2.7.93.

Council and Commission (Council and Commission of the European Communities) (1993) *The Treaty on European Union*. Luxembourg: OOPEC.

Crawford-Welch, S. and Tse, E. (1990) 'Mergers, Acquisitions and Alliances in the European Hospitality Industry', *International Journal of Contemporary Hospitality Management*, **4(2)**, 10–16.
Curran, J. (1993) *TECs and Small Firms: Can TECs Reach the Small Firms Other Strategies have Failed to Reach?* Paper presented to the All Party Social Science and Policy Group, House of Commons.
Curran, J., Kitching, J., Abbot, B. and Mills, V. (1993) *Employment and Employment Relations in the Small Service Sector Enterprise*. Kingston: Centre for Research on Small Service Sector Enterprises.
de Koning, A. and Snijders, J. (1992) 'Policy on Small and Medium-sized Enterprises in Countries of the European Community', *International Small Business Journal*, **10(3)**, 25–39.
Goss, D. (1991) *Small Business and Society*. London: Routledge.
Haughton, G. (1993) 'The Local Provision of Small and Medium Enterprise Advice Services', *Regional Studies*, **27(8)**, 835–42.
Keeble, D. and Walker, S. (1993) *New Firm Formation of Small Business Growth in the United Kingdom: Spatial and Temporal Variations and Determinants*. Research Series No. 15. Sheffield: Employment Department.
Keeble, D. and Wever, E. (1986) 'Introduction' in Keeble, D. and Wever, E. (eds) *New Firms and Regional Development in Europe*. London: Croom Helm, 1–34.
Korte, W. (1986) 'Small and Medium-sized Establishments in Western Europe' in Keeble, D. and Wever, E. (eds) *New Firms and Regional Development in Europe*. London: Croom Helm, 35–54.
Lauder, D., Boocock, G. and Presley, J. (1994) 'The System of Support for SMEs in the UK and Germany', *European Business Review*, **94(1)**, 9–16.
Litteljohn, D. (1993) 'Western Europe' in Jones, P. and Pizam, A. (eds) *The International Hospitality Industry*. London: Pitman 3–24.
Meager, N. (1993) 'From Unemployment to Self-employment in the European Community' in Chittenden, F., Robertson, M. and Watkins, D. (eds) *Small Firms, Recession and Recovery*. London: Paul Chapman, 27–53.
Mulhern, A. (1994) 'The SME Sector, the Single Market and the Appropriateness of DGXXIII Policies', *Small Business and Enterprise Development*, **1(1)**, 3–11.
Pickering, J.F., Greenwood, J.A. and Hunt, D. (1971) *The Small Firm in the Hotel and Catering Industry*. London: HMSO.
Rees, H. and Shah, A. (1994) 'The Characteristics of the Self-Employed: The Supply of Labour' in Atkinson, J. and Storey, D. (eds) *Employment, the Small Firm and the Labour Market*. London: Routledge, 317–27.
Restormel Economic Development Service (1994) *Business Needs Survey: Very Small Firms*. Cornwall: Restormel Borough Council.
Sharkey, G. (1992) 'Information Search by Small Firms', *Business Information Review*, **2**, 42–9.
Stanworth, J. and Gray, C. (1991) (eds) *Bolton 20 Years On: The Small Firm in the 1990s*. London: Paul Chapman.
Storey, D.J. (1988) 'The Role of Small and Medium-sized Enterprises in European Job Creation: Key Issues for Policy and Research' in Giaoutzi, M., Nijkamp, P. and Storey, D. (eds) *Small and Medium-sized Enterprises and Regional Development*. London: Routledge, 140–60.
—— (1994) *Understanding the Small Business Sector*. London: Routledge.
Storey, D., Keasey, K., Watson, R. and Wynarezyk, P. (1987) *The Performance of Small Firms*. London: Croom Helm.

Thomas, R. (1993) 'EICs and Sectoral Usage: The Case of Hotels and Catering', *EIA Review*, **2**, 18–23.

——(1994) 'European Union Enterprise Policy and the Hospitality Industry', *International Journal of Contemporary Hospitality Management*, **6(4)**, 10–15.

——(1995) 'Public Policy and Small Hospitality Firms', *International Journal of Contemporary Hospitality Management*, **7(2/3)**, 69–73.

Thomas, R. and Thomas, H. (1992) 'State Regulation and the Hospitality Industry: The Case of Hot Food Take-aways', *International Journal of Hospitality Management*, **11(3)**, 197–211.

—— (1994) 'The Informal Economy and Local Economic Development Policy', *Local Government Studies*, **20(3)**, 486–502.

Viceriat, P. (1993) 'Hotel Chains', *European Economy*, **3**, 365–79.

Von Moltke, H. (1993) 'The European Commission View' in Bennett, R.J., Krebs, G. and Zimmerman, H. (eds) *Chambers of Commerce in Britain and Germany and the Single European Market*. London: Anglo-German Foundation, 87–103.

Westrip, A. (1986) 'Small Firms Policy: The Case of Employment Legislation' in Curran, J., Stanworth, J. and Watkins, D. (eds) *The Survival of the Small Firm*. Aldershot: Gower, vol. 2. pp. 184–203.

Williams, C. and Thomas, R. (1996) 'Paid Informal Work in the Leeds Hospitality Industry: Unregulated or Regulated Work?' in Haughton, G. and Williams, C. (eds) *Corporate City? Partnership, Participation and Partition in Urban Development in Leeds*. Aldershot: Avebury, 171–83.

Zhao, J.-L. and Merna, K.M. (1992) 'Impact Analysis and the International Environment' in Teare, R. and Olsen, M. (eds) *International Hospitality Management*. London: Pitman, 3–30.

NINE

Social policy

Rosemary Lucas

INTRODUCTION

European social policy is based on the principle that a level playing field of good employment (social) rights, both legally and voluntarily based, will underpin an economically successful European Union (EU). Most early commentators on recent developments in European social policy have concurred on the point that the law in particular is likely to have a profound effect on UK employment practice now and in the future (for example, Wedderburn, 1990; Towers, 1992; Gold, 1993a, 1993b). The author has been rather more circumspect in relation to the effects of social policy in the hospitality and tourism industries (Lucas, 1991, 1993). Indeed, it is possible to point to some severe limitations of this policy where it is voluntary; for example, in regard to protecting and improving the lot of disadvantaged, low-paid workers, many of whom are found in industries such as hospitality (Lucas, 1993).

In spite of the UK government's publicly stated antipathy to the principles that underpin this social dimension, many of the policy measures have now been formally adopted by all the member states, although not all of these have yet been fully implemented. And as Gill (1994, p. 427) suggests, change will be gradual, from a 'weaving of a European dimension into national industrial relations systems'.

Additionally, decisions reached in the European Court of Justice (ECJ) over the last two decades have required UK governments to plug gaps in domestic legislation where this has been found not to comply with the UK's social obligations under the Treaty of Rome 1957. A number of key legal judgements, mainly given by the ECJ, are referenced to enable the reader to examine the facts and issues more closely. The impact of social policy is already inescapable in areas such as equality, pensions, and health and safety, although the practical effects of many new legislative measures, such as the extension of maternity rights, remain to be seen.

This chapter focuses on decisions reached among the member states themselves to implement key areas of social policy since 1989, many of which have been subsequently incorporated into national legislation. Additionally, we shall consider how earlier national legislation has been tested in the courts, and how decisions reached in the ECJ and elsewhere have found such legislation wanting and required the law to be amended.

The opening section of this chapter summarizes the historical development of European social policy. The second section outlines some of the legal complexities associated with policy implementation. The third section gives a broad overview of recent key social policy measures, and the final section considers the extent to which social policy is likely to impact on employment practice in the hospitality and tourism industries from an employment cost perspective.

HISTORICAL DEVELOPMENTS

A period of inertia: 1957–85

Since the Treaty of Rome 1957, the principle of economic integration has been underpinned by social policy provisions contained in Articles 117–23 of the Treaty. These provisions remained largely dormant during the early years of the Community, and it was only during the 1970s, shortly after the UK joined the then European Economic Community (EEC), that social policy was given a higher profile. Even so, attention was focused on a small number of areas such as employment protection, the equal treatment of men and women, and health and safety. One of the most significant early events resulted from the decision in the *Defrenne v Sabena (No. 2)* Case 43/75 [1976] ECR 455 ECJ, which ruled that Article 119 (equal treatment for men and women) was directly applicable (to public and private sector workers). This meant that claims for equal pay could be made under the Equal Pay Act 1970 and Article 119 (see Smith *et al.*, 1993, pp. 184–9, 211–30).

During the early 1980s, further attempts to develop the social dimension met with deadlock and disagreement among the member states. Proposals to improve the status of part-time workers and to require more formal worker participation arrangements under the controversial Vredeling (Fifth) Directive fell on stony ground. By contrast, proceedings instigated by the European Commission against the UK government in *Commission of the European Communities v United Kingdom of Great Britain and Northern Ireland* 61/81 [1982] IRLR 333 ECJ required that the Equal Pay Act 1970 be amended to allow equal pay claims for work of equal value where there was no job evaluation scheme in force. Similarly, the UK was also required to legislate for the transfer of undertakings in order to provide employment protection for employees in such circumstances. Such increased regulation stood firmly at odds with the Conservative administration's espoused policy of deregulating the employment relationship. Parliaments may have the power to legislate, but it is now the ECJ that is the ultimate arbiter over the meaning of employment law in the EU and what rights derive from it.

A flurry of activity: 1986–92

By the mid-1980s the Single European Act (SEA) 1986 affirmed all the member states' determination to secure more quickly the economic objectives of the Community through the completion a single internal market by the end of 1992. Achieving the single market was to be much more explicitly linked to social policy measures than before and, significantly, the Act introduced a new article into the Treaty of Rome. Article 118A gave the European Commission direct authority to take legislative action on health and safety matters, and for such proposals to be adopted by qualified majority voting (QMV), a procedure that was to become the object of some controversy.

Whilst all 12 member states had signed the SEA, thus endorsing both its economic and social objectives, a growing UK antipathy to the social dimension began to be more clearly articulated, although the UK could not escape its obligations. The Social Charter 1989 came into being largely as a statement of intent that social policy would be given real meaning at last, at least to 11 of the member states, although it had no legal force. A summary of the Charter's main principles is given in the appendix to this chapter. The UK government refused to sign the Charter, maintaining that the implementation of more social policy measures would increase the costs and burdens on businesses and create unemployment.

The Charter's accompanying Action Programme provided the vehicle for turning some, but not all, of the Charter's proposals into law (see below). The decision-making base for proposals is complex, but more details can be found in Industrial Relations Services (1992a, pp. 23–9). From the Action Programme, many proposals have now been adopted, some on the basis of unanimity and others, related to health and safety, by QMV.

In practice, the UK's antagonistic stance has had the following effects. First, proposals subject to unanimity have been modified and, indeed, a number have gone through on the basis of significant dilution. But a few have been vetoed by the UK, and remain to be finalized. Second, where proposals have been subject to QMV, dilution may also have occurred, but if the UK were to be the sole objector, the proposal would still go through. Events at Maastricht in 1991 led to changes in relation to the first of these procedural points.

Consolidation, confusion and uncertainty: 1993 and beyond

The Maastricht Treaty, signed in February 1992, aimed to finalize the European integration programme, with the Treaty on European Union (TEU) coming into force on 1 January 1993, although problems with ratification delayed implementation until 1 November 1993 (see Industrial Relations Services, 1993b, 1993c, 1994b). However, the UK continued with its antagonistic stance on social matters by opposing the substance of the 'social chapter' in the draft TEU. In particular, the UK opposed the extension of QMV to a wider range of issues and the establishment of a European-level mechanism to give employers and trade unions a greater role in formulating and implementing social policy – the 'social dialogue' (see, Hepple, 1993, pp. 9–11). This led to the UK's 'opt-out' from the social provisions, sometimes referred to as the 'social protocol'.

The implications of the opt-out have created a deal of confusion and uncertainty. The 'protocol', signed by all 12 member states, notes the desire of 11 member states (excluding the UK) to continue along the Social Charter path, and authorizes the 11 to take advantage of the appropriate institutions, procedures and mechanisms to make this possible. One effect is that whilst the two procedural routes to adopting proposals noted above remain, if the UK blocks a proposal that is subject to unanimity, the remaining member states (increased to 14 since Sweden, Austria and Finland joined the EU in January 1995) now have the option to reformulate and adopt that proposal among themselves. The UK no longer participates in discussions and, in theory, is not bound by the subsequent proposal. In practice, the position is not that simple. The recently adopted European Works Councils Directive – the first measure pursued by this 'fast-track' route

– will affect the UK to the extent that multinational companies with more than 1000 employees and employing at least 150 workers in more than two member states will be bound by the directive in those states outside the UK.

The UK's opt-out has generated considerable unease among the other member states, and the indications from the European Commission's Social Policy White Paper, issued in July 1994 (Industrial Relations Services, 1994d, 1994e, 1994f), are that this position is untenable and cannot be sustained (Carvel, 1994). The White Paper also outlined the EU's blueprint of social policy to the end of the century (this is summarized below). However, the new three-year social action programme for 1995–97, the successor to the 1989 Action Programme accompanying the Social Charter, contains few new proposals for legislation, particularly in the field of employment law. The main priorities are for consolidation and effective implementation of existing measures. The zeal for creating an even more level playing field by extending the platform of employment rights seems to have been replaced with a 'new orthodoxy': faced with the challenge of fighting unemployment, there is an agenda for growth, competitiveness and employment (Industrial Relations Services, 1994d, p. 13; 1995b).

LEGAL COMPLEXITIES

The effect of the Treaty of Rome 1957 was that Community law became overriding and binding in member states' courts, a position that became applicable in the UK when Parliament made it a member of the EEC by passing the European Communities Act 1972. Thereafter the ECJ in Luxembourg, not the House of Lords (HL), became the final court of appeal. 'The supremacy of Community law is essential to the very idea of a European Community' (Bourn, 1992, p. 12); hence the questionable validity of the UK opt-out at Maastricht. However, as will become evident, although Community law is important, it does not govern all aspects of social policy envisaged by the Social Charter.

The effect of Community law is a highly complicated subject (see for example Hepple, 1991; Steiner, 1994). The following brief summary inevitably glosses over the mass of technical legal complexities (for more general outline details, see Lucas, 1995). The summary concentrates on the fact that social principles contained in articles may be promulgated in directives; for example, Article 119 gave rise to the 76/207/EEC equal treatment directive and the 75/117/EEC equal pay directive.

EC regulations have *direct effect*, as do directives which are 'sufficiently precise', making them enforceable to individuals against organs of the states – that is, in the public sector. Directives do not apply directly in the private sector, but following *Frankovich v Italian Republic* 6/90 [1992] IRLR 84 ECJ, individuals may take action against the state for failure to implement a directive. The government may be liable to compensate those who have suffered loss where rights to compensation from a private sector employer are excluded.

EC directives with *indirect effect* have to be implemented into national laws, normally within a stated period. Many of the measures mentioned below that derive from the Social Charter have fallen into this category, including the protection of women at work directive (92/85), which has given rise to increased protection from dismissal on grounds of pregnancy and childbirth, and new maternity-leave provisions. These were enacted in the UK by the Trade Union Reform and Employment Rights Act (TURERA) 1993 (see below).

Where a state does not conform to Community law – for example, it does not pass legislation to implement a directive – the European Commission may take enforcement proceedings at the ECJ. This procedure was used in *Commission of the European Communities v United Kingdom of Great Britain and Northern Ireland* 61/81 [1982] IRLR 333 ECJ over the UK's failure to implement the requirements of the 75/117/EEC equal pay directive, which extended equal pay legislation to women working in situations and occupations in which no men were present (see above). Additionally the *Frankovich* principle may allow workers to claim compensation for the government's non-implementation of the acquired rights directive, which was highlighted in *Commission of the European Communities v United Kingdom of Great Britain and Northern Ireland*, C-382/92 [1994] IRLR 392 ECJ.

Directives are not the only legal mechanism available to the member states in order to give effect to the Social Charter's provisions, although these are among the most important. It has already been noted that Treaties themselves may have direct effect, as in the case of Article 119, which bans unequal pay between men and women who do equal work in the public and the private sectors. Other aspects of the Social Charter rely on decisions, which are binding on the parties to which they apply, and recommendations and opinions, which have no legal force. Here the European Commission has sidestepped tackling the low-pay problem, because it proposed and, ultimately, delivered an opinion on an equitable wage, which merely denoted the Commission's views without any kind of legal underpinning.

The view that 'wage-setting is a matter for the Member States and the two sides of industry alone ... in the context of collective agreements or by reference to them according to the practices in force of the Member States' (cited in Wedderburn, 1990, p. 14) illustrates what is meant by the Commission's principle of 'subsidiarity'. Abolition of wages councils and wages boards in the UK in 1993 removed the only wage-setting mechanism for hospitality workers; the earnings gap between the highest paid and the lowest paid has been widening over time (Gosling *et al.*, 1994). This opinion is likely to be of little benefit in protecting already low-paid hospitality workers, whose position appears to be deteriorating further since wages councils were abolished.

But subsidiarity is 'a principle with "several faces"' (Hepple, 1993, p. 20), which may also be applied by allowing 'derogations' from directives in particular circumstances, such as has already been allowed for in the working time directive, importantly influenced by the UK's active presence. To assume that social policy imposes a blanket imposition of stringent regulations is simply misleading.

Finally, in most cases, infringements of individual employment rights are raised and dealt with through normal UK procedures that start at an industrial tribunal and may be appealed to the Employment Appeal Tribunal (EAT), the Court of Appeal (CA) and the HL. However, if any case raises issues of Community law, such as the interpretation of a Treaty, it may be referred to the ECJ for clarification. For example, from a reference by the EAT in *Marshall v Southampton and South-West Hampshire Area Health Authority (Teaching)* 152/84 [1986] IRLR 140 ECJ and [1983] IRLR 237 EAT, the ECJ held that it was contrary to the equal treatment directive to require women to retire earlier than men. As a result the Equal Pay Act 1970 and the Sex Discrimination Act 1975 were amended to extend unlawful discrimination against women in relation to retirement.

In regard to matters for which there is no obvious legal remedy, it would seem, as Wedderburn (1990) has exhorted, that trade unions could attempt to seek redress for non-legal deficiencies through the mechanism of collective bargaining. However, this is not a realistic option for the vast majority of hospitality and tourism workers, where trade union density, recognition and collective bargaining arrangements are very marginal (see Lucas, 1995, pp. 98–101).

AN OVERVIEW OF SOCIAL POLICY

The nature and scope of envisaged European social policy are contained in the appendix to this chapter, but a number of these intentions have not been fully realized, and others have been subjected to considerable compromise in the decision-making process.[1] For the purposes of this chapter, the main areas of social policy with legal force in an employment context are now summarized, although gaps in the legal coverage are also mentioned. These legal issues do not fall into easily definable, discrete parts. But it is necessary to classify the law in some way in order to simplify what is an extremely complex scenario. Three broad classifications used to inform a fuller discussion elsewhere (Lucas, 1995) are also used here in order to summarize the main features of European social policy: these are health and safety, equality, and the workplace. Areas of social policy that do not easily fit into these classifications are discussed under 'Other aspects'. Matters outstanding are summarized at the end of this section.

Health and safety

'Mainstream' measures

Among the least contentious measures have been those concerned with 'mainstream' health and safety, which have been progressed along the qualified majority route under the new Article 118A. The most important measures include the framework directive on measures to improve the health and safety of workers, and the 'daughter' directives dealing with matters such as display screen equipment, manual handling of loads and personal protective equipment, which have have been introduced into British law by six sets of regulations from 1 January 1993 (Health and Safety Executive, 1992a, 1992b, 1992c, 1992d, 1992e, 1992f), although the implementation of some will not be completed until 1997. There is a broad consensus that the new measures are an improvement (Smith *et al.*, 1993; James, 1993a, 1993b). Details of other proposed health and safety measures still in the pipeline are given by Industrial Relations Services (1995a, p. 29; 1995b, p. 14; 1995c, p. 28).

'Ancillary measures': working time and young people

Other 'ancillary' health and safety measures have proved to be extremely contentious, because Article 118A has been used to progress more controversial directives on working time and the protection of young persons. (The arguably rather less controversial health and safety rights of pregnant workers, also progressed along this route, are discussed under equality.) The working time directive adopted in November 1993 seeks to limit the maximum average working week (including overtime) to 48 hours. Workers are to be entitled to 11 consecutive hours of rest in 24 hours, and 35 consecutive hours of rest a week, in principle including Sundays. The directive also provides for a rest break whenever the working day exceeds six hours, restrictions on night work, and four weeks' paid annual leave (for more details and discussion, see Industrial Relations

Services, 1994a, pp. 24–5; Bercusson, 1994a, 1994b).

The directive on the protection of young people at work, eventually adopted in June 1994, requires employers to carry out risk assessments before any worker under 18 starts work. For those aged 15 to 18 and no longer in compulsory full-time education, the working day is to be limited to 8 hours and the working week to 40 hours. Some night work is prohibited, and a rest break of 30 minutes is to be given after four-and-a-half hours' work. The over-13s still in full-time education are subject to a maximum 12-hour week (for more details, see Industrial Relations Services, 1994c, pp. 27–8).

The UK government's opposition, both to the principle that these are actually health and safety measures and to the substance of the proposals themselves, has been a consistent feature of the debate of the last few years. The upshot is that proposals in each area have been diluted significantly. For example, in regard to the working time directive, annual leave is fixed at three weeks' paid leave for the first three years (to 1999), and voluntary opt-out of the 48-hour week will be allowed for seven years after implementation (to 2003). There are also substantial derogations; for example, for certain types of worker and particular activities. For those young people aged 15 to 18 and no longer in full-time compulsory education, the maximum 8-hour day and 40-hour week will not apply to the UK for four years after implementation (until 2000). The same period of delay has also been secured in regard to the maximum 12-hour working week for over-13s in full-time education.

The UK government has challenged the validity of the base of the working time directive as a matter of health and safety, although the case appears to be rather tenuous (see Harrington, 1993). A decision of the ECJ, due in the summer of 1996, is expected to dismiss the UK's challenge. Whatever happens, it is clear that UK legislation to implement the directive by November 1996 will not be in place. Individuals may then seek redress for non-implementation of the directive via the *Frankovich* route. Employers would be well advised to keep timekeeping records.

Equality

It has already been noted that the Community has had a profound influence on the development of equal treatment between men and women, although little has been achieved on the front of differences related to race or ethnicity. The most notable recent equality developments relate to the rights of pregnant workers, equality in pension schemes, and achieving a more just outcome in some equal treatment cases.

Pregnant workers

From October 1994 all pregnant workers, regardless of hours worked or length of service, were given the right to take 14 weeks' paid maternity *leave* (TURERA 1993, Section 23). The contract of employment (except remuneration) continues throughout the period of leave. Pregnant workers also have increased protection from dismissal on grounds of pregnancy and childbirth and no longer need two years' service (TURERA 1993, Section 24). The longer period of maternity *absence* of 40 weeks, introduced by the Employment Protection Act 1975, which is subject to having two years' continuous service, still remains. The view of most commentators is that the maternity regulations are unnecessarily complicated, and that the opportunity to rationalize the whole situation has been missed.

Decisions reached in the ECJ relating to pregnancy dismissals have also been important, particularly in rejecting the notion that a pregnant woman had to find a 'comparable male' in order to establish that direct sex discrimination had taken place. The key cases are *Dekker v Stichting Vormingscentrum Voor Jong Volwassen (VJV-Centrum) Plus* 177/88 [1991] IRLR 27 ECJ; *Hertz v Aldi Marked K/S (sub nom Handels-og Kontorfunktionaerernes Forbund i Danmark v Dansk Arbejdsgiverforening)* 199/88 [1991] IRLR 31 ECJ; and *Webb v EMO Air Cargo (UK) Ltd*, C-32/93 [1994] IRLR 482 ECJ (for more details, see Lucas, 1995, pp. 224–6).

In December 1994, Schedule 3 of TURERA 1993 and the Management of Health and Safety at Work (Amendment) Regulations 1994 came into effect. Pregnant women, those who have recently given birth and those who are breastfeeding have been identified as special groups requiring measures for their protection. Risk assessment requirements are laid down, and women may refuse to undertake risky work (for more details, see Aikin, 1995).

An attempt to introduce parental leave and leave for family reasons was vetoed by the UK, and this matter has been progressed along the 'social protocol' route by the other 14 member states (Industrial Relations Services, 1995c, pp. 29–30; Milne and Wolf, 1995, p. 20).

Pensions

Equality in pension schemes has both an equal pay and a sex discrimination dimension, and it is in this area that the ECJ has played a major role, rather than the member states themselves. In the landmark case of *Barber v Guardian Royal Exchange Assurance Group* 262/88 [1990] IRLR 240 ECJ, the ECJ ruled that benefits paid out under a contracted-out private occupational pension scheme were pay under Article 119, which required the equalization of pensionable ages under private occupational pension schemes with effect from 17 May 1990. Thus:

> While the differential state of pensionable age is outside the scope of Article 119, retirement benefits (indeed retirement ages) which are based on the state pensionable age are not, which means that the exclusion in the domestic legislation for provisions relating to death or retirement does not comply with EC law.
>
> (Smith *et al.*, 1993, p. 228)

The Barber case posed a number of difficult, complex questions (for more detailed discussion, see Lucas, 1995, pp. 222–4), which were largely answered in six key ECJ judgments delivered at the end of 1994 (*Bestuur van het Algemeen Burgerlijk Pensioenfonds v Beune*, C-7/93 [1994] *IDS Brief 527* ECJ; *Coloroll Pension Trustees Ltd v Russell and others*, C-200/91 [1994] IRLR 586 ECJ; *Fisscher v Voorhuis Hengelo BV and another*, C-128/93 [1994] *IDS Brief 527* ECJ; *Smith and others v Avdel Systems Ltd*, C-408/92 [1994] IRLR 602 ECJ; *Van den Akker and others v Stichting Shell Pensioenfonds*, C-28/93 [1994] IRLR 616 ECJ; and *Vroege v NCIV Instituut voor Volkshuisvesting BV and another*, C-57/93 [1994] *IDS Brief 527* ECJ). Two key outcomes from these judgments are that women's pension age can be equalized upwards – this will eventually become 65 for both sexes in the UK. Additionally, part-timers have been unreasonably excluded from pension schemes, and retrospective claims from part-timers are allowable to 8 April 1976 (see Incomes Data Services, 1994). These judgments led to the sole proposal for social policy legislation covering the entire EU (including the UK) being submitted in 1995, in the form of a draft directive amending the 1986 directive on equal treatment for men and women in occupational social security schemes (Industrial Relations Services, 1995c, p. 29).

Equal treatment

The upper limit for damages for injury to feelings in sex discrimination cases of £11,000 was removed as a result of *Marshall v Southampton and South-West Hampshire Area Health Authority (Teaching) (No. 2)* 271/91 [1993] IRLR 455 ECJ. Awards in excess of £100,000 were made in the rash of retrospective sex discrimination claims lodged by ex-service personnel unable to continue their employment on becoming pregnant. Although the EAT laid down guidelines for assessing compensation in *Ministry of Defence v Cannock and others* [1994] IRLR 509 EAT, sex (and race) discrimination will inevitably become more expensive.

The proposal to shift the burden of proof from applicant to respondent in equal treatment cases, initially opposed by the UK and Denmark, is now being progressed along the 'social protocol' route (Industrial Relations Services, 1995c, pp. 29–30).

The workplace

A range of new workplace rights has come about from implementation of the Action Programme and from other decisions which are outlined below. The new workplace rights contained in TURERA 1993 all became effective in 1993. The decision reached in *R v Secretary of State for Employment, ex parte EOC* [1994] IRLR 176 HL reversing [1993] IRLR 10 CA ruled that the treatment of part-timers was incompatible with Community legislation. As a result the UK government has removed the minimum hours' qualification (16 hours, or 8 hours and above after five years' service) for employment protection rights. This change took effect from 6 February 1995 as a result of the Employment Protection (Part-time Employees) Regulations 1995, made under the European Communities Act 1972, Section 2(2). Although the appropriate service qualifications remain (typically between one month and two years), the two years' service qualification for unfair dismissal claims has been challenged in the courts with the consequence that the position remains unclear (Merrick, 1995).

Written statement of terms and conditions

There are important changes to the documentation that employers must provide relating to the written statement of terms and conditions of employment (TURERA 1993, Section 26 and Schedule 4). This must now be issued to all new employees, regardless of hours worked, within two months of commencing employment. Employers must provide all the principal statements relating to the main terms. In excepted cases employees may be referred to accessible documents; for example, certain aspects relating to grievance procedures and disciplinary rules and procedures, particulars of sick pay and other terms relating to sickness or injury, and particulars of pensions.

Pay

Itemized pay statements (pay slips) must now be issued to all employees regardless of hours worked (TURERA 1993, Section 27).

The Social Charter's provisions about an 'equitable' wage are in the form of an opinion, which has no legal force. This has had no effect on the decision to abolish British wages councils in August 1993 (TURERA 1993, Section 35). The prospect of there being a comprehensive system of minimum wages in the UK, in the form of a statutory national minimum wage, is dependent on the election of a Labour government.

Transfer and redundancy

The Transfer of Undertakings (Protection of Employment) Regulations (TUPE) 1981 contain provisions relating to the dismissal of employees as a consequence of a transfer, the continuity of contracts, and consultation requirements. The concept of automatic transfer and what constitutes an undertaking are still not wholly clear, in spite of the attempt by TURERA 1993 (Section 33) to remedy some of the defects of TUPE. As a result, TUPE applies to any undertaking (or part) whether or not it is a commercial venture.

Subsequent judgments given in *Commission of the European Communities v United Kingdom of Great Britain and Northern Ireland*, C-382/92 [1994] IRLR 392 ECJ and *Commission of the European Communities v United Kingdom of Great Britain and Northern Ireland*, C-383/92 [1994] IRLR 412 ECJ ruled that the UK had failed to implement the acquired rights directive 1977 and the collective redundancies directive 1975. TUPE has been held to cover contracting out under compulsory competitive tendering (Thatcher, 1994), and employees' representatives are to have been consulted prior to the transfer: in other words, consultation is not restricted to trade union representatives. These cases suggest that additional provisions in TURERA 1993 (Section 34) designed to broaden redundancy consultation requirements with trade unions at the workplace involved, even if the redundancy decision had been taken outside the member state, were insufficient to comply with the acquired rights directive 1977. While a new directive is being proposed to replace the 1977 directive (Industrial Relations Services, 1995a, p. 28), the Collective Redundancies and Transfer of Undertakings (Protection of Employment) Regulations (Amendment) Regulations 1995, introduced in October 1995, attempts to clarify UK law in regard to redundancy consultation, redundancy consultation prior to a TUPE transfer and unfair dismissals connected with a TUPE transfer.

European Works Councils and participation

Provision for European Works Councils was the first measure to be adopted (September 1994) under the 'social protocol' route by 11 member states, excluding the UK. It is effectively 'a procedure in Community-scale undertakings and Community-scale groups of undertakings for the purposes of informing and consulting employees' (Industrial Relations Services, 1994g, p. 27). However, UK multinationals with more than 1000 employees and employing at least 150 workers in more than two member states will be bound by the directive in those states outside the UK. A number of multinationals, including Bass, which has hospitality businesses, have announced their intention of introducing similar arrangements in the UK.

There are other proposals relating to information, consultation and participation (see Industrial Relations Services, 1995a, p. 28; 1995b, p. 15). Some have argued that increased employee consultation and participation are inescapable features of workplace practice in relation to a range of different workplace issues (Aikin and Mill, 1994; Welch, 1994).

Atypical workers

Attempts by the member states to extend part-timers' (in EU terms, usually staff working over 8 hours a week) rights in regard to pay, holidays and other employment rights on a pro-rata basis remain unsuccessful. Following the UK's opposition to these matters, the other 14 member states have announced their intention of progressing this issue along the 'social protocol' route in 1996 (Industrial Relations Services, 1995a, p. 28; 1995c, p. 29).

Other aspects

Arrangements to provide for the mutual recognition of vocational qualifications are in progress. The member states have yet to adopt a common position on the freedom of movement (Industrial Relations Services, 1995a, p. 30; 1995c, p. 28). The UK has come under some criticism from other member states for its refusal to abandon passport checks at entry points to the UK entirely. Political agreement has been reached in the form of a decision on vocational training for the implementation of a community-wide vocational training policy, LEONARDO (Industrial Relations Services, 1995a, p. 30). However, proposals that public and employer-provided transport should be adapted to accommodate disabled workers in order to facilitate transport to and from work have made slow progress. So too has the issue of the transfer of occupational pensions between member states. Provisions related to the posting of workers and their working conditions are continuing towards a common position.

Matters outstanding

The White Paper of 1994 identified the outstanding issues of social policy that remained to be implemented, including those mentioned above under 'Other aspects'. Concrete proposals fall into seven areas as follows, many of which are not legally enforceable (see Industrial Relations Services, 1994d, p. 15):

- jobs – employment and labour policy;
- training – measures on vocational training;
- labour standards – including employee participation and proposed directives on working time in sectors and activities excluded from the 1993 working time directive;
- European labour market – including an extension of mutual recognition of diplomas to professions not yet covered, and an adaptation of EU rules on unemployment benefits for people looking for work in another member state;
- equal opportunities – including parental leave and the reversal of the burden of proof;
- social protection – including a modification of the 1986 directive on equal treatment in occupational social security schemes, in line with the *Barber* judgment and subsequent ECJ rulings;
- social dialogue – including a tripartite Standing Committee on Employment.

Details of the Commission's planned work in the employment and social field over the period 1995–97 were subsequently set out in a new action programme and during 1995, as noted above, progress was made in relation to parental leave, the burden of proof and modifying the 1986 directive on equal treatment (Industrial Relations Services, 1995b; 1995c).

SOCIAL POLICY AND EMPLOYMENT PRACTICE IN THE HOSPITALITY AND TOURISM INDUSTRIES

The reality and potentiality of EU social policy on employment law and employee relations in the UK are undoubtedly significant. There is a much extended framework of individual employment legislation now in place, although there are still doubts in some areas whether this fully conforms to EU requirements. But how all this translates into changing employment practice in the hospitality and tourism industries is much more difficult to predict. This final section considers the relationship between social policy and employment practice from an employment cost perspective.

'Good' practice: frustrated by ignorance?

Price (1993, p. 16) has noted that employment legislation has the dual purpose of providing protection to employees against unscrupulous employers and encouraging the development of good employment practice. Yet managers can only develop good practice if they know what recommended practice is, and how this relates to their establishments (Price, 1994, p. 52). Price found that proprietors and partnerships, which are highly significant forms of ownership in the hospitality industry, were least aware of legal standards. From this it follows that they must stand a greater chance of breaking the law, although ignorance is no defence, and that they are less likely to have appropriate practices/procedures in place (see also Lucas, 1995, pp. 147–51; 201–7).

Employees can only seek legal redress about employment issues if they know their rights and the means to seek redress where they believe those rights have been infringed. As the vast majority of hospitality employees do not enjoy the support of trade unions, they are not in a strong position to press employers to implement good practices. Non-unionized employees are also less likely to be well informed about their employment rights than employees in other sectors. So ironically, an employment sector which has considerable potential to 'improve' employment practice as a result of a more comprehensive coverage of employment protection legislation may still remain a 'poor' practice industry because of the employer and employee 'problems' noted above.

The points addressed above consider only one dimension of approaches to social policy. The perspective that underpins Price's argument is based on the point that 'poor' employment practice is damaging to quality, efficiency and, ultimately, competitive advantage. This is the fundamental stuff of EU social policy. But it is also possible to hold an alternative view, which states that 'good' employment practice is damaging because it is too expensive, and the only basis on which some businesses can compete is on 'low-cost, low-price' employment.

'Cheap' practice and the employment cost dimension

The 'low-cost, low-price' approach is essentially the line of argument that has been taken by the UK in challenging a number of EU social policy measures. This strategy has probably been closely espoused by many hospitality and tourism employers for a long period of time. In an attempt to test its validity more fully, it becomes necessary to refine the cost dimension of employment practice by disaggregating employment or labour costs into 'direct real' costs and 'indirect perceived' costs, a point which has been developed more fully by the author elsewhere (Lucas, 1993, pp. 93–7).

Briefly, it is proposed that 'direct real costs' of basic pay, national insurance contributions and fringe benefits dominate the employment decision, rather than 'indirect perceived' costs of employment protection (see also Disney and Szyszczak, 1989). However, there is some overlap between these cost areas, which may have become even more marked in some cases as a result of EU social policy developments, noted below.

Many hospitality workers are low paid, and often employed on temporary, casual or short-term contracts, thus excluding them from some key employment protection rights that depend on a service qualification. Additionally, managers seek to perpetuate high labour turnover to maximize flexibility and to ensure that employees do not build up the necessary service qualification required for some rights, particularly unfair dismissal protection. If Price's evaluation of proprietors and partnerships as being relatively ignorant of the law holds true on a larger scale, then it follows that managers of such businesses are unlikely to pursue employment strategies that seek to circumvent the law's requirements.

Furthermore, putting any kind of price per employee on the cost of a potential unfair dismissal claim is unlikely to be the way that most managers actually 'cost' employment decisions. Costs will be driven by the basic hourly rate of pay and other benefits, by actual numbers of staff employed, and by hours of work. Therefore, employment rights are not perceived as real costs and will not dominate managerial decision making on employment. Thus, much of EU social policy is unlikely to make a lot of difference to employment decisions and practices, because it falls into the 'indirect perceived' cost category.

Returning to the 'direct real' costs of employment, it is also possible to suggest that EU social policy will have relatively little impact because there is no compunction on the UK to do anything about low pay. Since wages councils were abolished, employers have effectively been given *carte blanche* to pay even lower basic pay. But even if there were to be some legislative underpinning of minimum wages in the future, unless this were to be well publicized and enforced effectively, the opportunity for employers to ignore legal requirements, particularly for 'ignorance' reasons noted above, could be considerable. However, the wider application of national insurance contributions and other fringe benefits to more part-timers, and the application of this to the UK, remains to be decided.

To return to the issue of overlap between 'direct real' and 'indirect perceived' employment costs, it is possible to identify some significant areas of social policy which may lead employers to alter employment practice because a quantifiable cost is easy to identify. Maternity leave is perhaps the most obvious example, because it is an employment right with a directly identifiable cost dimension. It is probably likely to have been better publicized than some of the other new rights. The hospitality and tourism industries employ large numbers of women, many of whom are probably of childbearing age. So employers could avoid the 'cost' of losing an employee for 14 weeks' paid maternity leave if they targeted older women and male workers. There are potential sex discrimination implications, at least if employers are going to prefer men to women, but while the burden of proof remains on the applicant, this is still a difficult area for individuals to succeed in proving their case.

CONCLUDING COMMENTS

Of course it is easy to 'blame Brussels' for adding to employment costs, but the reality is that the UK government itself has probably done rather more of this in the area of 'direct costs' than 'Brussels' has, by requiring employers to fund the full cost of statutory sick pay and state redundancy pay, and by increasing national insurance contributions. It should also be noted that many of the provisions in the working time directive were in force for many hospitality workers until the remaining parts of the Shops Act 1950 were repealed in January 1995. Some provisions of the young person's directive are similar to those contained in the Children and Young Person's Act 1933, so there is arguably little that is new in 'direct' or 'indirect' cost terms with regard to directives that remain to be implemented. In other words, it is necessary to be a little cautious about the impact of EU social policy on employment practice. It is still early days, and although the potentiality of the social policy appears to be considerable, the reality may turn out to be less so in hospitality and tourism, because the policy contains relatively little substance to deflect employers from pursuing 'poor', low-cost employment strategies.

NOTE

1. The Industrial Relations Services's *European Industrial Relations Review* offers one of the most comprehensive coverages of social policy developments in an understandable and succinct format, including a twice-yearly social policy state-of-play review. These reviews report, relatively quickly after the event, a summary of decisions reached (or not reached) at the twice-yearly meetings of the Council of Ministers in order to implement the Social Charter's Action Programme. The *Review* should be consulted for more details, and the most informative at the time of writing are Industrial Relations Services 1992a, 1992b, 1993a, 1994a, 1994c, 1995a, 1995b, 1995c. *People Management*, the newly titled bi-monthly magazine of the Institute of Personnel and Development, and its predecessors *Personnel Management* and *Personnel Management Plus*, also offer good contemporary coverage of EU social policy developments.

REFERENCES

Aikin, O. (1995) 'Taking Care of Pregnant Workers', *People Management*, 9 February, 30–3.

Aikin, O. and Mill, C. (1994) 'No Escape From Consultation', *Personnel Management*, October, 54–7.

Bercusson, B. (1994a) *Working Time in Britain: Towards a European Model. Part I: The European Union Directive*. London: Institute of Employment Rights.

—— (1994b) *Working Time in Britain: Towards a European Model. Part II: Collective Bargaining in Europe and the UK*. London: Institute of Employment Rights.

Bourn, C. (1992) *Sex Discrimination Law*. London: Institute of Employment Rights.

Carvel, J. (1994) 'Brussels Guns for UK Opt-out', *Guardian*, 27 July.

Disney, R. and Szyszczak, E. (1989) 'Part-time Work: A Reply to Catherine Hakim', *Industrial Law Journal*, **18**, 223–30.

Gill, C. (1994) 'British Industrial Relations and the European Community', *International Journal of Human Resource Management*, **5(2)**, 427–55.

Gold, M. (1993a) (ed.) *The Social Dimension – Employment Policy in the European Community*. Basingstoke: Macmillan.

——(1993b) 'Overview of the Social Dimension' in Gold, M. (ed.) *The Social Dimension - Employment Policy in the European Community*. Basingstoke: Macmillan, 10–40.

Gosling, A., Machin, S. and Meghin, C. (1994) *What has Happened to Wages?* London: Institute of Fiscal Studies.

Harrington, J.M. (1993) *The Health and Safety Aspects of Working Hours - A Critical Review of the Literature*. University of Birmingham: Institute of Occupational Health.

Health and Safety Executive (1992a) *Display Screen Equipment at Work: Health and Safety (Display Screen Equipment) Regulations 1992, Guidance on Regulations L 26*. London: HMSO.

——(1992b) *Management of Health and Safety at Work: Management of Health and Safety at Work Regulations 1992, Approved Code of Practice L 21*. London: HMSO.

——(1992c) *Manual Handling: Manual Handling Operations Regulations 1992, Guidance on Regulations L 23*. London: HMSO.

——(1992d) *Personal Protective Equipment at Work: Personal Protective Equipment at Work Regulations 1992 Guidance on Regulations L 25*. London: HMSO.

——(1992e) *Work Equipment at Work: Provision and Use of Work Equipment Regulations 1992, Guidance on Regulations L 22*. London: HMSO.

——(1992f) *Workplace Health, Safety and Welfare: Workplace (Health, Safety and Welfare) Regulations 1992, Guidance on Regulations L 24*. London: HMSO.

Hepple, B. (1991) 'Institutions and Sources of Labour Law: European and International Standards' in *Encyclopedia of Employment Law. Vol. 1*. London: Sweet and Maxwell, 1052–1061.

——(1993) *European Social Dialogue - Alibi or Opportunity?* London: Institute of Employment Rights.

Incomes Data Services (1994) 'Post-Barber Confusion Over?', *IDS Brief* **527**, October, 2–6.

Industrial Relations Services (1992a) 'Social Charter State of Play', *European Industrial Relations Review*, **221**, 23–30.

——(1992b) 'Social Charter State of Play', *European Industrial Relations Review*, **227**, 25–31.

——(1993a) 'Social Policy State of Play', *European Industrial Relations Review*, **234**, 20–5.

——(1993b) 'Maastricht and Social Policy - Part One', *European Industrial Relations Review*, **237**, 14–20.

——(1993c) 'Maastricht and Social Policy - Part Two', *European Industrial Relations Review*, **239**, 19–24.

——(1994a) 'Social Policy State of Play', *European Industrial Relations Review*, **240**, 23–9.

——(1994b) 'Maastricht and Social Policy - Part Three', *European Industrial Relations Review*, **241**, 28–36.

——(1994c) 'Social Policy State of Play', *European Industrial Relations Review*, **247**, 26–32.

——(1994d) 'Social Policy White Paper Part One', *European Industrial Relations Review*, **248**, 13–18.

——(1994e) 'Social Policy White Paper Part Two', *European Industrial Relations Review*, **249**, 24–8.

——(1994f) 'Social Policy White Paper Part Three', *European Industrial Relations Review*, **250**, 28–31.

——(1994g) 'European Works Council Directive', *European Industrial Relations Review*, **251**, 27–32.

——(1995a) 'Social Policy State of Play', *European Industrial Relations Review*, **252**, 26–32.
—— (1995b) 'The New Social Action Programme', *European Industrial Relations Review*, **257**, 12–19.
——(1995c) 'Social Policy State of Play', *European Industrial Relations Review,* **259**, 26–30.
James, P. (1993a) *The European Community: A Positive Force for UK Health and Safety Law?* London: Institute of Employment Rights.
——(1993b) 'Occupational Health and Safety' in Gold, M. (ed.) *The Social Dimension - Employment Policy in the European Community*. Basingstoke: Macmillan, 135–52.
Lucas, R.E. (1991) 'Some Thoughts on the European Social Charter', *International Journal of Hospitality Management*, **10(2)**, 174–7.
——(1993) 'The Social Charter - Opportunity or Threat to Employment Practice in the UK Hospitality Industry?' *International Journal of Hospitality Management*, **12(1)**, 89–100.
——(1995) *Managing Employee Relations in the Hotel and Catering Industry*. London: Cassell.
Merrick, N. (1995) 'Unfair Dismissal Ruling Opens Way for Fresh Claims', *People Management*, 10 August, 10–11.
Milne, S. and Wolf, J. (1995) 'Parental Leave Depends on Charity of Employers', *Guardian,* 8 November, p. 20.
Price, L. (1993) 'The Limitations of the Law in Influencing Employment Practices in UK Hotels and Restaurants', *Employee Relations*, **15(2)**, 16–24.
——(1994) 'Poor Personnel Practice in the Hotel and Catering Industry: Does It Matter?' *Human Resource Management Journal*, **4(4)**, 44–62.
Smith, I.T., Wood, Sir J.C. and Thomas, G. (1993) *Industrial Law*, 5th edition. London: Butterworths.
Steiner, J. (1994) *Textbook on EC Law*. London: Blackstone Press.
Thatcher, M. (1994) 'Has the Government Finally been Defeated over TUPE?', *Personnel Management*, July, 13.
Towers, B. (1992) 'Two Speed Ahead: Social Europe and the UK after Maastricht', *Industrial Relations Journal*, **23(2)**, 83–9.
Wedderburn, Lord (1990) *The Social Charter, European Company and Employment Rights*. London: Institute of Employment Rights.
Welch, R. (1994) 'European Works Councils and their Implications', *Employee Relations*, **16(4)**, 48–61.

CASES

Barber v Guardian Royal Exchange Assurance Group 262/88 [1990] IRLR 240 ECJ.
Bestuur van het Algemeen Burgerlijk Pensioenfonds v Beune, C-7/93 [1994] *IDS Brief 527* ECJ.
Coloroll Pension Trustees Ltd v Russell and others, C-200/91 [1994] IRLR 586 ECJ.
Commission of the European Communities v United Kingdom of Great Britain and Northern Ireland 61/81 [1982] IRLR 333 ECJ.
Commission of the European Communities v United Kingdom of Great Britain and Northern Ireland, C-382/92 [1994] IRLR 392 ECJ.

Commission of the European Communities v United Kingdom of Great Britain and Northern Ireland, C-383/92 [1994] IRLR 412 ECJ.
Defrenne v Sabena (No. 2) Case 43/75 [1976] ECR 455 ECJ.
Dekker v Stichting Vormingscentrum Voor Jong Volwassen (VJV-Centrum) Plus 177/88 [1991] IRLR 27 ECJ.
Fisscher v Voorhuis Hengelo BV and another, C-128/93 [1994] *IDS Brief 527* ECJ.
Frankovich v Italian Republic 6/90 [1992] IRLR 84 ECJ.
Hertz v Aldi Marked K/S (sub nom Handels-og Kontorfunktionaerernes Forbund i Danmark v Dansk Arbejdsgiverforening) 199/88 [1991] IRLR 31 ECJ.
Marshall v Southampton and South-West Hampshire Area Health Authority (Teaching) 152/84 [1986] IRLR 140 ECJ and [1983] IRLR 237 EAT.
Marshall v Southampton and South-West Hampshire Area Health Authority (Teaching) (No. 2) 271/91 [1993] IRLR 455 ECJ.
Ministry of Defence v Cannock and others [1994] IRLR 509 EAT.
R v Secretary of State for Employment, ex parte EOC [1994] IRLR 176 HL reversing [1993] IRLR 10 CA.
Smith and others v Avdel Systems Ltd, C-408/92 [1994] IRLR 602 ECJ.
Van den Akker and others v Stichting Shell Pensioenfonds, C-28/93 [1994] IRLR 616 ECJ.
Vroege v NCIV Instituut voor Volkshuisvesting BV and another, C-57/93 [1994] *IDS Brief 527* ECJ.
Webb v EMO Air Cargo (UK) Ltd, C-32/93 [1994] IRLR 482 ECJ.

APPENDIX: SUMMARY OF THE MAIN PRINCIPLES OF THE SOCIAL CHARTER 1989

Collective rights

Collective rights are as follows:

- the right to freedom of association in trade unions;
- the right to join and not to join a trade union;
- a right to bargain collectively with an employer;
- rights to information and consultation;
- rights of participation in decision making;
- the right to strike and settlement of disputes.
  Some exclusions permitted, for example, that of the right to strike in the armed forces.

Individual rights

Young workers

Young workers' rights are:

- a minimum age for work;
- 'equitable remuneration';
- a limit on working hours.

The disabled

The disabled are entitled to firm measures to improve integration in the labour market.

The elderly

On retirement, the elderly must have resources for a decent standard of living. Those without a pension or other means have the right to adequate social security.

Equality and discrimination: sex, race and beliefs

There must be equal treatment and opportunities for men and women regardless of race and beliefs – including access to employment, pay, training and development of careers.

Working and living conditions

- The internal market must bring an improvement in living conditions.
- There is to be approximation between countries on duration of working hours and atypical types of employment, including part-time and temporary work.
- There is a right to a weekly rest period and an annual holiday.

Pay, employment status and placement services

- Everyone must be free to choose an occupation and have free access to public placement services.
- All employment must be 'fairly remunerated' with an equitable wage to provide a 'decent standard of living'.

Health and safety

- Workers must have satisfactory health and safety conditions.
- Workers must have training, information, consultation and 'balanced participation' on risks at work and steps to reduce them.

Training

- Every worker must have access to vocational training throughout his or her working life.
- Public authorities or the two sides of industry must set up continuing, permanent systems for retraining, with leave from work, especially on new technology.

Freedom of movement

- Every worker has the right to freedom of movement in the Community (subject to public order laws and health and safety).
- Equivalent qualifications must be recognized.

Social protection

- Workers have the right to adequate social protection and an adequate level of social security benefits.
- Those unable to work must receive sufficient resources.

The worker and the labour market

- Employment development and job creation must be given first priority.

TEN

Education and training policy

David Parsons

INTRODUCTION

Skill capacity and its development became important issues in the rapidly expanding tourism industries of the European Union (EU) in the mid- and late 1980s. This was led by growing recruitment and retention problems in some member states, in a sector which was emerging early from the effects of depressed consumer spending through the early 1980s. It was fuelled also by new dynamics in the use of human capital in this sector – productivity pressures to contain labour cost and the emergence of robust quality and customer-care initiatives led by larger employers and marketing and sectoral bodies.

Something more deep-seated was also involved in many member states. Industry leaders were coming to accept that the success of their business, in a tourism market increasingly open to new concepts and more global competition, was being compromised by inflexible employment practices and outdated or unconstructive attitudes to investment in human capital, particularly among the independent operators and family firms which dominated provision in much of the sector. To this was added industrial concern in some member states about the relevance and responsiveness of relevant external education and training facilities to support the development of skills in the sector.

This chapter looks at the background to some of these issues and the practical responses. It reviews the contribution of public policy, and the role and focus of other policy initiatives. The findings draw on a range of data sources, but in particular on a comparative review across four member states conducted by the author for the National Economic Development Office in the UK.[1] The chapter centres on intermediate and management level skills and training, where many of the concerns of the tourism and hospitality sectors have focused.

THE POLICY CONTEXT

The last 10 years have seen a resurgence of interest in public policy across much of the EU in the competitive significance of human capital in economic performance. A less tangible effect has also been variously reported in corporate policy (Derr, 1992; Brewster and Hegewisch, 1993). In public policy this has been led by the persistence, throughout the 1980s and since, of historically high levels of unemployment, which policy makers increasingly recognize as having a large structural element. In macro-economic policy this is seen as under-utilized capacity, which in the developed economies of the EU imposes high social costs. Measures to address these have until recently focused on a variety of wage subsidy and labour market measures, taken at national or sub-regional level by individual member states. At European level, measures have been limited, but following the policy stimulus of the Maastricht Treaty, proposals for pan-European measures have been formulated in social policy and in labour market measures (Commission, 1994).

At national level, policies also continue to evolve. The available evidence on labour market measures has suggested these have increasingly emphasized supply-side policies. These have in general been aimed at reducing supply through assisted early retirement and related programmes, or building capacity and adaptation within disadvantaged groups - including the longer-term unemployed and new entrants to the labour market.

Demand-side measures have been less widespread. Where they have been seen to play an important role, notably in France and the Netherlands, this has been through measures of direct or indirect subsidy of labour cost to employers recruiting those unemployed - and the long-term unemployed in particular. In general, analysts and policy makers have increasingly seen these measures as costly and ineffective. In the UK and Ireland, for example, early experiments with subsidies and assisted measures were shown to have high substitution elements (Rajan, 1985), and were thought to have little direct effect on enhancing job opportunities that would not otherwise have been developed through the normal operation of the labour market.

Supply-side measures in the UK to promote more flexible approaches to labour supply, such as job sharing or job splitting, were also seen to be of doubtful effectiveness. Throughout Europe in this period, national supply-side measures have come increasingly to emphasize vocational education and training (VET) initiatives. These have variously focused on new entrants to the labour market, the long-term unemployed, social groups seen to be affected more strongly by exclusion within the labour market, and those affected in contracting sectors.

EU policy in this area is being radically reshaped. A variety of transnational and national EU support programmes in VET and higher education were consolidated at the end of 1994 into two composite programmes, LEONARDO and SOCRATES, concerned respectively with vocational and prevocational education. This includes the Community Action Programme for Education and Training in Technology (COMMET II), which has helped to shape transnational institutional development in hospitality and tourism management courses (Parsons, 1991a). Specific priorities within both the LEONARDO and SOCRATES programmes were unclear at the time of writing, but under the principle of subsidiarity, activity is likely to remain peripheral to national measures. SOCRATES will incorporate the ERASMUS and LINGUA programmes specifically concerned with EU student mobility and language competence.

SKILL CAPACITY AND UTILIZATION IN THE HOSPITALITY SECTOR

The sectoral effects of these broad and shifting national public policy measures in VET across Europe are difficult to measure. This goes deeper than measurement effects and any problems in data comparability and context. In practice, the focus of any national-level VET initiatives in the tourism and hospitality sectors has been highly fragmented. In member states with a strong sectoral tradition of shaping employment policy, such as Germany, the low levels of unionization characteristic of this sector have militated against sectoral innovation through social dialogue.

In general, labour market measures focused on the sector have been uncommon, and dedicated VET initiatives have rarely been associated with them. An important exception has been the employment development initiatives usually associated with sectorally targeted regional or local economic development measures. Here European-level policies have established a long track record of support of reskilling or youth training measures under the European Social Fund (ESF) in assisted areas. Evaluation of these interventions has often been patchy and focused on narrow output measures, such as trainees' completion and placement records, with little evidence on which to judge substitution effects or impact on local development. The scale and utility of ESF-supported VET initiatives across member states (and within them) are consequently uncertain. Overall, the effect seems to be to have driven further fragmentation of VET policy response to below national level.

Across all member states, the most coherent sectoral approach to VET policy has been in the UK (HMSO, 1989). Here 129 Industrial Training Organizations (ITOs) have evolved following the reorganization of industrial training policy in the early 1980s, to provide for convergence in determining and shaping sectoral VET initiatives. These are likely to be the subject of some amalgamation and convergence of VET development following a recent government initiative to encourage the formation of National Training Organizations (DfEE, 1996). Some seven ITOs represent various elements of the tourism and hospitality sectors.

Co-ordination across these agencies has generally been limited. Superimposed on this have been contrasts in resourcing and VET priorities, which have together provided for a highly fragmented approach to VET policy development and implementation across the tourism and hospitality sectors. The effects of this fragmentation, reinforced by contrasting traditions in diverse employer and sector groups, have been profound. Externally developed co-ordination initiatives, such as the UK-government-sponsored Tourism Training Initiative of 1987–9, were unable to secure a consensus for VET development priorities across the diverse interest groups, despite the backing of senior industrialists and the industries' national marketing bodies (NEDO, 1990). More broadly based policy developments in VET in tourism and hospitality have consequently evolved outside of the ITOs and employer bodies – usually within individual or collaborating institutions.

In Europe, tourism and hospitality have been recognized as important engines of job growth to all member states, but with some important exceptions this has not commonly stimulated initiatives to review skill implications of growth and change at national level. The UK example is illustrative.

Reports such as *Competence and Competition*, published by the National Economic Development Office (NEDO, 1984), drew attention to the narrowness and relatively poor performance of the UK's VET system. As the 'productivity miracle' of the mid-1980s started to lose impetus, the economic pundits came to see these skills deficiencies as a serious constraint on UK competitiveness in globalizing and turbulent markets.

Although much of this research has focused on operative-level, craft and technician skills, the UK's performance in general management education and training has also been shown to fall some way behind that of its major competitors.

This general concern has been slow to translate into concern within the sector with tourism skills. Tourism in the UK established itself as the fastest-growing area of the economy in job terms in the mid- and late 1980s, but surprisingly little attention was paid to the impact of this on the demands for and supply of intermediate and higher-level skills in this sector (Parsons, 1987). As early as 1986, tourism employers in some parts of the country were reporting accelerating difficulties in recruiting and retaining a range of general and functional management skills. By 1990, the industries' leaders were recognizing this and related skill problems as a brake on the performance and competitiveness of UK tourism. These problems have eased since, as UK tourism has been squeezed by domestic recession and depression in international travel, but the underlying weaknesses remain. As early as 1994 (IFF, 1994) research was showing skill shortfall starting to accelerate.

These difficulties should not be seen in isolation. They need to be set against a background of an under-trained and often inefficiently used workforce in many tourism businesses in the UK. Research looking at small and medium-sized hotels in the UK and (West) Germany has suggested that low skill attainment levels of hotel employees in the UK was a major contributor to what was then diagnosed as a 40 per cent productivity gap between hotels in these countries (Prais *et al.*, 1989). More broadly based research has also suggested that the low attainment levels of managers in these activities may be a major barrier to further improvement of the general skills base of the tourism workforce in the UK (Parsons and Cave, 1992). Unfortunately, detailed comparative studies of this nature are unusual.

This is an imperfect diagnosis. In Europe, surprisingly little is known about the pattern and determinants of skills shortages at management or operative level. Even less is known of the precise relationship between attainment levels in the workforce and productivity improvement. Yet evidence from the UK, at least, shows there is reason to be concerned (Berry-Lound *et al.*, 1991). Recruitment and retention problems for skilled operative staff, supervisors and managers in tourism have been (and remain) subject to the vagaries of domestic and international demand, but have been seen generally to intensify in the late 1980s. With the number of young people entering the UK workforce set to shrink further in the mid-1990s, and then likely to recover only slowly, these problems are projected to intensify without adequate corporate or public policy responses (Metcalf, 1994).

COURSE INFRASTRUCTURE AND CO-OPERATION

Against this background of fragmented policy responses at EU and national levels, what have been the institutional policy responses to growth and skill change for the tourism and hospitality sectors? To understand the pattern of institutional response, it is important to recognize the contrasting national foundations which underpin this. For example, hospitality management and tourism-related VET programmes have a more recent origin in the UK and Ireland than in many of the continental European countries. In Germany, the Netherlands and Switzerland, the origins of the hospitality management education systems are employer collaborations from the late nineteenth century. In the UK, the provision of higher-level hospitality education dates from the late 1940s and comes mainly from institutional initiatives, although craft-level training has earlier responses. Later development has some advantages. Although more recently developed courses (especially in integrated tourism studies) have yet to develop the maturity, or the market presence with employers, of established programmes, they are less likely to follow traditional approaches to management development, which are now losing favour with major recruiters (Parsons and Cave, 1992).

The development of the UK system has more in common with that of the USA, where higher-level hospitality programmes grew rapidly from the mid-1970s and where integrated approaches to tourism management education have been more recent developments. The situation is similar in France, where higher-level courses in the sector (unlike craft-level training) have mostly developed quite recently. Unlike the US developments, however, the UK and French ones have not been bolted onto established, lower-level food-processing, nutrition and travel operations courses. They have consequently not suffered from the plethora of low-calibre courses which has characterized the US experience. The approach in the UK and France has more recently placed an increasing emphasis on degree-level provision. This reflects the particularly innovative role of the 'polytechnics',[2] colleges of higher education and central institutions in the UK. The distinctions between university and polytechnic – the UK dual system – have been lost in the reshaping of UK higher and further education in the 1990s, but they had played an important role in the development of hospitality management and related tourism courses. The Ecole de Commerce and some state-funded universities have played a similar role in France.

Intermediate-level courses[3] in the UK have related to the Higher National Diploma (HND) and in France to the Brevet de Technicien Superieur (BTS). In both countries these have remained an important feature of hospitality management, but in the UK, unlike France, enrolment trends suggest that the expansion of first-degree courses is now starting to erode the academic intake at intermediate level. This could be a fundamental weakness, leading perhaps to falling quality or even quantity of output from HND courses in the early 1990s. This might have a profound effect on recruitment to line and trainee management positions in larger employers, and to functional and general management in smaller organizations. In France, enrolment on the intermediate-level BTS courses has not suffered from the expansion of higher-level courses and they have generally established an important and valued presence in the labour market (Parsons and Cave, 1992).

Industrial analysis has suggested that education and training programmes at post-experience level are set to play an important role in an industry where many managers and owners are not formally qualified and have practical experience that may be narrow. These programmes have also been relatively slow to develop in the UK, France, Germany, the Netherlands and probably elsewhere in member states. In Europe in general, integrated and certificated approaches to post-experience management education in tourism are in their infancy. The situation in the USA is different. Here such programmes have gained widespread acceptance by the industry. The focus for policy developments here have been the hospitality industry's quasi-independent Educational Institute, through which the hotels and restaurant trade bodies have worked, together with leading faculty associations, to produce integrated programmes of hospitality management and certificate modules aimed fundamentally at personnel in post.

Close and productive institutional partnerships such as those in the USA are unusual in the UK. In continental Europe it has been more common for such partnerships to focus on full-time course provision. Post-experience courses have been a low priority.

The European Union's COMMET programme, in particular, has been the focus for the cross-institution student transfers which cement these cross-national co-operations. In this sector the VET-focused FORCE programme (the 1990–94 Community Action Programme for Continuing Education in Europe) has been less influential.

It is also in the USA that post-experience management education and certificate programmes have been most extensively developed for managers in tour organization and travel operations, although there is concern about the quality of some of these programmes. This is now being tackled by more rigid entry and assessment criteria and mechanisms, and provides a cautionary lesson for evolving partnerships in Europe (Hawkins and Hunt, 1988).

Poor integration and late development of post-experience programmes in much of Europe are weaknesses in an industry where competitive pressures, market and technological change will put great pressure on existing managers to 'stay qualified'. In some countries, such as the UK, the situation may be a double constraint, since so few managers are professionally qualified or have a sound basis of management education.

Overall, the structure of course provision in the UK does not suffer the gaps of that of some countries (notably Switzerland) or the inflexibility of that of others (such as Germany). However, the UK system which has evolved is poorly integrated, and both accreditation and certification remain fragmented, leading to apparent confusion for students and recruiters alike (Parsons, 1993). Credit accumulation, transfer mechanisms and wider access routes are being developed, but are only slowly being integrated into relevant courses in the UK. The evolving National Vocational Qualification (NVQ) system in the UK is having important effects on the integration and standardization of courses up to and at intermediate level, but is not expected to have an early effect on professional-level courses. In this situation, the policy impetus for structural change has come from outside the system rather than within it.

YOUNG PEOPLE AND ENROLMENT

Where policy developments have impacted on VET provision in the tourism and hospitality sectors, these have in general been targeted at young people and in particular at prospective new entrants to the industry. New advanced-level courses for both tourism and hospitality management have proven particularly popular with students. In the UK, for example, bachelor-degree courses in hospitality management have been popular and vastly oversubscribed (HMI, 1991; Parsons, 1991a).

Even if allowance is made for students making multiple applications, available places in the late 1980s and early 1990s could have been filled two or three times over by entrants. For bachelor-degree-level tourism courses, this figure was even higher (CNAA, 1993). At intermediate level the situation was less encouraging, as more of the traditionally qualified school-level entrants (with appropriate GCE A-level passes) apparently switched their sights to the expanding number of bachelor-degree-level places.

The popularity of advanced-level courses developed by institutions has been apparent elsewhere in Europe. In Germany, demand for the now well-established relevant *Fachhochschulen* diplomas, specializing in tourism or hospitality management, has remained buoyant. A similar picture has emerged in the Netherlands and Switzerland. In France, comparisons are confused by the different access system for higher education, but early indications are for a high level of student demand for the more recently established Magistere and MST (Maîtrise de Sciences et Techniques) courses in those areas (Parsons, 1991b).

In general, a review of initiatives in advanced-level hospitality and tourism courses shows the following:

- Policy developments below national level, through individual institutions or more occasionally through cross-national collaborations, have seen the number of student places in hospitality management and related tourism studies at bachelor-degree level in Europe expand sharply since the early 1970s.
- It parallels similar trends in North America.
- The rate of expansion in hospitality management programmes in the UK has been more cautious. Almost uniquely among those member states reviewed in the NEDO study, this has not capitalized on high levels of student and industrial demand. This seems to have been a failure more of the higher-education planning system in the UK and in particular of its market intelligence than of institutional policy development (Parsons and Cave, 1992).

Tourism and related management studies have shown a different pattern. Integrated advanced-level courses in tourism and management in Europe were established earliest in Germany (Kempten, Munich, Heilbronn, Worms and others) and in the Netherlands (Hill, 1988). However, the expansion in course provision in France and the UK, although later, has been much more extensive. In each of these countries, student demand for the new courses has been demonstrated by remarkably high applicant–admission ratios to most of the new courses. Unlike the case with hospitality management, however, industrial demand remains uncertain. Despite this, recent trends throughout Europe have seen institutions favouring the development of integrated bachelor-degree-level and postgraduate tourism studies. Experience in the longer-established programmes in the Netherlands and Germany suggests industrial demand for such courses is at best exaggerated, and in some cases has led to high levels of graduate unemployment or underemployment among graduates and diplomates.

Institutions of higher education providing hospitality and related tourism management courses in Germany, France and the Netherlands (and Switzerland) generally have applicant-admission ratios which are low by UK standards. High applicant-admission ratios are shown in the UK to have benefits in keeping the quality of student intake high and maximizing graduate employment prospects. However, this is at the expense of a relatively low level of qualified personnel supply. There is also some evidence that this approach may stimulate in students unrealistic expectations of career opportunity and progression on entering employment. Such problems are not unique to the UK, but they do seem to be more acute.

Student enrolment patterns in the UK are different in another important way. A remarkably high proportion of the intake to hospitality management and related tourism courses at both intermediate and degree level is of 18–19-year-old students. In France there is a similar focus. By international standards, this breadth of student intake is limited. In Germany and Switzerland, deferred entry to higher education and credit systems for industrial experience result in many of the intake in higher-level courses being in their mid-twenties. At intermediate level in Germany, the proportion is even higher, with many advanced-level courses reserving up to half of available places for what would be classified in the UK and France as ‘mature’ enrolments. Entrants in their late twenties are not unusual.

These are important differences. In the UK, many of the influences which underpin institutional developments are beyond the control of providers. In particular, the system is based on a much lower level of student participation in post-compulsory education, which has led to generally lower levels of academic or vocational qualification attainment in the 'mature' workforce. However, the tradition of entry to higher education at or soon after completing secondary education in the UK is also a product of institutional 'marketing' programmes and the structure of course provision, which is predominantly geared to younger entrants. This rigidity is a weakness in broader skill-supply terms.

CAREERS PATHS AND JOB CHOICE

What effect are these various developments having on skill supply at advanced and intermediate level? Comparative data is limited, but the NEDO study has provided a seven-country contrast valid at the start of the 1990s, following a decade seeing the emergence of most of the key VET developments for the sectors.

Table 10.1 Estimates of graduations from advanced-level hospitality management and tourism related studies in selected countries (output per capita)

Number of completing students per million population

	Great Britain (1988)	Canada (1989)	Federal Republic of Germany	France	Netherlands (1987)	Swizerland	US (1989)
Hospitality management							
Graduate & first degree programmes	14.9	25.0	5.2	3.1	22.3	188.3	52.2
Intermediate-level diploma & certificate programmes	25.4	N/A	29.8	12.7	71.4		N/A
Total	**40.4**	N/A	**35.1**	**15.8**	**93.7**	**188.3**	N/A
Tourism studies							
Graduate & first degree programmes	1.4	N/A	6.0	8.0	16.0	20.0	4.3
Intermediate-level diploma & certificate programmes	1.7	N/A	–	8.0	–		N/A
Total	**3.1**	N/A	**6.0**	**16.0**	**16.0**	**20.0**	N/A
All advanced-level	**43.5**	N/A	**41.1**	**31.8**	**109.7**	**208.3**	N/A

Source: NEDO, 1990

Overall, Table 10.1 shows that the scale of UK student supply is somewhere in the middle of the observed countries. It lags behind the high level of student throughput in North America, Switzerland and the Netherlands (despite high student drop-out rates in both Canada and the USA), but holds up well in contrast to Germany and France.

Some account needs to be taken of the determinants of these differences. The scale of provision in the USA and to a lesser extent in Canada stems mainly from much higher overall participation rates than in the member states reviewed here. This is exacerbated by student preferences, which increasingly emphasized professional and management programmes over technology and liberal arts (Parsons, 1993).

In Switzerland and the Netherlands, the high level of output is related more to a relatively high proportion of students entering higher education choosing hospitality management or tourism-related courses. Both countries aim for a substantial degree of over-supply of management skills in these specialities. The funding system for higher education and students in the UK makes this policy approach unrealistic.

The balance of supply is also important. In the UK, employers have reason to be concerned about the mix of courses and the proportion of graduates who choose to enter careers in the industry. Information from bachelor-degree-level hospitality management courses in the UK suggests that of those graduating an average of 90–95 per cent go directly into employment or further study, but available data suggests that in the late 1980s only just over half took up jobs in hotels, catering or related tourism activities, although there were important institutional variations. More recent data on destination may be distorted by the labour market consequences of recession – and are not reviewed here – but by European standards this is low. In Germany, Switzerland and France, an average of over 80 per cent of those graduating go into hospitality or related tourism jobs. In the Netherlands, it is also much higher than the UK average. The situation for graduates from the recently established 'tourism' courses in the UK is not yet clear. Employment patterns for the earliest graduates from these courses have been distorted by the recent recession, but early indications are not favourable.

Some allowance needs to be made for the generally high UK completion rates, but it none the less seems almost uniquely in the UK that institutional developments are failing to 'convert' sufficient of those proposing to take up careers in the industry into actual entrants. This is a long-standing issue (Airy and Nightingale, 1981), but on current levels of student throughput it suggests that the hospitality and tourism industries are 'losing' about 40 per cent of potential supply to other industries. This – rather than insufficient enrolments – may account for much of the reported skill-supply deficiency in the UK. There is, however, no detailed research evidence on the career choice of hospitality management graduates in the UK, and little research elsewhere. This is urgently needed if policy makers and educators are to understand and address the destination issue. In the UK at least, informal evidence suggests that intense competition in the graduate labour market in the mid- and late-1980s (Pike and Pearson, 1990), combined with the often poor-quality work experience, may be key issues.

Given the difference between UK and other countries' 'conversion' rates, a key policy issue is whether graduates of hospitality management programmes are being attracted away from jobs in hotels and catering or are rejecting careers in the industry. In the UK, there is evidence that the poor quality and limited supervision of the extended work experience which is an integral aspect of most courses may be leading to early disillusionment with the industry (Hughes, 1990). Although this issue is particularly acute in the UK, it is becoming evident elsewhere in Europe. As a result, in Germany and France some institutions have developed more rigorous control procedures for placements, including internship or externship 'contracts', agreed work experience schedules or contracts, student 'log books' and closer academic supervision. These have stemmed from institutional concerns and not from wider policy developments.

In North America, co-operative education concepts have also become increasingly important, and this is set to be a precedent for Europe. The larger number of employers offering placements in Germany and France enables a greater degree of quality control by placement tutors themselves. This more systematic approach to controlling the quality of work experience, and its value to recruiter and student, is generally uncommon in the UK. Ironically, hospitality management programmes in the UK usually have more extended work experience elements than in other countries.

This remains a complex issue. Some account needs to be taken of student expectations. Through the 'dual' system in Germany and similarly in Switzerland, a high proportion of advanced-level students enter courses with substantial experience of the industry – five or six years in operational or supervisory posts is not uncommon. Such entrants have already expressed a commitment to careers in the industry and are likely to hold more realistic expectations of it than those entering direct from school.

Student selection methods have a similar effect. In Switzerland, some institutions apply a pre-admission selection semester, which is thought to act as a realistic job preview, and ensures that more of those entering direct from secondary education understand better what the industry has to offer. A similar mechanism has been developed by *Fachhochschulen* in Germany.

Under the stimulus of a tightening graduate labour market in the late 1980s, considerable progress had been made on 'systemizing' graduate recruitment programmes in many of the major hotel and travel groups in the UK as elsewhere, in Germany and France. Among the multinationals, this often builds in a cross-national dimension, notably for hospitality management development and most notably in the French ACOR group. In general, however, too often the bachelor-degree graduate or intermediate-level diplomate – especially in the UK – continues to be faced with an abrupt transition to a 'learning by doing' culture, supplemented with sparse induction training and few continuing education opportunities. This may dissuade many from entering the industry, and inflate turnover rates for those that do – particularly when they are faced with the sophisticated, fast-track management training posts offered in the clearing banks, major insurance groups, retail distribution and other service industries.

This makes special demands of tourism and hospitality recruiters in Europe. Other evidence has proposed (NEDO, 1990) that there is much more that recruiters should learn from the sophisticated graduate recruitment and careers programmes of the best-practice hotel and travel corporations in the USA, and to a lesser extent in Canada, Germany and France. With few exceptions, careers programmes even among the European multinationals are up to five years behind their more sophisticated corporate competitors in North America. However, with graduate labour markets now less tight and recruitment targets widening to other disciplines, it is doubtful whether the labour market itself will provide sufficient corporate policy stimulus.

CROSS-NATIONAL PERSPECTIVE

Each of the seven countries involved in the 1990 NEDO study sees higher education and training for tourism management and related studies in or approaching a state of flux. Expansion, restructuring of the tourism industry, changing student preferences and demand have stimulated an increase in course provision in all the countries, although with mixed effects. This has generally boosted course provision, particularly at higher levels and in integrated or combined tourism studies. A wider range of providers has also become involved, and in continental Europe the pattern of course provision is spreading well beyond the confines of the dedicated 'hotel schools' which have often been the foundation of specialized business and management education for these industries.

In all seven countries, these changes have involved a painful transition. In many there is evidence of rising tensions between the new range of providers and many sectors of the industry, particularly on the scope and quality of higher-level courses. Quality of provision is everywhere a major issue.

The approaches taken towards management education for the tourist industry vary considerably between – and often within – each of these countries, but the research has indicated many common challenges. In general, intermediate-level management education is well (and often long) established, providing in most countries an effective mix of professional and practical education. In continental Europe, there is widespread industrial and academic concern about the quality of 'commercial' courses in the tourism and travel sector, but in general the foundations are strong. The challenges here relate mostly to broadening the educational and technological content of established courses without compromising their practical component. In some countries, and notably in the UK, there are also rising problems with the credibility of intermediate-level courses with young people.

Specialized education and training at bachelor-degree level or graduate study has in most countries been a comparatively recent innovation in tourism management, adopted especially in France. Elsewhere, many of the programmes remain in their infancy. The level and quality of academic and institutional investment in these programmes have been variable, but much of the tourism industry has as yet uncertain expectation of, and demand for, higher-level qualifications.

In each of these countries, the labour-market credibility of many of the higher-level tourism management programmes has yet to be established. This parallels early experience in North America. Some parts of the industry have been quick to appreciate the value of specialized higher-level courses – public sector agencies and destination management in particular – but elsewhere, in independent hotels, catering, and especially travel and tour management and facilities operation, the resistance has often proved persistent. Much of this may stem from the structure of the European tourism industry and in particular the preponderance of small firms. Certainly many European providers have found that, in integrated tourism studies, effective and broadly based industry–institutional partnerships are much more difficult to achieve and sustain at higher level than at intermediate level.

Policy makers may need to consider whether member states could profit from a more constructive synergy between the public and private sector to harness the clear evidence of rising academic and student interest in the business of tourism management. This might focus in particular on the need for the following:

- Realistic and labour-market-related balance between intermediate and higher-level course provision. There is already some evidence that student demand for intermediate-level courses, which have a firm labour-market base, may be being compromised in some countries – but not all – by the rapid expansion of higher-level courses, which as yet do not have such a base.
- Effective mechanisms of 'market mediation', in particular at higher levels, to establish better the role for higher-level courses in different sectors of these industries, and to relate this more effectively to student selection and assessment, curriculum design, student guidance, and revised career paths in industry.
- Systematic approaches to co-operative education in both theoretical education and work experience programmes. In some countries, notably the UK, there is evidence that the poor quality and industrial management of work experience programmes are leading many students to turn away from the industry. Others might also profit from looking again at the scope for co-operative education processes.

- Less rigid mechanisms for access to higher level courses. In particular, urgent attention needs to be paid to the more effective integration of post-experience and continuing management education with existing approaches to course provision, and to the promotion and take-up of new or established post-experience courses in industry.

Management education and training in Europe's hospitality and tourism industries seem to be at a watershed. Substantial progress has been made by individual institutions in many countries in developing new advanced-level courses, but tensions have arisen between providers and some sectors of the industries, and these must be urgently addressed. On one side lie moves towards a better consensus by providers and employers on the routes towards greater professionalism, and on the other a retreat into the spirit of amateur business management, which often holds back the performance of the industry.

The internationalism of the tourism business has led to calls for greater standardization and integration of provision between and within both developed and developing economies. This may be difficult to articulate and even more so to achieve. There is much to be learnt from a better understanding of the diversity of national approaches towards management education in the tourism industry in the developing economies of Europe. The earlier NEDO study has made a cautious start. What seems to be missing is a convergence of policy interest and diagnosis to take this forward.

NOTES

1. The programme was developed by the Tourism and Leisure Industries Sector Group, which brought together the industries' corporate and trade union leaders, key agencies and government. Its focus was on reviewing practice and policy developments in the then Federal Republic of Germany, France, the Netherlands and the UK. Parallel studies - not reported in detail here - were conducted in the USA and Canada. The results of the programme were published in 1992 (Parsons and Cave, 1992).
2. In the UK since 1991 most of the former polytechnics, and some of the former locally-funded institutions of higher education, have sought and been granted charter status as 'new' universities.
3. Here classified as advanced-level studies below bachelor-degree level.

REFERENCES

Airy, D. and Nightingale, M. (1981) *Tourism Occupations, Career Profiles and Knowledge*. London: Tourism Society.

Berry-Lound, D., Battersby, D. and Parsons, D.J. (1991) *Jobs in Tourism and Leisure: A Labour Market Review*. London: British Tourist Authority.

Brewster, C. and Hegewisch, A. (1993) *European Developments in Human Resource Management*. London: Kogan Page.

CNAA (1993) *Review of Tourism Studies Degree Courses*. Committee for Consumer and Leisure Studies. London: Council for National Academic Awards.

Commission (Commission of the European Communities) (1994) *European Social Policy: A Way Forward for the Union*. Brussels: CEC.

Derr, B. (1992) *The Emerging Role of the Personnel/Human Resource Manager in Europe*. Lausanne: Institute of Management Development.

DfEE (1996) *National Training Organization: A Consultation Paper*. Department for Education and Employment. London: HMSO.

Hawkins, D.E. and Hunt, J.D. (1988) 'Travel and Tourism Professional Education', *Hospitality and Tourism Education*, **11**, 191–207.

Hill, R.W. (1988) 'Cross-cultural Approaches to the Teaching of Tourism' in *Proceedings of the 1st International Conference on Teaching Tourism*. Guildford: University of Surrey.

HMI (1991) *Hospitality First Degree Provision*. Report of Her Majesty's Inspectorate, Department of Education. London: HMSO.

—— (1992) *Hotel, Catering and Tourism Management: Higher Education in the Polytechnics and Colleges*. Report of Her Majesty's Inspectorate, Department of Education. London: HMSO.

HMSO (Her Majesty's Stationery Office) (1989) *Employment for the 1990s*. Employment Department. London: HMSO.

Hughes, H. (1990) *Hotel and Catering Degree Courses*. London: Council for National Academic Awards.

IFF (1994) *Skills Needs in Britain, 1994*. London: IFF Research Ltd.

Metcalf, H. (1994) *Recruitment Challenges: Tackling the Labour Squeeze in Tourism and Leisure*. Tourism and Leisure Sector Group. London: National Economic Development Office.

NEDO (National Economic Development Office) (1984) *Competence and Competition: Training and Education in the Federal Republic of Germany, the United States and Japan*. London: National Economic Development Office.

—— (1990) *Working for Pleasure: Tourism and Leisure Tomorrow*. London: National Economic Development Office.

Parsons, D.J. (1987) 'Jobs in Tourism', *Employment Gazette*, **95**, 336–46.

—— (1991a) 'Managing for Pleasure: Some Lessons from a Comparative Review of Management Education Programmes in Tourism', *Revue de Tourism,* **1**, 11–17.

—— (1991b) 'The Making of Managers: Lessons from an International Review of Tourism Education Programmes', *Tourism Management*, **11**, 197–207.

—— (1993) 'Developments in the UK Tourism and Leisure Labour Market' in Lindley, R. (ed.) *Employment: Britain in the Single European Market*. London: HMSO, pp. 101–12.

Parsons, D.J. and Cave, P. (1992) *Developing Managers for Tourism*. London: National Economic Development Office.

Pike, G. and Pearson, R. (1990) *The Graduate Labour Market in the 1990s*. Brighton: UK Institute of Manpower Studies.

Prais, S., Jarvis, V. and Wagner, K. (1989) 'Productivity and Vocational Skills in Services in Britain and Germany: Hotels', *National Institute Economic Review*, **27**, 52–7.

Rajan, A. (1985) *Training and Recruitment Effects of Technical Change*. Aldershot: Gower Press.

ELEVEN

Environmental policy

Richard Welford

INTRODUCTION

Since the 1960s, there has been a growing interest in the environment, or more specifically in the damage being done to the environment, in Europe and North America. The process of European integration has brought the transnational nature of the environmental problem to the forefront. The hole in the ozone layer and global warming are the result of not one country's action but that of many. Acid rain, which is polluting rivers and lakes and damaging forests, often emanates from one country and is deposited in another. European integration therefore offers an opportunity for transnational co-operation, and this has been reflected in a multitude of European environmental legislation, much of which is already in place.

The effects of different industrial sectors upon the environment vary enormously. At one end of the spectrum we might put the oil companies, whose very business is environmentally damaging, and towards the other end we might put the hospitality industry, which has less of a direct impact on the environment. The latter nevertheless, in most cases, could still make environmental improvements through energy usage reduction, recycling, customer awareness initiatives and other internal systems. However, there is still much confusion for both consumers and companies about what constitutes an environmentally friendly operation, and the 'green revolution' to date has provided few answers.

This chapter therefore attempts to provide some of those answers in the context of the tourism and hospitality industries. It begins by looking at the European Union (EU)'s policies which impact on the environment and particularly at the Fifth Environmental Action Programme. It goes on to consider the important concept of sustainable development and to discuss what a more sustainable tourism industry might look like. Lastly, it examines some of the more practical things which firms can do in the hospitality industry to improve their environmental performance. This includes carrying out environmental audits.

Everything which consumers, companies and other institutions do will have some impact on the environment. Even substances which in their final form are environmentally benign may have been unfriendly in their manufacture, especially if that manufacture was energy greedy. They may have been produced using non-renewable resources and may also pose problems after they have been used and come to be disposed of. If we take what is commonly called a cradle-to-the-grave view of products and services, where we examine their environmental impact through their life-cycle from raw material usage to disposal, then there are few, if any, activities which will not have some negative impact on the environment (Fabrycky and Blanchard, 1991). The key question is therefore not how we eliminate environmental damage completely, but how we reduce it over time and how we achieve a state of balance such that the amount of environmental damage done is reparable and therefore sustainable.

It is generally accepted that the world cannot go on using the resources of the planet at the present rate. But there is a 'free rider problem' at work. Everyone thinks that there should be something done, but many people just assume that everyone else will do it, and since their individual impact is minute it will not matter to the environment. The trouble is that when too many people or firms think in that way then nothing is ever achieved. The world has scarce resources and only limited capacity to deal with the pollution caused through production, service provision and consumption.

The success of tourism relies to a great extent on the quality of the environment where it takes place. Tourism is therefore influenced by the environment, but it must also be recognized that the environment is equally influenced by tourist activities. Tourism therefore requires proper planning and management, and the industry itself has a responsibility to respond to the environmental challenge for its own well-being, as well as for the well-being of society as a whole. Moreover, tourist activities today can destroy the potential earning capacity of a tourist destination in the future. Evidence from Germany suggests that up to 20 per cent of tourists who consider that the environment of their destination is damaged are unlikely to return (Boers and Bosch, 1994).

The European Commission represented the EU in the United Nations Conference on the Environment and Development (UNCED) in Rio de Janeiro in 1992. The 'Earth Summit' agreed a range of conventions and actions which the Commission has begun to implement since then. Amongst these was the adoption of 'Agenda 21', which aims at providing the foundations for sustainable development; the Rio Declaration, which sets out the fundamental principles to ensure sustainable development; and the Declaration on Forests, which calls for national policies on the management of forests.

Within Agenda 21, particular emphasis is placed on the need to manage land sustainability, to combat desertification, to manage mountainous areas, to protect oceans and fresh water, and to strengthen the role of indigenous populations in determining their own futures (Keating, 1993). These are all areas where tourism has a direct impact, usually in a negative way. Agenda 21 stresses the need for all groups to work together to move towards increased sustainability, but emphasizes the role of industry in developing policies that result in operations, products and services which have lower environmental impacts.

The hospitality industry, particularly in the developed world, must therefore take into account the costs of the effect of its operations on the environment, rather than regarding the planet as a free resource. In the past, few companies have counted the costs of the pollution which they discharged into the atmosphere, and the debate has now turned to legislation aimed at forcing companies to comply with certain standards and taxing firms which pollute. The so-called 'polluter pays' principle is now central to legislation in the EU. The implication here is clearly that prices will rise for consumers as firms experience increased costs associated with environmental improvements. Less energy consumption and more efficient use of resources are obvious targets for improvement and should not conflict with industry's aims, since their attainment can actually reduce costs.

The rapid growth of public environmental awareness in recent years has placed new pressures on all types of business. These pressures can take many forms as individuals collectively exercise their environmental conscience as customers, employees, investors, voters, neighbours and fellow citizens. Increasingly, environmental performance is seen as an integral part of a company's wider social responsibility (Zenisek, 1979). However, whether it is due to intellectual fatigue with environmental issues, a lack of conviction that an individual's own actions will have an impact, or a reluctance to reduce private consumption for public welfare, many individuals seemingly prefer to pass their responsibilities on to those parties that they feel can make a significant impact. The two major such parties are government and industry. Given an inherent reluctance in the public to reduce their own levels of consumption, it is apparent that government and industry must respond in order to protect the environment effectively.

EUROPEAN INTEGRATION AND THE ENVIRONMENT

The original Treaty of Rome of 1957 was concerned with stimulating economic growth and contained no specific reference to the environment. Since then, though, EU environmental policy has developed in line with general concern in Europe and the deteriorating environmental position in which Europe finds itself. By 1990, 160 pieces of environmental legislation had been passed covering pollution of the air and water, noise pollution, chemicals, waste, environmental impact assessment, the prevention of industrial accidents and wildlife protection.

However, few member states have been able to enforce EU legislation fully. Denmark is probably the only country with a consistently good record, and the Southern European countries have consistently bad records. Once again, this highlights the emphasis often given to economic growth rather than environmental protection, with the primary aim of countries such as Spain and Portugal being the attainment of similar living standards to the rest of the Community.

The Single European Act (SEA) of 1986 gave environmental policy a boost, stating not only that there is a need for such legislation but that the laws should meet three key objectives:

- preservation, protection and improvement of the quality of the environment;
- protection of human health;
- prudent and rational use of natural resources.

These objectives must be met by applying four principles:

- prevention of harm to the environment;
- control of pollution at source;
- payment by the polluter;
- integration of environmental considerations into other Community policies (all EU policies are now required to take the environment into account).

The Internal Market Programme has added a new note of urgency to environmental problems. The relationship between economic growth and the environment has returned to centre stage. Clearly, there exists a major opportunity with industrial and legislative restructuring to put into place the appropriate financial and regulatory mechanisms that would make the internal market environmentally sustainable. The extent to which this happens will be seen over time, but the SEA also provides the necessary constitutional basis for a forceful environmental response. Perhaps the strongest part of this is the requirement that policy makers should make environmental considerations a component of all the Community's other policies.

In 1992 the European Union's Fifth Environmental Action Programme was introduced. The first environmental action programme in 1973 set out a number of principles which have formed the basis of environmental action in the EU ever since. The aims are clearly set out, stating that:

1. Prevention is better than cure.
2. Environmental effects should be taken into account at the earliest possible stage in decision making.
3. Exploitation of nature and natural resources which causes significant damage to the ecological balance must be avoided. The natural environment can only absorb pollution to a limited extent. Nature is an asset which may be used but not abused.
4. Scientific knowledge should be improved to enable action to be taken.
5. 'The Polluter Pays' principle; the polluter should pay for preventing and eliminating environmental nuisance.
6. Activities in one Member State should not cause environmental deterioration in another.
7. Environmental policies of Member States must take account of the interests of developing countries.
8. The EU and Member States should act together in international organisations and also in promoting international environmental policy.
9. Education of citizens is necessary as the protection of the environment is a matter for everyone.
10. The principle of action at the appropriate level; for each type of pollution it is necessary to establish the level of action which is best suited for achieving the protection required, be it local, regional, national, EU-wide or international.
11. National environmental policies must be coordinated within the EU without impinging on progress at the national level. It is intended that implementation of the action programme and gathering of environmental information by the proposed European environment agency will secure this.

(*Official Journal of the European Communities* C112 20.12.73)

The main activities of the EU in the environmental policy arena until 1987 were centred on the application of nearly 200 command and control directives in areas as diverse as lead in petrol and aircraft noise. More recently, in realizing that environmental policy is of little use unless enforced, EU environmental policy has given increased emphasis to the improved enforcement of existing legislation. Emphasis has also shifted from the use of traditional command and control instruments in environmental policy to the application of economic-market-based instruments, such as the proposed carbon tax, and voluntary agreements. The aim of such measures is to encourage change in all sectors of industry and society, in a more general way than can be achieved through the use of tightly defined legislative instruments. The use of economic instruments and voluntary measures is seen as a complement rather than a substitute to the more traditional application of command and control measures.

The EU view of the future of environmental policy and its interface with industrial development is clear. With some 340 million inhabitants, the Community is the largest trading bloc in the world, and is therefore in a critical position to take the lead on environmental issues. The Commission accepts that tighter environmental policy will impact on the costs of industry; however, increasingly a high level of environmental protection has become not only a policy objective on its own but also a precondition of industrial expansion. In this respect, a new impetus towards a better integration of policies aiming at consolidating industrial competitiveness and at achieving a high level of protection of the environment is necessary in order to make the two objectives fully mutually supportive.

These views are given more substance within the Fifth Environmental Action Programme. This sets out the likely developments of EU environmental policy in a general sense, and includes a number of specific measures relating to industry. Perhaps most importantly, the commitment of the EU to strengthen environmental policy is underlined. The EU shares the view that urgent action is needed for environmental protection, and that many of the great environmental struggles will be won or lost during this decade. Further, it states that achieving sustainability will demand practical and political commitment over an extended period and that the EU, as the largest trading bloc in the world, must exercise its responsibility and commit itself to that goal (Fleming, 1992).

For industries and companies that are facing a rising tide of environmental legislation, it is essential that attempts are made to find out about and then positively address the legislative pressures which they are under. However, the Fifth Environmental Action Programme focuses on the improved enforcement of existing legislation rather than the adoption of new legislation. To some extent, this should allow industry to take stock of the rapid increase in environmental legislation that has taken place in recent years and to focus on achieving compliance with existing legislation (Welford and Gouldson, 1993). Despite the stated objective of concentrating on the effective implementation of existing policy, there are many pieces of environmental legislation in the EU policy pipeline which are awaiting final adoption. Many of these measures have fundamental implications for business, and the need to track forthcoming legislation therefore remains essential.

Furthermore, the Maastricht Treaty and the Fifth Environmental Action Programme require that environmental policy should be fully incorporated into all other Community policies. Therefore, while it may become easier to track the development of policies which are explicitly environmental, it will become more difficult to monitor the development of environmental policy throughout the activities of the Commission as a whole. The establishment of the European Environment Agency, which will collect data and monitor compliance throughout the Community, could help to disseminate information to all interested parties. In the meantime, the delay between the release of EU legislation and its subsequent implementation in member states offers vital time for planning, for those companies that monitor the development of European environmental policy, in order to avoid the costs and exploit the opportunities which are undoubtedly generated.

Tourism has been selected as a priority area within the Fifth Environmental Action Programme, both because of the industry's significant environmental impact, and because of the relevance of the action at a Community level. For tourism there are three key areas of action which the European Commission would like to encourage:

- better planning, development and management of mass tourism, especially in coastal and alpine areas;

- sustainable tourism development and the development of different types of activity and product in other areas;
- changes in tourist behaviour and raising visitor awareness.

As part of this plan a number of initiatives have taken place within the LIFE programme, established by the Commission in 1992. Projects which contribute to the development and implementation of environmental policy are still encouraged, particularly where these include innovative demonstration projects, such as land-use planning and the use of 'clean' technologies, awareness campaigns and the provision of technical assistance. Within this framework the LIFE programme seeks to stimulate a planned approach to tourism development, especially in supporting actions which respect the natural environment.

The strategic significance of the EU's views cannot be overstated. By taking a long-term, Community-wide perspective and accepting that industrial competitiveness is enhanced by tight environmental legislation, they will make the policy framework within which all European companies must participate reflect these views. Some companies, some regions and some nations will benefit. If the views of the EU are correct, the economic prospects of the Community as a whole will benefit and the environment certainly will. However, at the company level, realizing these benefits will not be automatic, strategic planning and proactive responses to the changing policy climate are imperative if success is to be secured. Information must be gathered, its implications assessed, and the necessary action taken in a systematic and integrated way.

Tackling environmental problems always requires a concerted and co-operative effort, and in the EU success will depend on the extent to which member states are not only politically committed to the environmental philosophy but also willing to co-operate. The balancing of the economic growth/environment trade-off is likely to determine the Europe-wide success of any policies. But there also needs to be concerted and co-operative political motivations. There will be those who will therefore argue that the attainment of an effective and concerted environmental policy in Europe will require political and economic union. However the EU and national governments legislate over environmental protection and police offenders, significant environmental improvement will only be attained with the co-operation and commitment of producers.

In the future we will see more initiatives to encourage environmentally sensitive tourism. For example, member states are being encouraged to draw up inventories of tourism resources within their own borders. Such inventories will then be used to draft regional and tourism development programmes which protect the environment better. Between member states, regions with similar geographical characteristics are being encouraged to work together to identify solutions to mounting environmental degradation. For example, coastal regions and mountainous areas are being encouraged to co-operate to identify forms of tourism and hotel provision which can contribute to regional environmental improvement plans.

Within the tourist industry, the European Commission is also encouraging information networks, where hotels, restaurants and the transport sector can share solutions and strategies for overcoming damage caused to the environment. This voluntary co-operation is very important if the whole tourist industry is to become more environmentally responsible. Nevertheless, there will still be a great emphasis placed on governments and local authorities to ensure that future planning applications for new tourist facilities meet newer and tougher environmental requirements.

Another specific action the EU will support is the drawing up of a code of behaviour for tourists. The aims of such a scheme would be to get service providers to educate their customers and ensure that they are aware of the environmental impact of their activities. In effect it requires the industry itself to take more responsibility for visitor management. Moreover, by having a practical guide drawn up, tourists can feel more of a part of the environment they are enjoying, and help to protect it for future generations. It is likely that such a strategy, involving the industry and its consumers, will be central to devising and delivering new tourist products and facilities.

SUSTAINABLE DEVELOPMENT AND SUSTAINABLE TOURISM

The belief which lies behind the concept of sustainable development is that there is a trade-off between continuous economic growth and the sustainability of the environment. Over time, growth causes pollution and atmospheric damage. The concept of sustainable development stresses the interdependence between economic growth and environmental quality. It is possible to make development and environmental protection compatible by following sustainable strategies and by not developing the particular areas of economic activity that are most damaging to the environment.

The Brundtland Report, commissioned by the United Nations to examine long-term environmental strategies, argued that economic development and environmental protection could be made compatible, but that this would require quite radical changes in economic practices throughout the world. It defined sustainable development as 'development that meets the needs of the present without compromising the ability of future generations to meet their own needs' (World Commission, 1987). In other words, mass consumption is not possible indefinitely, and if society today acts as if all non-renewable resources are plentiful, eventually there will be nothing left for the future. But more importantly than that, mass consumption may cause such irreparable damage that humans may not even be able to live on the planet in the future.

The challenge that faces the economic system is how to continue to fulfil its vital role within modern society whilst working towards sustainability. Compliance with the principles of sustainability cannot be achieved overnight. However, both for entire economies and for individual businesses, there is hope that it can be achieved within the time scales which appear to be necessary if environmental catastrophe is to be avoided.

There is increasing concern that tourism can damage the environment. Holiday packages have led to overcrowding, over-exploitation and depletion of resources in many regions of Europe. This has led to both environmental and cultural damage in those regions where traditional industry has largely been replaced by tourism. The environmental situation is particularly disturbing in the Mediterranean, where coastal areas have seen rapid growth in both tourism and manufacturing industry.

However, the tourism industry will find itself having to respond to increasing pressure from the European Commission to improve its environmental performance. It will be directly affected by directives on environmental impact assessment, the quality of bathing water, waste management and control of emissions. The Commission's proposals for the urban environment stress the need to develop a planning strategy for urban tourism. Moreover, through the use of its Structural Funds, the Commission is able to support regional action programmes which improve the environment. Such programmes are increasingly integrated schemes which include participation from all industries including tourism.

According to the Tourism Society (1991), sustainable tourism challenges us to view the use of our precious natural and built resources in a creative way. It is important to recognize the real relationship between economic activity and environmental concern. In recognizing the 'polluter pays' principle, there is a need for new charges for tourism management purposes. In addition, however, we must recognize that the concept of sustainable development encompasses wider issues than just the environment.

According to Welford (1995), the concept of sustainable development is made up of three closely connected issues:

- *Environment:* The environment must be valued as an integral part of the economic process and not treated as a free good. The environmental stock has to be protected, and this implies minimal use of non-renewable resources and minimal emission of pollutants. The ecosystem has to be protected, so the loss of plant and animal species has to be avoided.
- *Equity:* One of the biggest threats facing the world is that the developing countries want to grow rapidly to achieve the same standards of living as those in the West. That in itself would cause a major environmental disaster if it were modelled on the sort of growth experienced in post-war Europe. There therefore needs to be a greater degree of equity, and the key issue of poverty has to be addressed.
- *Futurity:* Sustainable development requires that society, businesses and individuals operate on a different time scale to that which currently operates in the economy. While companies commonly operate under competitive pressures to achieve short-run gains, long-term environmental protection is often compromised. To ensure that longer-term, inter-generational considerations are observed, longer planning horizons need to be adopted, and business policy needs to be proactive rather than reactive.

The Brundtland Report concludes that these three conditions are not being met. The industrialized world has already used much of the planet's ecological capital, and many of the development paths of the industrialized nations are clearly unsustainable. Non-renewable resources are being depleted, while renewable resources such as soil, water and the atmosphere are being degraded. This has been caused by economic development, but in time will undermine the very foundations of that development.

The Brundtland Report calls for growth which is environmentally and socially sustainable rather than the current situation of unplanned, undifferentiated growth. This means reconsidering the current measures of growth, such as gross national product (GNP), which fail to take account of environmental debits like pollution or the depletion of the natural capital stock. While anxiety about the depletion of materials and energy resources has diminished since the 1970s, there is nevertheless now concern surrounding the environment's capacity to act as a sink for waste. For example, bringing developing countries' energy use up to the level of the developing world's would mean an increase in consumption by a factor of five (Welford and Prescott, 1996). Using present energy generation methods, the planet could not cope with the impact of sulphur dioxide and carbon dioxide emissions and the acidification and global warming of the environment which would result.

THE INDUSTRY RESPONSE TO SUSTAINABLE DEVELOPMENT

Companies are faced with the challenge of integrating environmental considerations into their production and marketing plans. There is always an incentive, however, for profit-maximizing firms seeking short-term rewards to opt out and become free riders (assuming that everyone else will be environmentally conscious, so that their own pollution will become negligible). We have seen that EU environmental legislation is increasingly plugging the gaps which allow this to happen, and firms attempting to hide their illegal pollution are now and will be subject to severe penalties. Even before then, though, businesses should recognize that not only is it ethical to be environmentally friendly but, with the growth of consumer awareness in the environmental area, it will also be good business.

Firms clearly have a role to play in the development of substitutes for non-renewable resources and of innovations which reduce waste and use energy more efficiently. They also have a role in processing those materials in a way which brings about environmental improvements. For many products (such as transport and washing machines), the major area of environmental damage occurs in their usage. Firms often have the opportunity of reducing this damage at the design stage, and when new products are being developed there is a whole new opportunity for considering both the use and disposal of the product.

According to the results of monitoring by the World Travel and Tourism Environmental Research Centre, there is evidence to suggest that many companies are adopting programmes to improve their environmental performance (Hawkins, 1994). This is partly motivated by a growing awareness that the industry's own interests are at stake and an increased emphasis put on environmental attributes as an element of non-price competition.

Given the internal and external demands to improve the environmental performance of a company, those companies that achieve high standards of environmental performance will benefit in a number of ways. In order to realize this competitive advantage, companies must seek to develop management strategies which will improve their environmental performance and address the environmental demands placed upon them by government, the EU and stakeholders. Welford (1994) shows, through practical examples, that by incorporating the increasingly important environmental dimension into the decision-making processes of the firm, managers can seek to reduce costs and exploit the opportunities offered by increased public environmental concern within a dynamic market place. Such a strategy must be proactive and honest and involve all those working in the hospitality and tourism industries.

The following seven principles for sustainable tourism were drawn up in May 1991 by the Secretary of State for Employment's Tourism Task Force. They form a useful basis for the growth and development of the industry:

- The environment has intrinsic value which outweighs its value as a tourism asset. Its enjoyment by future generations and its long-term survival must not be prejudiced by short-term considerations.
- Tourism should be recognized as a positive activity with the potential to benefit the community and the place as well as the visitor.
- The relationship between tourism and the environment must be managed so that it is stable in the long term. Tourism must not be allowed to damage the resource, prejudice its future enjoyment or bring unacceptable impacts.

- Tourism activities and developments should respect the scale, nature and character of the place in which they are sited.
- In any location, harmony must be sought between the needs of the visitor, the place and the host community.
- In a dynamic world some change is inevitable, and change can often be beneficial. Adaptation to change, however, should not be at the expense of any of these principles.
- The tourism industry, local authorities and environmental agencies all have a duty to respect the above principles and to work together to achieve their practical realization.

Recognizing the urgent need to support moral and ethical conviction with practical action, the hotel industry has established the International Hotels Environmental Initiative to foster the continual upgrading in the industry world-wide. With the co-operation and participation of individual companies, hotels and related organizations, the initiative endeavours to:

- provide practical guidance for the industry on how to improve environmental performance and how this contributes to successful business operations;
- develop practical environmental manuals and guidelines;
- recommend systems for monitoring improvements in environmental performance and for environmental audits;
- encourage the observance of the highest possible standards of environmental management, not only directly within the industry but also with suppliers and local authorities;
- promote the integration of training in environmental management among hotel and catering schools;
- collaborate with appropriate national and international organizations to ensure the widest possible awareness and observance of the initiative and the practice promoted;
- exchange information widely and highlight examples of good practice in the industry.

Clearly, every company within the hospitality industry can begin by improving its own environmental performance. In this first instance, organizations can develop environmental policies, assess their environmental impacts through reviews and audits, and develop comprehensive environmental management systems. It is to these practical issues that we now turn.

ENVIRONMENTAL POLICIES

Companies are beginning to realize that environmental issues need to be addressed for a number of reasons, including consumer pressure, potential cost savings, legislation and ethics. There is therefore growing interest in the area of environmental management. Environmental considerations are likely to be a source of quite profound changes in business practices.

The starting point for many businesses will be to write and distribute an environmental policy. This will set out the context for future action. There is no single model, and the policy will reflect a company's structure, location, industrial sector and business culture. If such a document is published then it is important that the plan is adhered to, thereby providing an all important environmental ethos within which the company must operate.

All aspects of a company's operations, from accounting and purchasing to service provision, sales and marketing, will have an impact on the environment, and the environmental policy should reflect a recognition of this. The policy needs to be comprehensive and detailed, but it should not contain statements or targets which the firm cannot hope to achieve. This will do more harm than good if exposed. The content of any policy will vary from firm to firm and be influenced by the activities of that organization.

Environmental policies should identify key performance areas and form a sound basis for setting corporate objectives. They need to be detailed enough to demonstrate that the commitment of the company goes beyond lip service. A clearly defined environmental policy should be implementable, be practical and relate to the areas in which the company wishes to improve its environmental performance. In particular, when designing an environmental policy the organization needs to think hard about how it is going to quantify its objectives and measure its environmental performance.

ENVIRONMENTAL AUDITING

The first environmental audits can be traced back to the USA, where corporations adopted this methodology during the 1970s in response to their domestic liability laws. Such audits are now common among US industry and growing in importance in Europe. Environmental audits are usually carried out by teams which include lawyers, economists, engineers, scientists and environmental generalists drawn from industry, government and consultancy. The US Environmental Protection Agency has been instrumental in promoting environmental audits in the USA, and has published policy guidelines which recommend going beyond the minimum legal requirements to identify actual and potential environmental problems.

There is some confusion over terminology still, but environmental auditing is generally seen as a check both on the environmental performance of a company and on the performance of the management system (see below), which should be designed to bring about improvements in that performance. In the first instance, the firm needs to establish a baseline against which to measure future audits, and this is commonly referred to as the environmental review. The environmental review follows many of the procedures of an audit as laid out below. However, strictly speaking an audit measures the attainment or non-attainment of some target objectives, whereas the environmental review simply provides an initial assessment of the environmental performance of the company.

The environmental audit consists of a regular, independent, systematic, documented and objective evaluation of the environmental performance of an organization. It should measure how well organizations, management and equipment are performing, with the aim of helping the company management to safeguard the environment. It also provides management information which can be used in the control of environmental practices and in assessing compliances with company policies, which includes meeting regulatory requirements. It should be stressed, however, that within the task of environmental management there is a role for everyone in the organization.

The overall aim of environmental auditing is to help safeguard the environment and minimize the risks to human health. Although auditing alone cannot achieve that, it is a powerful managerial tool. The key objectives of the environmental audit are:

- to determine the extent to which environmental management systems in a company are performing adequately;
- to verify compliance with local, national and European environmental and health and safety legislation;
- to verify compliance with a company's own stated corporate policy;
- to develop and promulgate internal procedures needed to achieve the organization's environmental objectives;
- to minimize human exposure to risks from the environment and ensure adequate health and safety provision;
- to identify and assess risk resulting from environmental failure;
- to assess the impact on the local environment of a particular activity or process by means of air, water and soil sampling;
- to advise a company on environmental improvements it can make.

There are a number of benefits to firms in having an environmental audit undertaken. These include assurances that legislation is being adhered to and the consequent prevention of fines and litigation, an improved public image which can be built into a public relations campaign, a reduction in costs (particularly in the areas of energy usage and waste minimization), an improvement in environmental awareness at all levels of the firm, and an improvement in overall quality. On the other hand, there are some potential disbenefits. These include the initial costs of the audit, the cost of compliance with it, and the temporary disruption of plant operations. It is also vital that management sees that the recommendations of the environmental auditor are adhered to, otherwise an audit report could be incriminating in a court case or insurance claim.

All environmental audits involve gathering information, analysing that information, and making objective judgements based on evidence and a knowledge of both the industry and relevant environmental legislation and standards. There is also the need to report the results of the audit to senior management, with recommendations and possible strategies for the implementation of the findings. This all needs considerable preparatory work, as well as follow-up time, in order for the findings to be accurate and comprehensive.

The environmental audit is more likely to be successful if the general ethos of the firm is supportive to the success of the programme and the welfare of the company. To this extent it is useful to consider some key characteristics which will provide the foundation for a successful programme. These factors will include:

- comprehensive support for the programme throughout management and particularly by senior management;
- acceptance that an auditing programme is for the benefit of management rather than a tool of individual performance assessment and is a function which, in time, will improve management effectiveness;
- recognition that useful information will come out of the audit programme and that information needs to be shared and acted upon;
- commitment to considering the comments and suggestions at each level of the organization's management and workforce and encouraging responsible participation;

- commitment to establishing systems for managing and following up on results;
- clearly defined roles, responsibilities and operational systems;
- recognition of an integrated approach where the auditing system is linked to a wider management system.

Much stress needs to be placed on the idea that audits should be seen by management as a positive help rather than a threatening or hostile exercise. The company must create a culture, led by its main board directors, which recognizes the positive benefits of the audit and sees it as good day-to-day management practice. Management must feel that they own the audit and, even though some external expertise may be used, it is an activity which is promoted and driven internally rather than externally (Callenbach *et al.*, 1993).

Fourteen specific activities which the business should consider are identified by the Hotel Catering and Institutional Management Association (HCIMA, 1993). These are simple and easily achievable, with little investment required:

1. *Communications.* Ensure appropriate communications channels exist to discuss environmental issues with guests, employees, suppliers, other businesses, tourist agencies, the local authority and environmental groups.
2. *Activities and products.* Ensure the company's main activities and products (accommodation and food) are ecologically sustainable and do the minimum amount of harm to the environment.
3. *Energy and water usage.* Devise written objectives for water and energy efficiency; their use should be monitored on a regular basis, and strategies for their reduction in use should be followed.
4. *Waste.* Develop policies for dealing with waste and the opportunities for either reuse or recycling. Food should not be wrapped in plastic.
5. *Materials and provision.* Assess whether supplies of raw materials (food, furnishings, decor, cleaning materials, etc.) can be sustained without damage to the environment. The objective should be to seek out less harmful materials where necessary and to buy products that are from sustainable sources or recycled material where practicable. Seek confirmation from suppliers on these issues.
6. *Purchasing.* List priorities for action, starting with those which will have the greatest environmental impact and/or cost saving. For those items where buying an environmentally sensitive alternative results in a cost premium, prepare a cost-benefit assessment.
7. *Suppliers.* Develop policies in all relevant departments for monitoring both suppliers and subcontractors and ensure that their environmental standards are as high as yours.
8. *Transport.* Where the transport of goods, staff and customers is concerned, develop plans designed to minimize the environmental impact.
9. *Site and buildings.* Prepare plans for enhancing the external attractiveness of the property and keeping the site as clean and tidy as possible.
10. *Health.* Develop plans which consider the health and well-being of staff and customers (such as healthy foods, non-smoking areas).
11. *Investment and banking.* Check pension, surplus capital investments and loan arrangements carefully to avoid involvement in businesses that have little or no care for the environment.
12. *Training.* Establish a means whereby an information exchange between staff can take place regarding green issues and new plans within the hotel. Try to get staff actively involved in local environmental initiatives.

13. *Guest participation*. Create ideas designed to encourage short-break, conference, dining and banqueting customers to be aware of green issues. This might include footnotes on menus, or inserts with the conference brochure or with bills.
14. *Sponsorship or product deals*. Consider giving financial or other support to environmental and community initiatives in the local area. It could well lead to increased popularity for the business through the positive public relations benefit.

ENVIRONMENTAL MANAGEMENT SYSTEMS

Management systems aim to pull a potentially disparate system into an integrated and organized one. An integrated system aimed at environmental improvement therefore covers not only management's responsibilities but the responsibility and tasks of every individual in an organization to improve its environmental performance. An integrated system which covers the totality of operations helps management and workers to see their place in the organization clearly, and to recognize clearly the interdependence of all aspects of an organization.

A management system should be developed and implemented for the purpose of accomplishing the objectives set out in an organization's environmental policy. Each element of the system will vary in importance from one type of activity to another and from one product or service to another. However, Welford (1992) points to some general characteristics which every management system needs to embody:

- The system needs to be comprehensive, covering all the activities of the organization. Gaps must not occur in the coverage of the system, since this is where errors and mistakes will occur and where accidents and environmental damage may occur. Every part of an organization must be involved in the implementation of the system, and every person must recognize his or her responsibility for putting the system into practice.
- The system and procedures within that system need therefore to be understandable to everybody involved. If roles and duties are not specified in an understandable way, they may not be carried out. This will usually involve documenting the system, training people fully in their tasks and responsibilities, and reviewing or auditing what is actually happening periodically. It requires that the system and all its elements are monitored, and that if the system breaks down it is rectified quickly.
- The system must be open to review, and there must be a commitment to a continuous cycle of improvement in the operations of the firm and in the quality of products or services it will produce. A continuous cycle of environmental improvement means that firms should aim for an ultimate goal of zero-negative impact on the environment.

An effective organizational structure of any management system is vital and should be clearly established within the organization. Clear lines of authority and communication channels need to be defined. The following are typical organizational aspects which need to be considered:

- All an organization's activities should be identified, defined and appropriately documented.

- General and specific responsibilities and authorities should be defined to particular groups and individuals, and where these are assigned to individuals somebody else should be made responsible in their absence.
- A management representative, preferably independent of other functions, should be appointed to resolve disputes and problems.
- The interface and co-ordination between different activities need to be clearly defined.
- Emphasis should be placed on the identification of actual or potential problems and risks, along with the initiation of remedial or preventive measures.

A central aspect of any management system will revolve around decision making. Senior management is ultimately responsible for making balanced judgements. But modern management methods highlight the need for flexibility and participation, and this usually involves decisions being taken further down the hierarchy. In arriving at decisions, the calibre and personal integrity of staff are of fundamental importance, and management needs to ensure that each person in the organization understands his or her role in decision making and the consequences of his or her actions. Decisions are often of a higher quality when they are participative, and systems need to avoid giving single individuals too much power. The quality of decisions is also closely linked to the availability of adequate education and training programmes for all employees, and such programmes need to be built into organization-wide systems.

CONCLUDING COMMENTS

The environmental revolution has been gathering momentum and speed since the 1960s and has developed rapidly in the 1980s and 1990s. Environmental considerations are likely to form an integral part of commercial normality, and indeed competitiveness, in the hospitality industry in the future. Definitions of business success are likely to include the assumption of zero-negative impact on the environment at the very least. A competitive advantage can be achieved not merely by keeping abreast of environmental developments but also by initiating change within an organization and responding with new, environmentally friendly products and services. Indeed, growing consumer awareness and environmental pressure groups are likely to ensure that firms which do not take action on the environmental front will lose market share.

Governments will increasingly seek to make the polluter pay, and the emphasis on sustainable tourism may mean that some branches of the industry may simply disappear. But ultimately, the success of environmental improvement will be determined largely by the responsiveness of business, and every organization operating in the tourism and hospitality industries has a responsibility to improve its own environmental performance.

Increasing environmental legislation at the European level will also act to stimulate research and technological innovation in the area of environmental improvement. For companies, the key to survival will be the development of environmentally sensitive products and services and a new emphasis on the responsibility of tourists. Companies looking to prosper in the 1990s are already rethinking their corporate policies ahead of legislation, which is inevitable. Using the tools of environmental auditing and introducing environmental management systems linked to environmental policies are the first practical steps which businesses in the industries can take. However, that is not the end of the imperative. In the future, successful businesses will develop their environmental strategies still further and be at the forefront of the search for more sustainable models of tourism development.

REFERENCES

Boers, H. and Bosch, M. (1994) *The Earth as a Holiday Resort: An Introduction to Tourism and the Environment*. Utrecht: Institute for Environmental Communication and Netherlands Institute of Tourism and Transport Studies.

Callenbach, E., Capra, F., Goldman, L., Lutz, R. and Marburg, S. (1993) *Eco-Management: The Elmwood Guide to Ecological Auditing and Sustainable Business*. San Francisco: Berrett-Koehler.

Fabrycky, W.J. and Blanchard, B.S. (1991) *Life Cycle Cost and Economic Analysis*. New York: Prentice-Hall.

Fleming, D. (1992) 'The Fifth EC Environmental Action Programme', *European Environment*, Special Supplement.

Hawkins, R. (1994) 'Towards Sustainability in the Travel and Tourism Industry', *European Environment*, **4(5)**, 3–7.

HCIMA (Hotel Catering and Institutional Management Association) (1993) 'Managing your Business in Harmony with the Environment', *Hotel Catering and Institutional Management Association*, February.

Keating, M. (1993) *The Earth Summit's Agenda for Change*. Geneva: Centre for Our Common Future.

Tourism Society (1991) *Sustainable Tourism: Development in Balance with the Environment*, Tourism Society Memorandum. London: Tourism Society.

Welford, R.J. (1992) 'Linking Quality and the Environment', *Business Strategy and the Environment*, **1(1)**, 16–24.

—— (1994) *Cases in Environmental Management and Business Strategy*. London: Pitman.

—— (1995) *Environmental Strategy and Sustainable Development: The Corporate Challenge for the 21st Century*. London: Routledge.

Welford, R.J. and Gouldson, A.P. (1993) *Environmental Management and Business Strategy*. London: Pitman.

Welford, R.J. and Prescott, C.E. (1996) *European Business: An Issue Based Approach*. 3rd edn. London: Pitman.

World Commission (World Commission on Environment and Development) (1987) *Our Common Future*. Oxford: Oxford University Press.

Zenisek, T.J. (1979) 'Corporate Social Responsibility: A Conceptualisation Based on Organisational Literature', *Academy of Management Review*, **4(2)**, 359–68.

TWELVE

Consumer policy

David Leslie

INTRODUCTION

The breadth and complexity of consumer policy precludes consideration of all aspects and attention to variations within member states, as is implied here by Schrivener (1993, p. 8): 'Following the removal of internal frontiers on 1 January 1993, the Community has set itself the aim of making the single market operate in a manner which is fully consistent with the interests of consumers.' Thus, the following discussion of consumer policy is not intended to be a detailed examination of the policies and associated regulations and practices relating to consumers, which are to be found in the various directorates of the Commission. Rather, the aim is to establish the general policy and direction of the Community and to review and examine initiatives, primarily in recent directives, directed towards the needs and interests of consumers of hospitality and tourism.

A substantial volume of European Union (EU) policies and regulation in one way or another directly impinges on, or has implications for, the consumer of hospitality and tourism services. Thus, the term 'tourists' is deliberately used here in order to aid both the focus and comprehensiveness of this discussion; tourists as consumers in this context serve well as the key link between such diverse services as air carriers and accommodation operators. Consideration is therefore not given to the plethora of regulations and guidelines, predominantly developed within each member state, relating to the specific operation of any one of the myriad of services involved in the supply of hospitality and tourism. A review of the Community's policy on consumers *and* these services serves to support this approach, due to the way in which attention is given to hospitality. In effect, this attention is on hotels and accommodation, clearly seen as an integral element of tourism, whilst other facets of hospitality services gain little attention. So in the interests of brevity 'tourism' and 'tourists' will by and large be used as generic terms, including hotel and accommodation operations and users as and where appropriate.

Although the EU for the majority of its life has given little direct attention to tourism, it has undoubtedly had an influence as a result of many initiatives in other areas (as is evident from discussion in the preceding chapters). Tourism, whilst not specifically mentioned in the Treaty of Rome of 1957, does come within that Treaty under the aegis of 'services'. This term is well used, accurately describing the myriad of business and operations that are considered, perhaps rather loosely, to constitute the 'tourism industry'. Tourism is thus perceived as a service and, as Davidson (1992, p. 25) expresses it, 'tourists are recipients of services'. Arguably, it is because of this perception that the EU until recently has had little direct impact on tourism *per se*; essentially, it: 'is located in an area of very weak common policy, that is the production and delivery of services' (Williams and Shaw, 1991, p. 265). This in part accounts for why little progress has been made in some areas of consumer policy, and why we can identify a recent rise in initiatives in this field.

The recognition and categorization of tourism under the umbrella of 'services' is a particularly important distinction, as it serves to account for the main thrust of the EU in that area of consumer policy directed at tourists. Overall, the main objective is to improve the operation, performance and quality of services (Commission, 1994a). This is underpinned by two key policy aims of the EU: to facilitate and encourage the free movement of people within the Community, and to improve consumer protection. In broad terms this comprises attention to the social security of tourists, tourist assistance, related insurance services and the protection of tourists' interests. These areas were identified specifically in the EU's initial guidelines on tourism, which cite in Article 2 the freedom of movement of persons and freedom to provide tourism services and transport systems, regulate development and protect the environment (Airey, 1983). Consumer protection directly relating to tourists comes under the umbrella of Directorate General XXIII Enterprise Policy, Distributive Trades, Tourism and Co-operatives (DGXXIII, created in 1989), along with small firms and crafts. It is noteworthy that prior to this it was located in DGVII, the transport section, which probably accounts for the apparent bias towards transport and related services; other directorates general (DGs) also highlight consumer protection, such as DGXI, which includes the environment and nuclear safety.

The Maastricht Treaty through Article 3a sought to reinforce consumer protection throughout the market. This aim is further reflected in other spheres: for example, Article 129 addresses public health; Article 130 indicates that whilst policy on the environment is directed towards preservation, protection and quality it also includes promotion of 'use'; Article 127a, with reference to Article 100a, considers consumer protection, specifically including attention to the health, safety and economic interests of consumers and the provision of adequate information (Woods *et al.*, 1993). These are recurrent themes across the whole spectrum of EU policy.

THE SIGNIFICANCE OF THE 'SERVICES' CATEGORIZATION

Key aspects of tourist services are that they are intangible, inseparable, heterogeneous, non-transferable, and invariably requested or reserved in advance. In essence the tourist is therefore purchasing something that has little or no material presence at the time of purchase. It cannot be seen, touched, or experienced except in terms of any information, promotional material, etc., provided. In order to consume the product, the tourist needs to go to the point(s) of supply. Moreover, the tourist in many cases will be purchasing a variety of services, such as a package holiday, which may include a range of providers and 'products' based in another country. Overall, the tourist is purchasing an experience: a domestic or overseas holiday, a short break, a weekend's golf. Although experience of what might be purchased may be nil, the tourist in most instances will have prior expectations of the quality of the services involved, which will include certain minimum standards. In the case of a general package holiday, these will include the quality of the airport, airline and associated services/facilities, means of transfer to accommodation, type of accommodation, contents of the bedroom, etc. These may be taken for granted on the basis of prior experience and knowledge gained from a range of sources, including the means of promotion and the services and destination(s) involved.

Overall, and to varying degrees, tourists trust that their expectations will be, at the least, reasonably met. Often what is the minimum standard for a service provided is based on the organization's policy, built up on past experience, influenced by the level of competition, and perhaps 'policed' by professional and trade associations, allied organizations and, as appropriate to the situation, legislation. However, the standard of the service and associated practices may vary according to the country and even within a country. Thus, when venturing into 'new territory' there is not necessarily any guarantee that any one service will meet the tourist's expectations or that what is actually presented meets the minimum standard. For example, tourists may select a hotel in a different member state on the basis of that country's hotel classification scheme, and discover too late that their interpretation of the scheme is in error. Alternatively, tourists may correctly believe on the basis of the information provided by the agent that they are reserving accommodation in a five-star hotel, only to find that they have been misled. In both cases, tourists do not have the opportunity to undertake a prior inspection and are thus dependent on the information provided. What happens if in the second case the hotel is in a different country, with an unfamiliar language, and it is clear that the misrepresentation lies with the owners of the accommodation? What can tourists do about this, what rights do they have, and what avenues of redress are open to the consumer?

From the foregoing we can identify three key areas:

- standards of services;
- quality and accuracy of information;
- consumer rights and facilitating the right of redress.

To these we can add safety and the protection of the consumers' economic/financial interests. It is these areas that we are most concerned with here.

OVERVIEW OF CONSUMER POLICY FOR TOURISM AND THE HOSPITALITY INDUSTRY

In any consideration of consumer policy in this field, account should be taken of the overall context within which it developed, in particular any aims of the Community which may serve as the bedrock for all initiatives relating to consumer policy. Thus, due note should be taken of the following key aim of the Community:

> to establish a core of legislation complemented and backed up by a number of information and education measures aimed at increasing awareness of how important the

'consumer' dimension is in the context of the single market.

(Commission, 1994a, p. 12)

Consumer policy can be considered to take two forms, namely legislation and guidance – the encouragement of what is considered to be best practice. This encompasses such diverse areas as trade descriptions, standards, promotion, etc., which attend to the safety, security and economic interests and rights of the tourists. Although it has been said (Mayhew, 1990) that it is not the intention of EU policy on tourism to regulate this sector, nevertheless it is in this area that the scale and potential influence of EU activity are greatest, due to the implications and/or domino effects of regulations and measures introduced in other areas. These may more often than not be the result of action introduced to promote competition, as in air transport – deregulation, the promotion of 'open skies', and policy on state subsidy to a national carrier. Others may be directed at health and safety, such as directives relating to the quality of bathing water. However, the areas with which we are most concerned are those directed at tourists. These are encompassed in the following broad aims:

- increasing the ease of crossing internal borders;
- improving the information available to, and for their protection as, consumers;
- promoting tourism as a basis for social integration – social tourism and 'Tourism for All' – and thus paying attention to access by the less abled.

Action on these policy aims has been on-going for some considerable time, though notably gathering momentum in recent years. The provision of accurate information and greater consumer protection for tourists is now considered to be a priority measure (Commission, 1994a). This encompasses a wide area, and includes attention to Computer reservation systems (CRS) in the code of conduct first presented in 1989, and to insurance issues (Council, 1992b). It is thus to the areas of information and protection to which we now turn our attention. To aid clarity these are considered under the following headings: consumer rights, information, safety, the Package Travel Directive, and the Timeshare Directive, and other measures and initiatives.

CONSUMER RIGHTS

The aim of the EU's policy on consumer rights[1] is summed up as follows:

> Helping and encouraging consumers and in particular, tourism consumers to be informed of their economic and legal rights and where and how they can access representation and consumer protection is an important role of the Community.
>
> (Commission, 1994a, p. 27)

The objective is twofold: first, for the tourist to benefit from a wider knowledge and availability of the increased range of services and competition resulting from the Single Market; second, and more pervasive, 'to heighten awareness of how the Community benefits its citizens directly and contributes to the improvement of their living standards' (Commission, 1993a, p. 8).

There is a wealth of communications, directives and measures which directly or indirectly support this aim. By and large the more specific of these – those primarily concerned with hotels/accommodation and travel – and their implications are examined in the following sections. The more pertinent general measures are as follows:

- The Council has drawn up a list of general criteria for contracts, and any non-negotiated contracts which are deemed by reference to this to be unfair are negated (Council, 1993).
- All products must meet certain minimum criteria as regards safety. Thus the Council has provided for a general safety measure applicable to all products in the absence of other relevant Community law (Council, 1992c).
- A proposal has been put forward covering liability for physical damage arising through the supply of services. This would be applicable to services which do not come within the scope of the EU's Package Directive. However, this is being reconsidered.
- Access to justice:[2] a potential problem for tourists is how they can obtain justice where appropriate for untoward events during their visit. In recognizing that this may be difficult, the Commission is keen 'to arrive at a situation where the consumer can seek redress whatever the circumstances, which is swift, effective and inexpensive' (Commission, 1993b, para. 1.6.6).
- Currently under consideration is attention to facilitating cross-border payments and the aim of reducing the costs involved.
- Other measures include directives on direct insurance (Council, 1992d) and airplane noise (for example, Council, 1989a).

INFORMATION

The Community Action Plan to Assist Tourism, implemented in January 1993, states as one of its aims 'to provide tourists with better information, a "Who's Who" of tourist organisations in Europe and including a manual on how to make Europe more accessible to the handicapped' (Council, 1992b, p. 26). The Council has initiated a pilot project setting up consumer information and advisory centres at a number of frontier regions, whose aim is to provide consumers with better information on the opportunities and problems of cross-border shopping, warranties, price comparisons and so forth. This serves to encourage visits to, and the purchase of goods offered in, other member states. This initiative reflects the wider context of the Commission's consumer policy, which overall is targeted at promoting consumers' physical health and safety, consumer information, representation and the protection of their economic and legal rights. This is evident in the Second Action Programme for Consumer Policy, adopted in July 1993 (Commission, 1993a), which comes under the sweeping title of 'Placing the Single Market at the Service of European Consumers'. The Community Action Plan to Assist Tourism 1993–95, under heading 4, identifies tourists as consumers and gives a number of projects to improve information for tourists about their rights or facilities.

Standardized system for information on hotels and accommodation

The potential for misunderstanding or even confusion on the part of the prospective tourist is considerable, given the different categories of accommodation and variations available within one country, let alone throughout the member states. The recommendation for a standardized information system for hotels was made in 1986 (Recommendation 86/665/EEC). It was proposed that there should be an official system of hotel guides, containing the information outlined in Table 12.1 for each entry, and that prices should be clearly displayed. The Council also launched a range of standardized symbols for hotel facilities (Figure 12.1).

Table 12.1 Proposed contents for standardized hotel information system

Name, address, telephone and telex numbers
Number of rooms and sanitary facilities
Opening period, including whether accessible at night
Maximum rate for a double room in the high season, including VAT
Distance from main transport terminal
Whether or not credit and payment cards are accepted
Information on languages available
The use of symbols

Note: This information should be presented in the host language and at least two other languages.
Source: Council (1986a)

The introduction of such a system with a correlating attention to standards may contribute to a general improvement in quality throughout the range. This would help address some of the evident weaknesses identified in a recent report (DNH, 1995).

Overall, progress in this area has been slow – notably so when one considers that a proposal was made by the European Parliament (EP) in 1984 to introduce a 'system of approval for tourist accommodation' (Downes, 1993, p. 70). More recently the Commission (1994a) has planned to review the matter, including the monitoring of the use of the symbols in different member states, and to consider what scope there is for development of the existing system.

SAFETY

The safety of tourists is a major plank of consumer policy. Given the potential for wide-ranging practices in attention to fire precautions, the Council (1986b) introduced the recommendation on 'fire safety in existing hotels'. Primarily this includes the provision of safe escape routes which will physically withstand a fire at least until evacuation of all personnel has been achieved. Other areas attended to are alarm systems, safety instructions, emergency fire-fighting equipment, the instruction and training of staff, and the need to limit the use of highly flammable materials.

The recommendation applies to all accommodation units of 20 rooms or more. As such it is not applicable to the majority of providers, which is possibly not in the best interests of consumers. Essentially, all efforts should be taken to reduce the risk of fire, prevent it spreading and to safeguard evacuation.

Progress in adoption and implementation of the recommendation is currently under review, and the undertaking of studies of fire safety in member states was put out to tender by the Commission at the end of January 1995. Even so, and given the importance of fire safety, especially in terms of consumer protection, it is perhaps surprising that the Community has not yet introduced appropriate legislation.

Building of historical or architectural interest

1

Green surroundings

2

Private car park

3

Indoor swimming pool

4

Outdoor swimming pool

5

Tennis courts at or near hotel

6

Sauna

7

Accessible at night

8

Telex available to clients

9

Lift

10

Meeting room available

11

Television room

12

Certain facilities for the disabled

13

Facilities for children

14

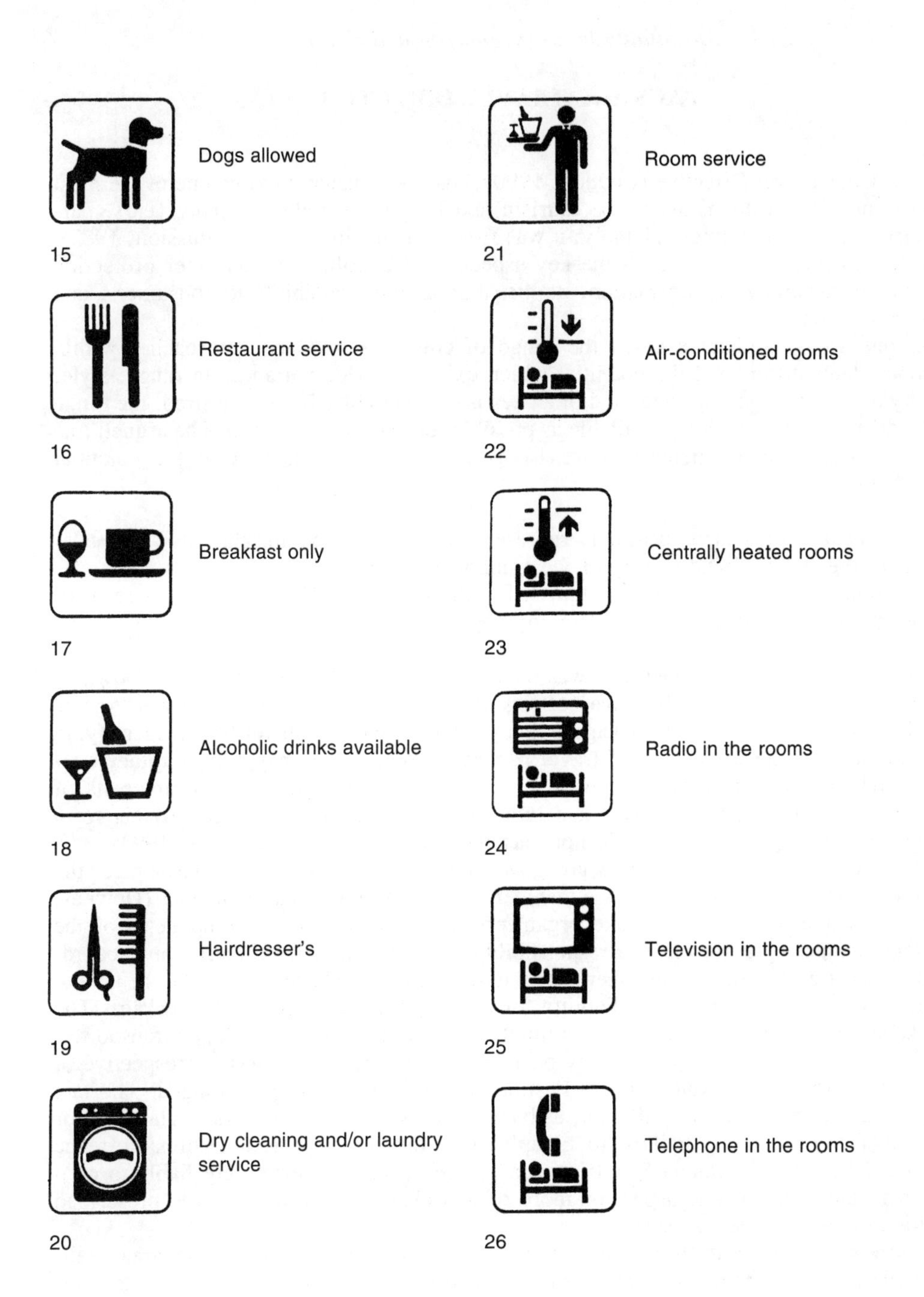

Figure 12.1 Standardized symbols for hotel facilities
Source: Council (1986a)

PACKAGE TRAVEL DIRECTIVE

The Package Travel Directive (Council, 1990b) may be considered to be one of the most significant EU developments in the tourism and hospitality field for many years, particularly for the travel trade. Notably, it was first signalled in 1982 (Commission, 1982). Manifest in this directive are all the key aspects of EU policy on consumer protection in tourism: accuracy of information, its distribution and availability to consumers, and their protection.

As one would anticipate given the range of countries involved, approaches within member states differ, and the potential which exists for wide variances in range, style, quality of information, packages and practices is considerable. If, as is desired, the range of products is to be as widely available as possible, harmonization can thus be argued for.

A potential further barrier to purchase is confidence on the part of the potential tourists that:

- the package presented accurately represents what is offered and they feel assured as to the standard and quality of the component elements;
- if something is remiss then the tourist has the right of redress, and that there is an easily accessed system to facilitate any appropriate action.

Arguably, it is this latter aspect that was the driving force behind the directive (Downes, 1993). In some ways the directive reflects the Association of British Travel Agents (ABTA) code of practice on package holidays, but it goes much further in identifying the liabilities of the organizers of travel packages. Whilst this may appear rather one-sided and predominantly biased towards consumers, it does attend to the interests of organizers, who hitherto may have had little protection against misfortune arising from a supplier's failings that they could not reasonably have foreseen (Downes, 1993).

The directive is designed not as a law governing package travel, which harmonizes the principles and practices evident in the member states, but rather as a set of rules (Downes, 1993). Essentially it seeks to make organizers legally liable for all components of the package; for example, they have a responsibility for their suppliers. Hitherto, and according to the varied practices in member states, tour operators and agents tended to be able to avoid contractual obligations and liability for other services included in the package. The 'package' itself may only have come within the rules on liability if it included transport.

Further, the directive applies to any package which meets the criteria, irrespective of the purpose (business or pleasure) or destination, as long as it is prearranged. The fact that it includes business is significant, as business persons are not generally classified or defined as 'consumers'. Failure to comply with the directive is a criminal offence (enforced by Trading Standards Officers in the UK), and organizers are liable to civil action in the event of one aspect or more of a package failing to meet the prescribed details or a reasonable standard.

Before we move on to discuss major elements of the directive, one other area needs to be clarified. The regulations apply to 'organizers', a term used in preference to 'tour operators' or 'travel agents'. Thus potentially anyone who organizes a package as defined within the directive is liable to come within the terms of the regulations. There are some exceptions; for example, those who only occasionally arrange packages are exempt, though this is subject to how 'occasional' is interpreted (BTA/ETB, 1993). What then is 'a package'? According to Article 2, it is:

> a pre-arranged combination of at least two of the following components, provided the

service covers a period of at least 24 hours or involves a night away from home:
- transport;
- accommodation;
- other tourist services not ancillary to transport or accommodation and accounting for a significant proportion of the package. [This is a key element for hoteliers and other accommodation operators.]

The package must be prearranged and offered for sale at an inclusive price (though separate billing of the components would not avoid the provisions: Downes, 1993). It is noteworthy that:

> the fact that a combination is arranged at the request of the consumer and in accordance with his specific instructions (whether modified or not) shall not of itself cause it to be treated as other than prearranged. (DTI, 1992)

We now turn our attention to the other key Articles of the directive.[3]

Article 3

This Article covers the provision of information on packages, such as brochures and advertising, though, notably, it is not actually a requirement to produce these. Those brochures that are produced should be accurate and comprehensive, and include the details presented in Table 12.2.

Table 12.2 Information brochures must contain

The destination and the means, characteristics and categories of transport used
The type of accommodation, its location, category or degree of comfort, its main features, and its approval and tourist classification under the rules of the member state concerned
The meal plan
The itinerary
General information on passport and visa requirements for nationals of the member state or states concerned, and of health formalities required for the journey and stay
Either the monetary amount or the percentage of the price which is to be paid on account, and the timetable for payment of the balance
Whether a minimum number of persons is required for the package to take place and, if so, the deadline for informing the consumer in the event of cancellation

Source: Downes (1993).

Compliance with this provision is not without problems, especially given the lead time between preparation and actual consumption, as suggested in the following extract:

> For some unknown reason the Commission has decided that a package holiday can work in the same way as, for example, a washing machine. This is a serious error and, if not corrected, will place an impossibly onerous burden on the tour operator. A tour operator sells a dream and, no matter how well or how factually described, the concept of a holiday is a product of the mind of the holidaymaker and will thus be differently perceived by each and every client. Issues such as how quiet a location is, how the food should taste, what constitutes luxury etc. are subjective opinions formed by the person's background, race and country of residence. To set minimum standards for a washing machine is child's play by comparison. (AITO, 1988)

Under this Article, agents may be liable if they provide a customer with an organizer's brochure or other promotional material which turns out to be inaccurate. However, material published prior to 1993 does not have to comply (see Regulation 15: BTA/ETB, 1993), though this may no longer be a valid defence.

Article 4

Article 4 covers the package travel contract. The consumer must be provided with specific information relating to passport and visa regulations (including the potential time required to obtain these), health formalities and insurance options before the contract is agreed. Tour operators may expect this to be carried out by their agent – in other words, it does not have to be in the brochure. The contract must also contain the information presented in Table 12.3, though obviously some of these points are not applicable to all packages and thus would not necessarily be included.

Table 12.3 Information which must be included in the contract

The travel destination(s) and, where periods of stay are involved, the relevant periods with dates
The means, characteristics and categories of transport used, the dates and points of departure and return
Where the package includes accommodation, its location, category, degree of comfort, main features, and compliance with the rules of the host member state concerned
The meal plan
Whether a minimum number of persons is required for the package to take place, and the deadline for informing the consumer in the event of cancellation
The itinerary
Visits, excursions and other services which are included in the total price of the package
The name and address of the organizer, the retailer and the insurer if appropriate
Details of the price, surcharge and taxes, fees, etc., not included in the price
The payment schedule and the means of payment
Special requirements which the consumer has communicated to the organizer or retailer when making the booking and which both have accepted
Periods within which the consumer must make any complaints concerning failure to perform or improper performance of the contract

Note: These terms must be set out in writing 'or such other form as is comprehensible and accessible to the consumer'. They must be communicated to the consumer before the contract is concluded and the consumer must be given a copy.

Source: Downes (1993).

The Article also allows for the possibility of a customer transferring a package to someone else if for some reason he or she is prevented from proceeding with the package, and provided reasonable notice of transfer is given to the organizer. It is understood that 'prevented' means by a valid cause – one which probably is outside the customer's control.

Article 5

This is a key Article which addresses the question of liability and just who is liable – basically the organizer. However, in the case of packages designed by tour operators and/or retailed or designed by travel agents, member states can define which one of these parties is liable. In the UK, the decision was taken to make the tour operator liable, and notably 'any clause by which the tour operator may seek to exclude his own, the travel agent's or third party's liability is void and ineffective' (Downes, 1993, p. 80). Thus the onus is on the tour operator to ensure that those services included are delivered in the appropriate manner and of expected standard, etc. If a tour operator is not involved, whoever organized the package is liable. Thus, organizers are liable for any failure on their own part or that of any supplier involved in the delivery of the package. This includes events outside the control of the organizer. A key question in establishing such liability is whether the organizer or supplier could reasonably have foreseen what might have happened. This is clearly open to interpretation and debate. The following examples illustrate the potential range of the liability involved:

- If an agent organizes a trip to the USA which includes air travel and hotel accommodation, and whilst at the hotel the client suffers injury in an accident caused by lack of due care on the part of the hotel, the agent is potentially liable.
- Should a tourist find himself or herself in a situation which could be described as unsuitable, contrary to reasonable expectation and thus contributory to an unsatisfactory experience, the organizer is liable. For example, a German couple found themselves in the company of the Swiss Union of the Friends of Folk Music throughout their Caribbean Cruise. This group, which included a brass band, accounted for approximately 85 per cent of the passengers and spent much of their time singing and playing musical instruments. The Frankfurt District Court found that the situation was not what a holiday cruise taker might reasonably expect, and ordered the package organizer to refund 30 per cent of the payment.
- If a fire breaks out in the accommodation and it is established that the supplier was negligent, the organizer will be liable.
- Should an accommodation operator fail to take reasonable precautions to secure the safety of the guests, for instance from assault, the organizer may be liable. For example, tourists in some accommodation localities might be prone to attention from persons of nefarious intent. If this were known and the manager took no steps to ensure such persons did not gain access to the premises and grounds, the organizer would be liable.
- If hoteliers offer a special activity weekend, or for that matter the traditional Christmas break package, they are liable if any element of the predetermined and qualified activities is not available or of lower standard than considered reasonable. The scope is potentially wide.
- If an hotel offers, as part of a prearranged package, guaranteed use of a range of defined leisure facilities within the hotel leisure centre during the guest's stay, and a number of these facilities are in fact not available, the hotel is liable. If the reason for their non-availability was that they were actually missing, the hotel would also be liable to prosecution.
- If at an in-house conference delegates find that an advertised service is not available, albeit due to the fault of the supplier – a round of golf every afternoon at the local course, say – the hotel is liable if it organized the conference. If the conference was organized by someone not connected with the hotel, the organizer could be liable.

Overall, and according to the BTA/ETB's guidelines (1993), the way to establish whether or not one is presenting a package is for the accommodation operator to ask 'Is the inclusion of the activity the main reason for the customer choosing to purchase the product?' If the answer is yes, then it would be safe to assume the package comes within the jurisdiction of the directive. A further noteworthy point is that the directive does allow the possibility for organizers to limit the level of damages that might be payable in compensation.

If the experience of similar regulations governing liability of organizers in Germany (see Downes, 1993) is anything to go by, there is clear potential for an initial flurry of complaints leading to both criminal and civil proceedings as a result of the implementation of this directive.[4] Once organizers have become well practised in its application to the development and organization of packages and the component parts, such claims are likely to decline. This is thus to the overall benefit of both tourists and organizers.

Finally, given the earlier attention to this matter, the Commission in formulating the directive rejected a proposal for a uniform classification system for tourist accommodation.

Article 7

This is concerned with the security of payments in advance on the part of customers. First, organizers must secure all prepayments; these must be placed in a situation that divorces them from being considered as assets. Secondly, organizers must have sufficient funds available for the repatriation of clients should the company collapse; in a number of situations this may be covered by the bonding arrangements already in existence, created as part of self-regulation by a professional agency such as ABTA. It should, though, be noted that not all operators within a certain sector are necessarily members of such a body. Such schemes may only be applicable to packages involving air travel; hence the need for arrangements to cover other types of package and contingency.

Organizers or retailers such as travel agents are to advise customers prior to contractual agreement of what arrangements have been made to protect any prepayments. This regulation has met with problems, and was under review at the request of the European Commission's Consumer Policy Service in 1994. The outcome is expected in early 1996.

TIMESHARE DIRECTIVE

The Timeshare Directive[5] was approved in the early autumn of 1994 by the Council. It primarily relates to timeshare contracts, and reflects the practice evident in other fields of allowing a cooling-off period of 10 days after a contract has been signed. Failure on the part of the company to identify all elements of the contract entitles the consumer to cancel the agreement. This may be of no more than passing interest to UK operators, given that the Timeshare Act of 1992 established, amongst other regulations, a 14-day cooling-off period. However, the same principles of good practice are not necessarily evident in other countries.

OTHER MEASURES AND INITIATIVES

Air travel

Flight reservations

The practice of over-booking seats and the subsequent possibility of 'bumping' ticket holders onto the next flight in the event of all persons with reservations turning up is to be discouraged (for example, Council, 1989b). Passengers so affected will be entitled to compensation, based on a sliding scale according to length of delay before the flight actually taken (Council, 1991a).

Baggage

With attention to furthering tourists' rights and facilitating travel within the Community, measures have been introduced to abolish controls and formalities on passenger baggage taken on intra-Community flights (Council, 1991b).

Competition

The Commission has been attentive to the advantages to consumers of increasing competition between airlines, aiming at deregulation and the promotion of 'open skies'. In July 1992, the Commission adopted a threefold package to liberalize what in effect was a closed market. Arguably, a more competitive market will lead to lower fares and greater flexibility. However, currently contributing to avoiding competition is the potential for different carriers to arrange mutual agreements, thereby reducing competition on agreed routes. This may not be in the interests of consumers, or for that matter any one country, in terms of their own planning. Certainly, it is contrary in spirit to the aims of the Commission, which have recently been reviewed (Commission, 1994b).

Sea and road transport have also been affected by measures to promote competition, namely allowing non-residents to enter these markets in other member states. Perhaps of passing interest is the removal of the applicability of Excise Duty to fuel in conventional tanks in the destination country (Council, 1992d).

Duty-free goods

The traditional activity of purchasing products with reduced excise duty, most commonly spirits and cigarettes, is perhaps one of the anomalies of the Single Market, particularly since the removal of tax frontiers (Council, 1992d). The high levels of revenue generated through the sale of duty-free goods contribute substantially to the overall profits of cross-border transport operators. The Community appears to consider this facility as rather an anachronism and would like to see it discontinued. However, in recognition of the contribution of these sales to operators' income, the practice is to be phased out by 1999. The traditional standard allowances for the most popular goods have not been relaxed, and the onus is on the duty-free outlets to apply the established limits.

Consumers potentially lose on two counts. First, they lose the opportunity to purchase (albeit limited) popular goods at below home-country prices. Second, as these sales potentially subsidize other areas of operations, it is probable that the loss of this revenue will lead to increases in passenger fares. However, there is a strong lobby in support of the continuance of the practice, which has led to the creation of the European Travel Research Foundation, launched officially in early 1995 and well supported by the organizations primarily involved (GJW, 1994).

Distance selling

This directive relates to those services or goods which are bought when the two parties involved – consumer and seller – are not both present face to face. Article 8 states 'no payment may be required by the consumer before delivery of the product or performance of the service'. If, for instance, a tour operator deals directly with a client at a distance, clearly this comes within the directive. However, if the client deals directly with an agent – that is, the principal's representative – this is not distance selling. Hoteliers may therefore not be allowed to request payments in advance, for example for Christmas breaks, when these are arranged directly with consumers but not in person. But if the hoteliers choose to promote such breaks through, say, travel agents, the directive apparently does not apply.

In the directive's original form, tourism services were excluded on the basis that they are 'services with a reservation attached'. The services identified were transport, accommodation, catering and entertainment. But in mid-1993 an amendment led to the inclusion of these services.

This directive has generated substantial concern over the implications of its implementation. It is potentially damaging for the sector, in that it implies that tourists could pay for their holiday after the event.

> The practical implications of this are enormous, and not just for travel package organizers. Accommodation operators could not insist on deposits for bookings; restaurants would not be able to require prepayments for functions; transport operators could not insist on payment until the journey is completed – unless, of course, the reservations were made on a face-to-face basis with the supplier. (Carey, 1993, p. 4)

However, this measure is gaining substantial support elsewhere in the EU (Anon., 1994b). The debate has continued, and it is understood in some quarters that these services are to be exempted from Articles 7–12; that is, a second amendment has been presented to exclude 'services with reservation' and designed to include exemption for credit cards (EIU, 1994).

VAT

This is a particularly complicated area, as manifest for example in Directive 77/388/EEC, which addresses VAT arrangements applicable to passenger transport, or in the debate on the applicability of VAT to tour operators. The latter point is not helped by the fact that VAT is not a consideration for organizers based outside the EU and thus, arguably, they have a competitive advantage.

However, the Commission appears keen to move towards harmonizing VAT throughout the market. The implications of this for the consumer will vary according to country. It could lead to increased transport and package-holiday costs due to VAT being applied on publications and promotional material. Transport appears to be one of the services where VAT is likely to be harmonized, and at rates between 4 per cent and 6 per cent. In the absence of such harmonization, practice within member states will continue to vary. For example, since April 1995 in the UK, VAT is applicable to transport which is considered as 'not going anywhere', so 'non-stop' round trips such as helicopter sightseeing trips, monorails in theme parks, or small-scale trains for children (as found in some parks) will become subject to VAT. Harmonization of VAT on tourist services throughout the EU could potentially lead to substantial reductions in the UK, due to its predominantly higher rates in most areas (Anon., 1994a). This outcome would be especially welcomed by hoteliers, who have been lobbying for it, but it appears to be a highly unlikely one. Significantly, it was ruled out by Viscount Astor (Business Travel World, 1995). Whilst the lobbying for change continues there appears little chance of any change, certainly under the present government, despite strong pressure from the BTA supported by a substantive report on the potential benefits of VAT harmonization (Touche Ross, 1996). This is evident from the Chancellor of the Exchequer's response to this question in the House of Commons on 16 May 1996 (Hansard) that the Government wish to keep the VAT system as simple as possible and thus with no variable rates.

CONCLUDING COMMENTS

The main thrust of EU policy on consumers for hospitality and tourism services is focused on the tourist and the key elements of transport and accommodation. This evidences the wider aim of seeking to promote the Single Market and the flow of tourists between member states. The main means to further this is a combination of attention to the provision and dissemination of accurate information with enhancement of consumer rights and ease of redress should something be wrong. More broadly, there are aims to promote the quality and availability of products and open competition. This has led to an array of measures including regulations which, as an examination of various approaches to regulation adopted by member states in these areas reveals, are invariably a compromise between extremes. Essentially, the EU takes a middle road. It should, though, be recognized that in areas where a member state has more stringent regulations, the directives are not to be taken as a dilution of these.

Whilst the policies identified help towards creating a 'level playing field' in terms of the products and suppliers of the member states, it may be argued that this will not significantly influence tourist flows, at least in the medium term. Further, these policies may have little impact on the role of key players in actual resort choice - that is, on the dominant role in the holiday market of intermediaries and tour operators.[6] Also, the measures introduced to improve the content and accuracy of information presented in brochures will not counteract the way such information is presented and used to influence consumer choice.

The steps that have been taken, perhaps most notably the Package Travel Directive, are certainly to the benefit of consumers, logically leading to the general enhancement of packages and professionalism on the part of all suppliers. What is significant, though, given the orientation to the protection of consumers, is the continuing absence of definitive action by the Community on classification schemes and the introduction of the proposed standardized information system for accommodation, and on fire safety.

Overall, there have been a number of major recent initiatives in consumer policy in this area in terms of direct action. Additionally, other directorates are also furthering the interests and needs of consumers and indirectly contributing to supporting consumers of hospitality and tourism services. The EU is thus becoming more pervasive in this field, and this will gradually increase as areas which hitherto have demanded greater attention become more settled. Evidence supporting such perceptions is not difficult to find: witness the expansion of activity since the formation of DGXXIII.

Finally, the evident orientation to encouraging tourist movements and expenditure reflects the wider aim of promoting the dispersal of 'wealth' from one area to another. This objective is seen to be being promoted through the increased attention given to consumer protection and the dissemination of information. There are indicators that this is also serving another, more subtle and overarching purpose of the Commission's, namely to encourage the direct support of consumers for the EU by demonstrating and actioning measures perceived to be in their direct interests over and above the approach of a member state.

NOTES

1. For a more detailed overall view on the Commission's attitudes towards, and aims for, consumer rights, see Commission (1993c).
2. For further discussion on access to justice, see Commission (1994c).
3. For a more detailed examination of the directive's Articles and particularly the legal implications, see Downes (1993). For interpretation and implementation in the UK, see BTA/ETB (1993).
4. For a well-informed and entertaining analysis of the potential for complaints and proceedings against organizers, see Nightingale and Stewart (1993).
5. For a detailed discussion of the role of the Timeshare Directive and recent developments, see RCI (1993).
6. For discussion of this area, see Goodall and Bergsma (1991).

REFERENCES

Airey, D. (1983) 'European Government Approaches to Tourism', *Management*, **2(3)**, 234–44.

AITO (Association of Independent Tour Operators) (1988) *Memorandum to the European Communities Committee (Sub-committee E) of the House of Lords*. Association of Independent Tour Operators. 19 July

Anon. (1994a) 'Touche Ross to Advise on Reducing VAT', *Tourism Marketplace*, **98**, 4–5.

Anon. (1994b) Quoted in 'No Pre-pay Proposal Gains Euro Ground', *Tourism Marketplace*, **98**, 6–7.

BTA/ETB (British Tourist Authority/English Tourist Board) (1993) *EC Package Travel Directive: Explanatory Notes for the Tourism Industry*. London: BTA/ETB in association with the Wales Tourist Board and Scottish Tourist Board.

Business Travel World (1995) *Briefing*, EMAP Response, **4**.

Carey, R. (1993) Quoted in 'EC Set to Launch Another Grenade', *Tourism Marketplace*, **96**, 4–5.

Commission (Commission of the European Communities) (1982) *A Community Policy on Tourism: Initial Guidelines*, COM (82) Supplement 4/82. Luxembourg.

—— (1993a) *Second Action Programme for Consumer Policy*, COM (93) 509 Final.

—— (1993b) *Access of Consumers to Justice and the Settlement of Consumer Disputes in the Single Market*, COM (93) 576.

—— (1993c) *Consumer Rights in the Single Market*. Brussels: ECSC–EEC–EAEC.

—— (1994a) *Report from the Commission to the Council, the European Parliament and the Economic and Social Committee on Community Measures Affecting Tourism*, COM (94) 74 Final.

—— (1994b) *Communication from the Commission: The Way Forward for Civil Aviation in Europe*, COM (94) 218 Final.

—— (1994c) *Access of Consumers to Justice,* Background Report ISEC/B4/94.

Council (Council of the European Communities) (1986a) 'Recommendation 86/665/EEC', *Official Journal*, L 384/54 31.12.1986.

—— (1986b) 'Recommendation 86/666/EEC', *Official Journal*, L 384/60 31.12.1986.

—— (1989a) 'Directive 89/629/EEC of 04.12.1989', *Official Journal*, L 363 13.12.1989.

—— (1989b) 'Regulation (EEC) No 2299/89 of 24.07.1989: Code of Conduct for Computerised Reservation Systems', *Official Journal*, L 220 29.07.1989.

—— (1990a) 'Regulation (EEC) No. 2349/90 of 24.07.1990', *Official Journal*, L 220 29.07.1990.

—— (1990b) 'Council Directive 90/314/EEC', *Official Journal*, L 158/59 23.06.1990.

—— (1991a) 'Regulation (EEC) No 295/91 on Establishing Common Rules for a Denied Boarding Compensation System in Scheduled Air Transport', *Official Journal*, L 36 08.02.1991.

—— (1991b) 'Regulation (EEC) 3925/91', *Official Journal*, L 374 31.12.1991, and 'Regulation (EEC) 1832/92', *Official Journal*, L 185 06.07.1992.

—— (1992a) 'Directive 92/49/EEC of 18.06.1989', *Official Journal*, L 228 11.08.1992.

—— (1992b) 'Second Community Three Year Action Plan 1993–1995', *Official Journal*, L 231 13.08.1992.

—— (1992c) 'Council Directive 92/95/EEC adopted 29 June 1992', *Official Journal*, L 228/24 11.08.1992.

—— (1992d) 'Directive 92/12/EEC 25.02.1992', *Official Journal*, L 76 23.03.1992.

—— (1993) 'Council Directive 93/13/EEC', *Official Journal*, L 95/29 21.04.1993.

Davidson, R. (1992) *Tourism in Europe*. London: Pitman.

DNH (Department of National Heritage) (1995) *Tourism: Competing with the Best*. London: HMSO.

Downes, J.J. (1993) 'Legal Liabilities and the Travel Trade: The EC Package Travel Directive Part II. Occasional Studies', *Travel and Tourism Analyst*, 69–87.

DTI (Department of Trade and Industry) (1992) *Implementation of EC Directive on Package Travel, Package Holidays and Package Tours (Articles 1–6). Consultation Document*. London: Department of Trade and Industry.

EIU (Economic Intelligence Unit) (1994) 'Travel Industry Monitor', *Travel and Tourism Analyst*, **52**, 23.

Garland, S. (1994) *EU Matters*, Briefing Notes produced by the Policy Department of the BTA/ETB. 22 December.

GJW (1994) *Report on Developments in the EU for the British Tourist Authority*, October–November. GJW Europe.

Goodall, B. and Bergsma, J.R. (1991) 'Tour Operators' Strategies: A Cross-Country Comparison' in Sinclair, M.T. and Stabler, M.J. (eds) *The Tourism Industry: An International Analysis*. CAB International.

Mayhew, A. (1990) 'Europe in the 1990s', *Tourism Industry 1990/1991*, 4–5. (NB: At the time of writing this article Mayhew was Deputy Director General of DGXXIII.)

Nightingale, L. and Stewart, P. (1993) *The Law of the Jungle*. London: Field Fisher Waterhouse Solicitors.

RCI (1993) 'Timeshare: The New Force in Tourism', Course Notes, 2nd edition. RCI Europe.

Schrivener, C. (1993) Member of the European Commission quoted in *Consumer Rights in the Single Market*. Brussels: Commission of the European Communities ECSC–EEC–EAEC.

Touche Ross (1996) *The Economic Effects of Changing VAT Rates on the British Tourism and Leisure Industry*. Report prepared for the BTA/VAT Working Group. London: Touche Ross & Co.

Williams, A.M. and Shaw, G. (1991) *Tourism and Economic Development: Western European Approaches*, 2nd edition. London: Belhaven Press.

Woods, T., Bird, L. and Williams, M. (1993) *European Studies*. London: Hodder and Stoughton.

THIRTEEN

Food safety policy

Richard North

INTRODUCTION

Although the future of UK food safety policy is bound up with the movement towards European integration, the country's national approach to food safety must be appreciated first. Without this background it is not possible to understand the full flavour of the current situation.

FOOD SAFETY POLICY IN THE UK

The best expression of UK government policy on food safety in the UK, as it affects the hospitality or any other food industry sector, is to be found in the White Paper on food safety (MAFF, 1989). Here the government claims that it is determined 'to encourage the widest availability of wholesome, attractive foods throughout the country. While encouraging freedom of choice, the Government gives the highest priority to the safety of the consumer' (p. 1). From this it can be deduced that the overt thrust of policy was (and is) directed towards ensuring consumer safety, although this absolute priority is tempered by the need to maintain freedom of choice. This policy has been given expression in a package of measures, including research, advice, legislation, monitoring and surveillance, and enforcement.

In pursuit of its policy objectives, the government claims to:

- carry out or commission research to provide a 'sound, up-to-date understanding of food safety';
- obtain expert advice to 'decide on action in the light of scientific, technical and medical evidence';
- promulgate legislative standards which 'lay down what the consumer has a right to expect' and 'how those standards are to be met', and 'impose penalties when they are not'.

In terms of monitoring and surveillance, the government commits itself to taking samples of food and packaging materials for examination and testing; monitoring food composition and its safety; and assessing changes and identifying necessary action. However – and this is especially relevant in respect of the current emphasis on risk assessment – the government has done little to improve the investigation of food-poisoning incidents, or the evaluation and widespread reporting of defects in food operations which might have given rise to food poisoning, so assisting the development of risk-based control models.

The importance of food-poisoning outbreak data in developing both local and national food safety policies cannot be over-emphasized. This is real data on which specific control models can be based, reflecting real risks, as opposed to models based on the theoretical appreciation of hazards. In any food-service operation, hazards are numerous, and not always easily identified or recognized. Thus, the lessons from failures, in a real-life situation which gave rise to actual illness, can give operators the best indications as to where to allocate their control measures and with what degree of priority, bearing in mind that resources are always limited.

According to Henry Petroski (cited in Wildavsky, 1988, p. 83), the continual study of failure is an important element in the maintenance of safety. Although written in an engineering context, his words have great relevance to the hospitality industry:

> I believe the concept of failure – mechanical and structural failure in the context of this discussion – is central to understanding engineering, for engineering design has as its first and foremost objective the obviation of failure. Thus the colossal disasters that do occur ... are ultimately failures of design, but the lessons learned from those disasters can do more to advance engineering knowledge than all the successful machines and structures in the world. Failures in turn lead to safety margins and, hence, new periods of success. To understand what engineering is and what engineers do is to understand how failures happen and how they can contribute more than successes to advance technology.

The government, in implementing its food safety policy strategies, has not recognized the value of this argument. As long as it seeks to maintain a high standard of food safety by the use of risk-assessment techniques, the lack of any initiative to maximize the flow of data on real risks will continue to represent a major failure of policy.

The only significant contribution made in this respect – largely as a result of prolonged and sustained criticisms from this author – has been the publication of revised guidelines on the management of outbreaks of foodborne illness (DH, 1994a). However, the content of the guidelines promotes methodology and techniques which gave rise to significant errors in reporting during 1988–92 (North, 1995), and they are unlikely to improve the flow of usable information, even if adopted. Moreover, there is no support for any training initiatives to promote better procedures.

As to the enforcement of food-safety legislation – another arm of policy – the government has committed itself to strengthening the powers of enforcement agencies, the functioning of which it acknowledges requires trained, expert enforcement officers, and practical and effective enforcement powers. In practice, this has amounted to the Department of Health (DH) launching a series of road-shows to introduce the Food Safety Act to environmental health officers. Government has done nothing specific to improve the skills or training of enforcement officers, even though the demands on their skills and expertise will increase as new legislation is introduced.

Nevertheless, some local authorities and professional groups within the Institute of

Environmental Health have undertaken audits of their own inspection procedures, and intend – on a voluntary basis – to continue monitoring their own performances, with a view to improving their effectiveness. The Institute itself has launched an on-going 'professional development' scheme, requiring all its members to take further and continued training, in which food safety matters are included.

THE FOOD SAFETY ACT 1990

The main plank of government policy is the Food Safety Act 1990, which applies from farm to plate and includes the hospitality industry. This Act owes its existence to the food scares of the late 1980s, and was introduced despite a government commitment not to introduce new legislation which increased the burdens of business (*Environmental Health News*, 23 September 1988). Nevertheless, the bulk of the requirements have not differed greatly from laws dating back to 1938.

Key additions have been:

- powers to register and license food premises (only the former have been taken up);
- stronger controls over unfit and contaminated foods;
- strengthened enforcement procedures, particularly in respect of closure of food premises;
- a provision for formal 'improvement notices' (see below);
- new powers to make regulations, especially those which implement European Union (EU) law as part of the single market programme.

One other addition has been the introduction of a 'due diligence' defence. This provides, in proceedings taken under the Act (specifically, the sale of food not complying with food safety requirements; food which is not of the nature, substance or quality of food; and falsely described food), a general defence to the owner or operator of food premises, providing all reasonable precautions have been taken and 'due diligence' has been exercised.

This concept has been much abused, in that it has been promoted by some industry pundits – with the tacit complicity of some regulatory authorities – as being mandatory. It is implied that operations *must* show due diligence, to which effect certain procedures not required by law are imposed simply to enable evidence to be submitted, in the case of failure, which might constitute a defence against prosecution. It must be recalled that such compulsion was not part of government policy and that 'due diligence' remains a voluntary option, to be invoked or not at the discretion of an operator in the event that he or she is threatened with prosecution. There is no *requirement* to show 'due diligence', and the costs of developing systems which will stand up in court – where the defence is ultimately tested – may well outweigh any benefits which might accrue in the rare event of a prosecution being threatened under the Food Safety Act. (The defence, of course, is not available in prosecutions under the general food hygiene regulations, to which hospitality operators are more frequently exposed.)

Of the mainstream additions, the 'improvement notice' provisions represented an acknowledgement of custom and practice in local authority environmental health departments, which enforce the legislation. Prior to the 1990 Act, it had been the practice to issue letters or 'informal notices' to proprietors of food operations, advising them of deficiencies in their operations, loosely based on legislative requirements. These 'notices' had no statutory basis or authority, but were nevertheless a useful device for promoting improved compliance, where inspecting officers judged that prosecution was not appropriate.

Augmenting the 1990 Act, the government issued a series of statutory codes of practice, applicable to enforcement officers. They required, amongst other things, a distinction to be made between legal requirements and those matters which - although they might be good practice - were not legally necessary. This heralded the pursuit of a more rational approach towards food safety enforcement. It was embodied in government policy, in a drive towards reducing the burden on businesses, as part of the then prime minister's deregulation initiative (a theme promoted by the European Commission - see Chapter 8).

These codes, issued as they were under the aegis of the Food Safety Act 1990, represented a development in government policy towards achieving greater consistency in law enforcement. Until the arrival of the Act, any codes of practice issued by the government were directed at firms in the food industry. It was therefore novel for the law enforcement agencies to be addressed in this way; and while the codes are not mandatory, they are a useful check on the excesses of enforcement officers, and can be used to effect by hospitality business operators to ensure that excessive demands are not made on them.

Another important aspect of the codes of practice was to introduce specific guidance on the enforcement procedures to be followed, and guidelines on such matters as the frequency of inspections relative to high- and low-risk foods. Frequency of inspection was no longer left entirely to the discretion of individual authorities, but founded on a basic form of risk assessment (although this has had its problems).

This rigid code tends to handicap the development of effective enforcement by tying local authority enforcement officers to a programme of inspections at specific frequencies based on a notional assessment of risk, which bears little relation to actual risk. It then requires quarterly returns on the inspections carried out, with the implicit threat of sanctions if inspection quotas are not reached. Enforcement priorities are therefore being driven to an extent by factors not wholly related to the protection of public health, bearing in mind that routine inspections by enforcement officials have been regarded as having little effect on improving health and safety in commercial and industrial operations (Robens, 1972). Moreover, there is no evidence that the current routine inspection model has any particular value in improving food safety. This author's own research has revealed that, frequently, offending premises have been inspected shortly before food-poisoning outbreaks. In two notable incidents, inspections were actually under way, with inspectors observing food preparation procedures while food was being served which subsequently poisoned consumers (North, 1995).

THE EUROPEAN INFLUENCE: THE FOOD HYGIENE DIRECTIVE

As well as the codes of practice, the Food Safety Act was followed by amendments to the Food Hygiene (General) Regulations 1970, which had remained essentially unaltered for over 20 years. These amendments introduced detailed temperature requirements and minor alterations, leaving the regulations otherwise unchanged. However, at the same time, a government-sponsored initiative to the European Community (EC) aimed at rationalizing general food hygiene legislation throughout the community, culminating in the promulgation of Council Directive 93/43/EEC on the hygiene of foodstuffs. This was adopted on 14 June 1993. The directive, together with aspects of Council Directive 80/778 on the quality of water intended for human consumption (as amended), has been implemented by the Food Safety (General Food Hygiene) Regulations 1995, which came into force on 15 September 1995, repealing the Food Hygiene (General) Regulations 1970. At the time of writing, agreement had yet to be reached on the temperature provisions of the amendment regulations.

The new regulations represented a watershed in food safety law and, thus, government policy. Since accession to the Treaty of Rome in 1972, all new food safety law has been based on detailed EC 'vertical' directives. These new regulations are based on a 'horizontal' directive. The difference is between a sector-specific instrument (such as the Fresh Meat Directive (91/497 EC), applicable to slaughterhouses and red-meat-cutting premises), which makes detailed, proscriptive provisions, and one which applies general principles to a wide range of establishments, leaving precise implementation to the proprietor. The directive on the hygiene of foodstuffs was thus seen as a deregulation measure (Murray, 1994), reflecting the UK view that 'overdetailed rules are not usually the right or necessary approach' (Acton, 1993, p. 1).

Being of general application, the nature of the directive – and the regulations derived from it – is such that the detailed requirements relevant to hospitality operations are not specified. The same law applies to food factories, retail outlets and a wide range of other establishments, and is confined to setting out general principles.

PRINCIPLES OF THE FOOD SAFETY (GENERAL FOOD HYGIENE) REGULATIONS

The central principle is a requirement imposed on the proprietors of all food businesses to identify steps in their activities which are critical to ensuring food safety. This is known as risk assessment. They must also ensure that adequate safety procedures are identified, implemented, maintained and reviewed. In particular, proprietors are required to:

- analyse the potential food hazards in their businesses;
- identify those points in the operations where hazards might occur;
- decide which of the points identified are critical to ensuring food safety (so-called 'critical control points');
- identify and implement effective control and monitoring procedures at those critical points;
- review the analysis of food hazards, the critical control points and the control and monitoring procedures periodically, and whenever the food business's operations change.

As to the construction, equipment and general conduct of operations, these requirements are set out in broad terms only. The detail is left to 'industry guides', provided for by the directive. These are required to provide the different industry sectors with guidance on compliance with the regulations and on practices which are necessary to secure the safety and wholesomeness of food. To ensure uniformity in framing the guides, a 'template' has been produced (DH, 1994b).

Completed guides may be submitted to the UK government for recognition. Where businesses then follow the advice in a recognized guide, this must be given due consideration by enforcers when assessing compliance with the regulations. However, there is no legal requirement for food business operators to follow the guides. It is open to them to demonstrate to enforcers that the objectives of the regulations have been achieved in other ways.

Another important aspect of the regulations is a requirement to 'ensure that food handlers are supervised and instructed and/or trained in hygiene matters commensurate with their work activities'. However, there are no specific courses or qualifications laid down, and training in food safety *per se* is not a legal requirement. Food business operators are responsible for identifying the detailed measures necessary for and relevant to their own operations.

The requirement to identify any step in the activities of a food business which is critical to ensuring food safety is a statutory translation of the principles of the Hazard Analysis Critical Control Point (HACCP) system, although it is not specifically identified as such. (It is more generally known as 'risk management'.) The HACCP system was first proposed in 1973 as the result of a joint effort by the Pillsbury Company, NASA and the United States Natick Laboratory to apply a nil-defects programme to the production of food for astronauts. It has since been used to establish effective safety-control systems in various sectors of the food industry, including chilled and frozen food manufacture, and canning (Sheard, 1986).

The implementation of HACCP, or some form of hazard analysis, is seen as a central plank of the government's food policy, and is described as a deregulatory measure. The theory is that, by focusing controls directly and specifically on risk factors, rather than imposing doctrinaire requirements which may or may not have relevance to food safety, the law enables food operations managers to determine their own priorities. By requiring specific risks to be addressed, the government satisfies its primary policy requirement, the maintenance of consumer safety.

However, experience has shown that implementation of the HACCP system requires considerable experience and skills, not readily available at all levels of the hospitality industry. In recognition of this, and to ease the way for small operators to comply with the provisions of the new regulations, the DH has issued guidance entitled *Assured Safe Catering* (ASC), styled 'a management system for hazard analysis' (DH, 1994c).

ASSURED SAFE CATERING

The use of ASC is regarded as an effective response in most catering units to the requirements of the directive, providing a framework for assessing, controlling and monitoring hygiene standards. Whereas HACCP proceeds on an individual food basis in identifying critical control points, ASC identifies generic critical control points (Knowles, 1994). Given the importance of 'risk assessment' to government policy, it is evident that the implementation of ASC will play a central role in relation to the hospitality industry.

Whether ASC will fulfil its promise is debatable: there are a number of clear defects in the system. Not least, it is evident from an analysis of the document that its authors appear unclear as to the distinction between hazard and risk, or their role in management programmes; yet risk management is the essence of HACCP and allied systems –

a process of making decisions and taking actions to control risk at an appropriate level.

In the ASC document, instructions are given to list hazards (as identified by the document) and to identify controls. This omits the vital stage of assessing risk, and effectively converts hazards into risks. Additionally, there are many references to the control of hazards, including the definition of 'critical control point', which refers to a step carried out to ensure a hazard is eliminated or reduced to a safe state. Identifying this confusion – or lack of appreciation of the implications of risk – is more than an exercise in semantics, because the difference between controlling 'hazards' and 'risk' is that between exercising non-specific and, therefore, onerous controls and controlling specific risk factors – that is, those which, if neglected, increase the possibility of food-poisoning to unacceptable levels.

The two concepts have been clearly identified and defined in a booklet issued by the Department of Trade and Industry as part of its 'deregulation' package (DTI, 1993). This publication is intended for the civil service, and commended to officials by no less a person than the current prime minister, John Major. In this document (p. 3), 'hazard' is defined as 'the situation that in particular circumstances could lead to harm'. 'Risk' on the other hand, is defined as 'the probability that a particular adverse event (i.e. a hazard) might occur'. Thus, a hazard is a situation where there is a potential of an undesirable outcome; risk is the probability or chance of that undesirable outcome happening.

When these concepts are applied to HACCP, in the context of controlling risk by focusing on critical control points (that is, those points in a process where failure would pose an unacceptable risk to the consumer), it becomes clear that the system is a means not of *maximizing* control, but of directing control measures to where they will have most effect. The net result of a properly designed system should minimize control effort, while improving its effectiveness. But because risk has been confused with hazard, in a context where there are many more hazards than risks, resultant systems will undoubtedly be more onerous than intended. To that extent, the DH, in its advice to caterers in ASC, has advised execution of its own policy on risk assessment in a way which seems designed to frustrate its own global intentions.

Any defects in ASC will be further exacerbated by a remarkable lack of any direct appreciation of the preconditions of effective risk management. In order to manage risk, it is essential that operations be predictable. Predictability of operations, however, requires standardization of procedures, something which is not always common in catering premises, but without which control measures may be inadequate or irrelevant. It is fruitless setting up a series of controls for various food-preparation processes if, for instance, different chefs go about making the foods in different ways. Equally, it is difficult to estimate risk, and therefore develop controls, if different operations are carried out together, and the range of operations varies from day to day.

INDUSTRY CODES OF PRACTICE

If the practical application of 'risk management' tends towards the over-complex, the hospitality industry might take comfort in the less rigorous detailed requirements of the new regulations, which allow interpretation to suit particular circumstances. However, there is some possibility that even this luxury might not be afforded. A draft code of practice, issued by the Joint Hospitality Industry Congress, working under the slogan 'uniting the industry' (JHIC, 1995), is considerably more onerous than anything required under the Food Hygiene (General) Regulations, much less the new legislation. For instance, while the regulations require drainage facilities adequate for the purpose intended, the code suggests that the direction of flow should be away from 'clean' areas to 'dirty' areas. Such a provision might, in existing premises, require the wholesale relaying of drainage systems and, in new premises, impose considerable restrictions on layout designers. Similarly, the code suggests it is 'good practice' to provide bactericidal soaps for hand washing, something which is neither good practice in all instances, nor required by law.

Although the provisions of this code, if finally approved, will not express statutory requirements, there are numerous examples of enforcement officials implementing guidelines as if they were law (Booker and North, 1994). It is not unreasonable to suggest that the code of practice could be likewise enforced, not least because the burden of proof rests with operators to demonstrate to enforcers that the objectives of the regulations have been achieved in other ways. In practice, this may be more difficult, time-consuming and costly than conforming with the provisions of the code which are not strictly necessary.

CONSISTENCY OF IMPLEMENTATION

Prior to the implementation of the new regulations, an important criticism of government food safety policy had been lack of consistency in implementation. This was particularly marked in the hospitality industry, especially from enterprises which operated premises in more than one local authority area. Many complaints were voiced about different requirements being imposed in different areas.

To an extent, this defect has been addressed not so much by central government as by the local authorities themselves. They have agreed that a co-ordinating body known as LACOTS (formerly Local Authority Coordination of Trading Standards) should extend its remit to food safety matters, the body now being known as the Local Authorities Coordinating Body on Food and Trading Standards, a title reflecting its wider role. Although a non-statutory body, LACOTS will, in effect, be part of the management system through which government policy in respect of local authority activities will be implemented. LACOTS executive instrument is a document on risk assessment issued in late July 1995 (LACOTS, 1995) advising local authorities on how to enforce the hygiene regulations. This states that it is not the role of inspecting officers to undertake the hazards analyses required by the regulations, or to develop the 'appropriate' systems. Instead, it advises officers to 'encourage and facilitate the proprietor's own assessment' by providing relevant advice and by taking 'appropriate enforcement action'. Balancing this, LACOTS warns that:

> A risk based approach must go beyond simply identifying hazards. Enforcement action taken to control hazards, without any consideration of the likelihood of the hazard being realised, can result in unnecessary controls being imposed on food businesses.
>
> (LACOTS, 1995, p. 7)

Should the LACOTS ethos prevail, somewhat in contrast with the DH's muddled approach to the subject of risk assessment, the hospitality industry can expect real improvements to devolve from current policy initiatives. For instance, inspectors are asked by LACOTS, possibly for the first time, to consider whether risks can be reduced to acceptable levels by allowing consumers to control their own exposure. (LACOTS cites an example of giving information such as guidance from the Chief Medical Officer relating to the risks for pregnant women concerning soft cheese and general risks associated with the cooking of eggs.) Moreover, in almost heretical mode, LACOTS actually asks inspectors to consider what might be the consequences of imposing no controls at all, clearly implying that while in some instances controls might be legally enforceable, they might serve no purpose.

This reflects the foreword to the DTI (1993) publication on risk assessment, attributed to John Major, which states:

> Regulation must be proportionate to the problem. New regulation will be justified where there is a clear risk of death or serious harm, but it is a mistake to try to regulate against all risks. Balanced risk assessment should be an integral part of the policy-making process.

Clearly, this ethos is being extended into the implementation of the current legislation, albeit only by an organization which has no statutory remit.

The provisions of the LACOTS guide have been designed to complement a revision of Food Safety Act Code of Practice No. 9, on the inspection of food premises (DH/MAFF, 1995), setting out matters to which enforcement officers *must* have regard in implementing the law. Of particular use in this respect is a provision which requires enforcement officers to distinguish, in their communications to operators, that which is a legal requirement and that which is merely advice or 'best practice', making it clear that only the legal requirements can be enforced. Prior to the codes this did not always occur in practice, leading some operators to spend large amounts on 'improvements' under the impression that they were required to do so, when this was not the case.

Another area with significant policy implications is the Deregulation and Contracting Out Act 1994, promulgated as part of the prime minister's deregulation initiative of 1993, and currently being pursued by first secretary Michael Heseltine. Of particular relevance are Sections 5 and 6, giving powers to the minister to improve enforcement procedures and make model provisions with respect to appeals.

Policy in this context is being developed to introduce statutory delays prior to the taking of enforcement action. This will allow informal consultations between enforcement officers and any business affected, and reduce the need for formal action. In tandem, appeal provisions are to be simplified and made more consistent and accessible. Also, appeal procedures will be introduced where no appeals are currently provided for, short of the highly expensive and uncertain High Court judicial review procedure.

In this context, some judicial processes may devolve from magistrates' courts, where they are commonly handled alongside criminal cases up to and including murder, to specialist tribunals such as the newly constituted Meat Hygiene Tribunals. These will consider appeals and other matters in a more informal and private environment.

CONCLUDING COMMENTS

There are positive and negative aspects of food safety policy as it applies to the hospitality industry. In theory, the move is towards a deregulated approach, devoted to self-regulation, and away from the proscriptive, inflexible regulatory model in use since World War II. This is supported at the European level and will (in theory at least) be applied throughout the EU. However, the implications of these new policy mechanisms do not appear to have been completely thought through by UK policy-makers, so that the support package for local enforcers is not as coherent or as complete as might be desired.

While no definitive view can be taken on the rest of the European scene, there is anecdotal evidence that the UK is more advanced in its implementation than any other member state. This is perhaps not surprising, since the UK has played a major role in developing initiatives in this area.

Nevertheless, while there is some scope for anticipating improvements in the implementation of food safety policy (in the UK at least), the seeds of confusion lie ready to germinate if enforcers and the industry alike fail to understand the implications of tailoring controls to risk, and develop hazard-based systems. Should this happen, the net effect of broadly-based measures, with a strong potential for improving safety without increasing the burdens on industry, could easily become a further mass of over-regulation, without yielding any measurable benefits.

In this context, it is a mistake for those involved in the hospitality industry to view food safety policy in the one-dimensional terms of safety law, much less European law. The UK situation has its own special attributes. A fuller appreciation of policy must take into account the impact of measures unique to the UK, such as the Deregulation etc. Act, as well as the technical implications of risk assessment, plus the various developments in enforcement. The lack of information as to real risk should remain an area of concern.

REFERENCES

Acton, C. (1993) 'EC Food Hygiene Directive on the Safety of Foodstuffs: 13 August 1993', Circular letter, Department of Health.

Booker, C. and North, R.A.E. (1994) *The Mad Officials*. London: Constable.

DH (Department of Health) (1994a) *Management of Outbreaks of Foodborne Illness*. London: Department of Health.

—— (1994b) *A Template – Industry Guides to Good Hygiene Practice*. Heywood: Health Publication Stores.

—— (1994c) *Assured Safe Catering*. London: HMSO.

DH/MAFF (Department of Health/Ministry of Agriculture, Fisheries and Food) (1995) *Food Safety Act Code of Practice No. 9 (Revised). Food Hygiene Inspections*. London: HMSO.

DTI (Department of Trade and Industry) (1993) *Regulation in the Balance – A Guide to Risk Assessment*. London: DTI.

JHIC (Joint Hospitality Industry Congress) (1995) *Food Safety (General Food Hygiene) Regulations 1995 – Guide to Compliance by Caterers*, draft. London: JHIC.

Knowles, T. (1994) 'Some Aspects of UK and European Food Legislation', *Hygiene and Nutrition in Foodservice and Catering*, **1(1)**, 49–62.

LACOTS (Local Authorities Coordinating Body on Food and Trading Standards) (1995) *Food Hygiene Risk Assessment – Guidance to Local Authorities on the Application of Risk Assessment Principles to Food Hygiene Inspections*. Croydon: LACOTS.

MAFF (Ministry of Agriculture, Fisheries and Food) (1989) *Food Safety – Protecting the Consumer,* Cmnd 732. London: HMSO.

Murray, T.W.S. (1994) 'MAFF/DH Food Law Deregulation Plan: Review of EC Food Hygiene Directives: 7 July 1994', Circular letter.

North, R.A.E. (1995) 'The Quality of Public Sector Food-poisoning Surveillance in England and Wales, with Specific Reference to Salmonellosis'. PhD thesis, Leeds Metropolitan University.

Robens, Lord (1972) *Safety and Health at Work. Report of the Committee 1970–72,* Cmnd 5034. London: HMSO.

Sheard, M.A. (1986) 'HACCP and Microbiological Quality Assurance in Catering', in *The HACCP Concept and Quality Assurance in Food Manufacture and Catering.* SOFHT Proceedings, 20–43.

Wildavsky, A. (1988) *Searching for Safety.* New Brunswick, NJ, and Oxford: Transaction Publishers.

FOURTEEN

Undertaking further research: a guide to official sources of information

Heather Smith and Rhodri Thomas

INTRODUCTION

It will be clear from reading the preceding chapters that European public policy is having an increasing impact on the business environment within which hospitality and tourism enterprises operate. The various stages of the policy-making process and any subsequent evaluations can generate a wealth of information, which will be of value to those with an interest in the development of these sectors. This chapter does not aim to be a bibliography, but rather to highlight some of the main forms of official publication so that individuals may more easily undertake their own research. It should be recognized, therefore, that *non-official* sources are excluded (for a review, see Thomas, 1992).

The major publisher of European Union (EU) documentation is the Office for Official Publications of the European Community (OOPEC/EUR-OP). In spite of efforts to improve access to documents, especially in recent years, many problems still remain for the researcher. This stems from the fact that information is produced as a by-product of the complex policy-making process rather than as part of a coherent publishing strategy. Hence, a knowledge of the institutional arrangements and the various stages of policy formulation is desirable before attempting to identify and trace relevant material (see Chapter 2).

Thomson (1989) provides a useful framework for understanding official documents, dividing them into four main categories:

- legislation;
- documentation of the legislative and judicial processes;
- research studies and reports; statistical titles;
- explanatory and background documentation.

The structure of this chapter broadly reflects Thomson's approach. It is worth noting at this point that European Documentation Centres (EDCs) and depository libraries are likely to be the easiest means of gaining access to the publications discussed below.

LEGISLATION

Primary legislation: treaties

These include the original founding treaties, the Merger Treaty, the Accession Treaties, the Single European Act (SEA) and the Treaty on European Union (TEU). Although specific reference to tourism is minimal, researchers obviously need to become familiar with their contents. The treaties are available in a variety of forms including monographs. In addition, they appear in the *Official Journal of the European Communities* (OJ), which is described in more detail below. Somewhat curiously, as Thomson (1995) points out, the TEU and the Acts of Accession for those countries joining in 1995 have appeared in the C series, rather than the L series of the OJ where legislation would normally be found.

Secondary legislation

Legislation adopted by the Council (or by the European Parliament (EP) and the Council under the co-decision procedure) appears in the L series of the OJ. The OJ is published at least once a day (excluding Sundays) and in several parts. It is regarded as *the* primary source of information produced by the EU. The C series contains background information and notices (including draft directives), and the Supplement contains details of public procurement notices. There is also an Annex, which contains the debates of the EP. Unfortunately, despite the frequency of publication, there may still be something of a delay between the adoption of a piece of legislation and its appearance in the OJ.

Each piece of legislation can be identified by a number, although confusingly the same number can be used for both a directive and a decision. Regulations are cited thus: ‘2343/90’, where 90 indicates the year (1990) and 2343 indicates the number of the document. Directives and decisions are cited as follows: ‘92/421/EEC’, where the year of publication is given first, followed by the directive or decision number.

The *Index to the Official Journal of the European Communities* can be used to trace legislation in the OJ. This is important, as legislation is not published in strict numerical order. The *Index* is broken down into an alphabetical and a methodological index. The latter can be used when the document number is known. If the reference numbers are not known, the alphabetical index can be used to find legislation by subject. However, it is still necessary to know the year of publication, as a cumulative index is not available.

Another means of tracing legislation is to use the *Directory of Community Legislation*. This is published twice a year and contains all EU legislation in force, with the appropriate OJ reference.

DOCUMENTATION OF THE LEGISLATIVE AND JUDICIAL PROCESSES

COM and SEC documents

Starting life as internal working papers, COM documents are given the extension ‘Final’ when they are made available to the public. This does not necessarily mean, however, that there will be no further amendments. There are two main forms of COM document.

The majority are proposals for legislation. Others are communications and memoranda which discuss policy objectives. Action programmes fall into the latter category. The Community Action Plan to Assist Tourism, for example, was published as COM(91) 97 Final.

It is much easier to trace COM documents when the numbers are known. The number in brackets indicates the year of publication and documents are then numbered sequentially. Otherwise it is necessary to rely on OOPEC's monthly *Documents* catalogue, which is divided into subject areas.

The texts of certain COM documents (minus the explanatory memorandum which accompanies legislative proposals) also appear in the C series of the OJ. Recently the C series has introduced a listing of Commission documents forwarded to the Council. These also state whether the proposal is of importance for small and medium-sized enterprises (SMEs), and whether it is going to appear in the OJ.

SEC documents are internal publications and, officially, are unavailable. Some are confidential but others can be obtained by writing to the appropriate directorate general (DG). There has been much criticism in the past over the difficulties of accessing these documents and recently greater efforts have been made to publish some as COM documents.

European Parliament reports and debates

EP reports (or *Session Documents: Series A*) contain the reports made by the specialist committees of the EP on a particular piece of legislation or policy, as well as EP recommendations. As these are presently only available on microfiche, tracing them is difficult without an accurate reference. The reports are debated in the EP and the subsequent discussions are reported in the Annex to the OJ (*OJ: Annex: Debates of the European Parliament*). EP resolutions, decisions and parliamentary questions appear in the C series of the OJ.

The EP has several publications which can be used to keep up to date with its activities; the *Week* summarizes its main decisions for a particular week, *EP Briefing* highlights issues to be discussed, and *EP News* contains features on the Parliament's activities. These three publications are available from the EP at no cost. The EP has also published six volumes of *Fact Sheets on the European Parliament and the Activities of the European Union*, which review the actions taken in particular fields.

The Economic and Social Committee

Economic and Social Committee Opinions and Reports give the Economic and Social Committee (ESC)'s view and recommendations on a proposal. For example, ESC (91) 1118 gave the ESC's 'Opinion on the proposal for a Council Regulation (EEC) on common rules for the allocation of slots at Community airports'. ESC opinions and reports also appear in the C series of the OJ. In addition, the ESC produces various publications which summarize its activities. These include its *Briefing*, *Bulletin*, *Info*, *Newsletter* and press releases.

The Committee of the Regions

The opinions of the Committee of the Regions appear in the C series of the OJ.

The Court of Justice and the Court of First Instance

Reports of Cases before the Court of Justice and the Court of First Instance contain the judgments of cases. Until recently the English versions of these publications were notoriously outdated, but they are now published during the same year as the judgment. A summary of cases brought and judgments reached is also available in the *Proceedings of the Court of Justice and the Court of First Instance of the European Communities* and in the C series of the OJ.

The Court of Auditors

The annual *Court of Auditors' Report* may be found in the C series of the OJ.

Finally, it should be noted that the *Bulletin of the European Communities* describes the progress of legislation through the various institutions.

RESEARCH STUDIES AND REPORTS; STATISTICAL TITLES

The Commission

The different DGs of the Commission offer a wide range of reports which may have been used to inform their deliberations. These are often written by external consultants and do not necessarily reflect the official view on a topic. Their value is that they assess the impact of particular measures.

The Statistical Office of the European Communities (Eurostat)

The *Eurostat Catalogue* lists the various publications available, usefully including an indication of content and format (not all are in paper formats). Informative general publications are *Europe in Figures*, the annual *Basic Statistics of the Community* and *Social Portrait of Europe*.

The various satellite bodies also produce publications and documents in accordance with their own areas of interest. Some of the major sources are discussed below.

European Centre for the Development of Vocational Training

The European Centre for the Development of Vocational Training (CEDEFOP)'s numerous research reports on vocational training include such titles as *Occupations in the*

Tourist Sector: A Comparative Analysis in Nine Community States (1994) and *Vocational Training in the Tourist Industry* (1991). Catalogues of recent publications are issued at regular intervals.

European Foundation for the Improvement of Living and Working Conditions

This organization produces numerous publications concerned with workplace-related issues.

European Investment Bank

The European Investment Bank (EIB) produces newsletters and publications relating to its activities, such as its *Annual Report*.

EXPLANATORY AND BACKGROUND DOCUMENTATION

The Commission publishes much useful material which is aimed at a general audience. The *European File* series, for example, is worth consulting for a concise introduction (about 12 pages) to issues. Thus, the now dated 'Tourism and the Community' (European File 17/82) gave an overview of initiatives associated with the industry. *European Documentation* booklets are more comprehensive, dealing with many of the same policy areas in more detail. Both series are now also published as *Europe on the Move*, and are available free of charge from the offices of the Representation of the European Commission.

The Commission offices in member states also publish material which is intended either to be introductory in nature or to keep readers up to date with developments. For example, the London offices publish a brief news bulletin entitled the *Week in Europe*, which, as its title suggests, alerts readers to what are considered to be the significant EU events of the week. The same bulletin may, therefore, have paragraphs on monetary union, agriculture and social policy. *Background Reports* are an attempt to overcome the brevity of these bulletins by offering a slightly more thorough explanation of official activity in individual policy areas. A number of fact sheets on various issues are also published occasionally.

In addition, the Commission publishes more specialist, subject-related periodicals, including *Social Europe*, *European Economy* and *Green Europe*. These can contain articles of direct relevance to the hospitality industry; for example, issue 3 of the 1993 volume of *European Economy* contained a chapter on trends within the European hotel industry. The annual *Panorama of EU Industry* also attempts to provide an overview of developments within various industries.

CONCLUDING COMMENTS

This chapter has attempted to explain the main forms of official publication which are likely to be useful for those with an interest in the implications of European integration for the hospitality and tourism industries. One of the difficulties faced by researchers is monitoring new initiatives and publications. The items listed below as further reading are valuable for keeping up to date with developments.

REFERENCES

Thomas, R. (1992) '1992 and the Hospitality Industry: A Review of Information Provision', *International Journal of Contemporary Hospitality Management*, **4(2)**, 3–7.

Thomson, I. (1989) *The Documentation of the European Communities: A Guide*. London: Mansell.

—— (1995) 'EU Institutions, Policy-making and the Legislative Process: Recent Developments and Impact for European Information Provision', *EIA Review*, **5**, 5–20.

FURTHER READING

Europe. Agence Europe, Luxembourg (daily).

European Report. European Information Service, Brussels (twice per week).

European Information Service. Local Government International Bureau, London (10 issues per year).

European Access, Chadwyck-Healey (six times a year).

INDEX